Indian English Fiction

Postmodern Literary Sensibility

Indian English Fiction
Postmodern Literary Sensibility

Vishwanath Bite

AUTHORSPRESS

Worldwide Circulation through Authorspress Global Network
First Published 2012
by
Authorspress

Editorial
Q-2A Hauz Khas Enclave
New Delhi-110 016

Marketing
E-35/103, Jawahar Park
Laxmi Nagar, Delhi-110 092

e-mails: authorspress@rediffmail.com; authorspress@hotmail.com
Website: www.authorspressbooks.com

Indian English Fiction: Postmodern Literary Sensibility
ISBN 978-81-7273-677-4

Printed in India at Sri Krishna Offset Press,

Dedicated to my father

Shri K.S. Bite

Who taught me to Rise...

Who taught me to Shine...

And

Who taught me to FLY hish in the Sky.

Preface

The present volume is a compilation of 26 well researched articles on Indian English fiction. These articles contributed by scholars, teachers, academicians and critics of repute, study indepth Indian English fiction exploring a variety of themes and aspects.

Dr. Vishwanath Bite in his insightful article "Beyond the National Allegory: Shashi Deshpande and Sunetra Gupta" discusses the fiction of two Anglophone women writers from India, Shashi Deshpande and Sunetra Gupta. He explores his idea that the novels of both Deshpande and Gupta are rich with distinctive modernist characteristics. He further argues that within this feminist tradition of postcolonial modernist fiction lie the unique power of its epiphanies, its ineluctable modality of otherness. Mrs. Madhuri Bite in her article regarding "Imagery of Goddess in Gita Mehta's *A River Sutra*: A Feminist Approach" explains the Narmada River is the first introduction of goddess imagery in the novel. Throughout the novel an imagery of goddess is considered as a driving force in various forms. She concludes that the use of goddess imagery in a *River Sutra* is used as a cultural agent and as a form of analysis. Sophia Jaychandran in her well researched article about "An Eco-critical Reading of Amitav Ghosh's *The Hungry Tide*" states that ecocriticism has emerged as a contemporary trend in the world of literary criticism. Her paper investigates how unrefined environmental preservation policies, ignoring the material reality of a landscape, are disadvantageous to the socially and economically backward classes, like indigenous people, forest dwellers, tribals and nomads.

Grishma Khobragade in her article "Women's Empowerment and Personal Mobility in the Novels of Shashi Deshpande and Nayantara Sahgal" makes an attempt to read certain selected novels of Shashi Deshpande and Nayantara Sahagal with the objective of locating the class and community structures embedded in them. She concludes that they have used class of women and their empowerment of Indian society effectively in their novels. Mohamed Hamoud Kassim Al-Mahfedi and Abdulmonim Ali Ben Ali in their research article, "Individuality and Space in Salman Rushdie's Fiction: A Postmodern Perspective" explore Rushdie's novels revolve around two strands or visions of human space: political domain and humane domain. They further state that through telling stories about imaginary realms and creatures freely entering the "painfully established" and systematized world order Rushdie wants to establish a new imaginary world without cultural pains.

In the article, "Interpreting Anita Desai's *In Custody* in the Light of Susan Sontag's Critical Essay *Against Interpretation."* Kirti B. Vitthani studies *In Custody* by Anita Desai and Susan Sontag's theory of interpreting any work of art comparatively. She states that Anita Desai insightfully narrates the aesthetics of art versus modern tools of comprehension. Pinaki Roy in her insightful article *"Postmodern Diasporic Sensibility*: Rereading Jhumpa Lahiri's Oeuvre" states that Lahiri's novel and short stories are mostly read for their precise presentation of the sentiments and disillusionments of Indians, settled especially in the United States. Further she explains that Lahiri presents strong female characters, but she has never have been an outright feminist.

Abdulmonim Ali Ben Ali's insightful article "Salman Rushdie's *Grimus* as an Alternative History" aims to question the efficacy of historical truth as factual knowledge in the light of his concept of history. Further he states that Rushdie's concern in this particular novel is the desire to offer an alternative version of history of the subcontinent and the postcolonial history in general by reworking the authorial view of historical experience and factual knowledge, and by simultaneously creating a fanciful image of historical realities similar to the postcolonial subcontinental history. Dr. Amit Shankar Saha studies Anita Desai, Bharati Mukherjee, Sunetra Gupta and Jhumpa Lahiri comparatively in his research article "The Spiritual Sense of Alienation in Diasporic Life: Reading Anita Desai, Bharati Mukherjee, Sunetra Gupta and Jhumpa Lahiri". In the article he also expresses his views on the concept of exile and how it reflects in the works of the selected writers. Dr. G.A. Ghanshyam in his well researched article, "Trimetric of Land, Culture and Identity in Indian English Fiction" studies Indian English fiction with a new perspective. He concludes that land, culture and identity are fused together to give a definite form and shape to the edifice of Indian English fiction, which characterizes it as a unique expression of the life, culture and ethos of India and its people.

Dr. Kiranjeet Kaur Bedi in her article analyses Nayantara Sahgal's *Rich like Us* with a thematic perspective. She further includes that the novels of Nayantara Sahgal deal with a wise gamut of themes ranging from personal dilemma and problems, joys and sorrows, fulfilment and frustrations of female protagonists to the political upheavals that India has experienced since Independence. Dr. Vimmie Manoj in her insightful article examines the fiction of Indian women writers with a postmodern feministic perspective. According to her, postmodern Indian women writers expose the root cause of inequality being sexuality that is constantly controlled to highlight women's subordinate position. Dr. D.G. Thakor evaluates sociological status of women in Gita Mehta's *A River Sutra*. He further states that the look reflects contemporary society by describing six stories through which people's money-minded attitude, indifference to the poor or low profile people, jealousy, anti-socialness, in-safety of women, optimism, kind full nature, women empowerment, metaphysis, etc. are well brought out G. Gulam Tariq expresses his views in the article "The World of Marginalised in Mahasweta Devi's Play

Mother of 1084." In his article he examines and compares the status of women in a male-dominated society through the role of Sujata who has been relegated to the position of a neglected, suppressed, ill-treated, mechanical and marginalized being in all forms in the male-dominated society which considers woman as an object of sex, only to reproduce, bring money when needed. She does not possess even a voice to express her own concerns.

Mrs. G. Sundari and Dr. K. Sandhya, in their contributing article "Nergis Dalal's *Skin Deep*: Sister-Knot in Conflict?" explain the role of women writers in Indian English literature through the work of Nergis Dalal. They analyse the novel with a psychological point of view and portray the relationship between two sisters. In her article, "Poile Sengupta's *Thus Spake Shoorpanakha, So Said Shakuni* As A Postmodern Text", Dr. L.V. Padmarani Rao describes the dramatic technique of the play. She further discusses that both the characters, Shakuni and Shoorpanakh,a played an important role in the respective epics, *the Ramayana the Mahabharata* but are not given due importance in the epics; on the contrary they are portrayed as vicious, villainous and neglected. R. Jothilakshmi. and Dr. G. Meenakshi Sundaram in their article explain the Soul-Body Concept in *The Selected Novels of R.K.Narayan*. According to them R. K. Narayan points out that the human body is perishable, whereas the soul is eternal. The novels *The English Teacher*, *A Tiger for Malgudi*, *The Man-Eater of Malgudi* and *Mr. Sampath* become all the more popular among the Indian readers for this philosophy of life which is a part of the mass consciousness of the Indian people. In their article, Dr. Kapil Dev Sharma and Dr. Pradeep Kumar Talan explore the theme of East-West encounter in Narayan's *The Bachelor of Arts*. Their paper portrays the dilemma and social inequality, economic and racial exploitation due to the East-West encounter.

Dr. K.K. Sunalini in her well-researched article, "Theme of Love in Manjul Bajaj's *Come, Before Evening Falls* "points out that Manjul Bajaj makes a difference in the portrayal of the theme of love. She further says that the writer deals with the theme of love in a pragmatic way and discriminates the men and women's attitude towards love. In his insightful article "Shiv K Kumar's *A River with Three Banks*: Revisiting Partition", Dr. P.R. Shewale discusses the tragic consequences of the partition. The merciless killing and bloodshedding in the wake of communal violence, the abduction of young girls, the loss of faith, and the migration of a large number of people from both sides of the border are some of them. He further says that Shiv K.Kumar has deeply explored the theme of partition in his novel, *A River with Three Banks.* Janmejay Kumar Tiwari in his article, "From Routes to Roots: Diaspora in the Novels of Salman Rushdie", shows that Salman Rushdie is the author who inaugurated the field of postcolonial diasporism with his debut novel *Grimus.* He deeply studies all his novels from the diasporic point of view. Ved Mitra Shukla in his research article states that Salman Rushdie is a children's writer and he proves his statement with the help of Rushdie's selected novels, *Haroun and the Sea of Stories* and *Luka and the Fire of Life.* Further, he examines that in both these novels there are also some common themes which have been popular in the world of children's literature.

In the article, "Interrogating the Metanarratives on Indian Independence with Reference to Partition Narratives", Raj Sree foregrounds the incoherence of partition narratives which very well express and interpret the cataclysmic event. He observes that typical of postmodernist fiction, partition narratives too seem to reflect the fact that the writer has become tired of trying to explain a disjointed and godless universe. Nancy S. Rethinam's article, "Theorizing the Saga of Lost Dreams from the Perspective of Post Modernism", attempts to place *The God of Small Things* in perspective within the larger framework of postmodernism and Indian Literature in English. She concludes that others allege *The God of Small Things* is simply a story about love, caste, and sexuality in India. But it is above these things. It is a counter discourse on the metanarratives of caste, gender, patriarchy and sexuality. Yatri D. Dave in her insightful article, "Culture of Consumerism as Reflected in Chetan Bhagat's *One Night @ Call Center*", focuses the trends and techniques of modern world. She describes that the novel deals with consumerism which shows how to attract customers for their selling of products. Paula Hayes in her scholarly article observes the avant-garde experience of silence in Ambai's short story *Yellow Fish.* This story is positively simplistic, elegant, and shorn of any unnecessary words; as a minimalist narrative it could easily be classified as avant-garde. The narrative vision of the story is driven forward primarily by images, not action.

I must record my deep sense of indebtedness to Mr. Akshay Jain and the whole team of Avishkar Publishers and Distributors, Jaipur for pursuing me to bring out the present volume. I must not forget to express my deep sense of gratitude to my respected father, Shri. K. S. Bite, my beloved wife, Madhuri Bite for her help in editing and her constant support in my literary activities. I must thank my brother Ramdas Bite for his love, affection and constant support.

The present anthology has strictly followed blind peer-review procedure while selecting the papers. I am thankful to Dr. Pradnya Ghorpade, Associate Professor in English, K. R. P. Kanya Mahavidyalaya, Islampur (M. S.), Dr. Lata Mishra, Editor, *Labyrinth: An International Refereed Journal of Postmodern Studies* (Gwalior), Dr. Ashok Babar, Principal, PVP, Mahavidyalaya, Kavathemahankal (M.S.), Dr. Dinesh Panwar, Chief Editor, *Lapis Lazuli: An International Literary Journal* (Ghaziabad) for reviewing, selecting papers, making suggestions and sharing with me critical arguments.

I must record my deep sense of indebtedness to Mr. Sudarshan Kcherry, Managing Director, and the whole team of Authorspress, New Delhi for encouraging me to edit the present volume.

Dr. Vishwanath Bite

Contributors

Vishwanath Bite, Assistant Professor in English, Govt.of Maharashtra's Ismail Yusuf College, Jogeshwari, Mumbai.

Madhuri Bite, Research Scholar, Department of English, Shivaji University, Kolhapur.

Sophia Jaychandran, Assistant Professor in English, Vanita Vishram Women's College of Commerce, Athwa Gate, Surat, Gujarat.

Grishma Manikrao Khobragade, Assistant Professor, Department of English, Birla College, Kalyan Maharashtra.

Mohamed Hamoud Kassim Al-Mahfedi & Abdulmonim Ali Ben Ali, Department of Studies in English, University of Mysore, Mysore.

Kirti B. Vitthani, Assistant Professor in English, R. K. Shah Women's Arts College, Saraswati Shaikshanik Sankul, Chhapra-bhatha Road, Amroli, Surat Gujarat.

Pinaki Roy, Assistant Professor of English, Malda College, Rabindra Avenue, Rathbari More, West Bengal.

Abdulmonim Ali Ben Ali, Research scholar, Department of Studies in English, University of Mysore, Mysore.

Amit Shankar Saha, Independent Researcher, Kolkata, India.

G.A. Ghanshyam, Professor of English, Govt. Arts College,

Seepat, Bilaspur (C.G.)

Kiranjeet Kaur Bedi, Assistant Professer [English], Department of Humanities & So. Sciences, NIT Raipur

Vimmie Manoj, Independent Researcher, Madhya Pradesh.

D.G. Thakor, Associate Professor in English, Shah N. H. Commerce College, Valsad, Gujarat.

G. Gulam Tariq, Associate Professor & Head, Department of English, Yogi Vemana University, Kadapa, Andhra Pradesh.

G. Sundari, Assistant Professor of English, Vijaya Institute of Technology for Women, Enikepadu, Vijayawada, Andhra Pradesh.

K. Sandhya, Associate Professor of English, Department of English, Maris Stella College, Vijayawada Andhra Pradesh.

L.V. Padmarani Rao, Assistant Professor, Department of English, Yeshwant Mahavidyalaya, Nanded, Maharashtra

Jothilakshmi R. & Dr. G.Meenakshi Sundaram, Department of English, CSI College of Engineering, Ketti The Nilgirs District, Tamil Nadu.

Kapil Dev Sharma & Dr. Pradeep Kumar Talan, Assistant Professor, AIMT, Greater Noida, Uttar Pradesh.

K.K. Sunalini, Assistant Professor of English, Ramappa Engineering College, Warangal, Andra Pradesh.

P.R. Shewale, Associate Professor & Head, Department of English, Shri Shahaji Chh. Mahavidyalaya, Kolhapur, Maharashtra.

Janmejay Kumar Tiwari, Independent Researcher, Allahabad.

Ved Mitra Shukla, Assistant Professor, Department of English, Rajdhani College, University of Delhi, New Delhi.

Raj Sree, Ross Mount, Kunnapuzha, Aramada P.O. Trivandrum.

Nancy S. Rethinam, Noah's Ark, Kunnapuzha, Aramada P.O. Trivandrum, Kerla.

Yatri D. Dave, Lecturer in English, Nirma Institute of Technology, Nirma University, Ahmedabad,Gujarat.

Paula Hayes, Strayer University, Memphis, Tennessee.

Contents

1

Beyond the National Allegory: Shashi Deshpande and Sunetra Gupta

— Vishwanath Bite

My example of postcolonial modernist aesthetics is the fiction of two Anglophone women writers from India, Shashi Deshpande and Sunetra Gupta. Attridge's claim of the potential relation of modernist aesthetics and the ethics of alterity can be seen as especially relevant in this tradition of women's writing, but what is perhaps more intriguing is the way an essentially modernist foregrounding of subjectivity is held in a delicate tension with a constantly vigilant awareness of what I call the ethics of 'otherness' inherent in such discourses, in a luminal state where one is indeed indistinguishable from the other. Of the two, Deshpande has been writing since the mid-eighties, and Gupta published her first novel in the mid-nineties, but they can be seen together as having projected a distinctly modernist aesthetics in their fiction, which has amounted to an implicit and silent critique of this dominant tradition in South-Asian Anglophone fiction. This is also no doubt the reason behind their marginalization in the current hype and attention South-Asian Anglophone writing has been receiving of late, as such aesthetics as writers like Deshpande and Gupta espouse in their fi ction is clearly disfavored by the current Rushdie-Jameson tradition of postmodernist postcoloniality.

The novels of both Deshpande and Gupta are rich with distinctive modernist characteristics, as, for instance, the importance of a sense of place, one that is both situated in, and disperses the idea of a nation, as opposed to the larger, unified, pan-Indian imaginative topos of the post-Rushdie national narrative. Indeed, the Bombay and Bangalore of Deshpande's fiction is as really rooted and sensually evoked as some of the most memorable locales in the vernacular literary traditions of India – Bibhuti Bhushan Bandopadhyay's Nischindipur, Quarratulain Hyder's Lucknow, London, or Sylhet. Here Sunetra Gupta is poised in an interesting space, delicately suspended between the sensual concreteness of places and their heavy memories which linger over her work on one hand, and a strong pull towards a psychological interiority which often inclines towards an emotional and philosophical abstraction. The physical spaces enclosed by London, New York, Princeton, Calcutta, the house Mandalay in *A Sin of Colour* are at the same time real and ethereal, and this tension between physicality and interiority is also a strikingly modernist one.

Another significant element of this aesthetics of postcolonial modernism relates to the use of ordinary English words like "door," "bus," "station" to achieve the creation of a way of life that has naturalized the cultural hybridity of colonial and post colonial life, especially in its urban, middle-class incarnation to the extent that it renders redundant, even spuriously faddish the Rushdiesque "chutnifi cation" of English and its scattering of untranslated Indian words and phrases and odd sentence constructions. With regard to the issue of linguistic and cultural hybridity in the context of (post)colonial life, the Indian novelist Amit Chaudhuri writes in his insightful introduction to *The Picador Book of Modern Indian Literature*: "Hybridity, however, can frequently enter texts in subtly disruptive, rather than obvious ways; it need not be worn like a national costume" (Chaudhuri xv). Such a belief in the evocative ability of everyday words and their encoding of deep-rooted cultural history, nowhere better expressed in Anglophone Indian fiction than in the fictions of Gupta and Deshpande (and a handful of others) is clearly a modernist assertion, a rebuttal of a Sausseurean loss of faith in the power of words to capture a real physical world. This strongly felt yet subdued hybridity in ordinary English words also echoes Raja Rao's identification of the subtle balance of alienness and familiarity of the language in the context of Indian life, as also of the creation of the kind of 'otherness' Attridge sees modernist aesthetics uniquely sensitive to.

The crucial idea here is 'ordinariness,' as I feel that it's modernism's commitment to the dailyness and the banality of the world, the 'cotton wool of daily life' that forms the fabric of its unique and subtle sensitivity to modes of 'alterity'. The radical replacement of the worthwhile, 'grand' subjects by epiphanies of ordinary train rides and purchase of breakfast-bread seems to be a significant step in the foregrounding of the ineffable 'other.' The strangeness of the chronicling of such base matter is followed by an inexplicable wonder at its beauty, leading to a destabilization that is both pleasant and eerie. And this is the juxtaposition such postcolonial modernist fictions always achieve with a remarkable degree of success. The shy hybridity of cultural translation, as of the colour and texture of traditional Bengali dishes, into not only the English language but something of the impersonality of a globally intelligible discourse is paralleled by the delicate celebration of the ordinary as extraordinary—a maidservant mopping the floor, seen in a frieze of classical dance, the pattern of *mehendi,* a colourful dye, on the hands of a young Marathi girl's hands, wet hair sticking to one's legs after a drenched tour through a monsoon shower in Calcutta.

Indeed, born, brought up and educated in several different continents, Sunetra Gupta's background is highly cosmopolitan, and one may add, diasporic, as much as any author of Indian-English fi ction, and so are most of her protagonists, but that has not detracted from the importance of the local, the concrete evocation of specific times and places in all their physicality in her fiction. The diasporic, somewhat dislocated perspectives of the protagonists, and in certain cases, those of the invisible narrator, creates relationships with the locale that are at once intense and distanced, deep with affection and humor, on part of a viewer-participant who is both an integral part of and peripheral to such atmospheres. Above and beyond the 'otherness' of English in the context of Indian life noted by Raja Rao, there are added distances to be bridged – the mind-boggling cultural diversity within India, and this deepens the dislocation in the perspectives and sensibilities of the sensitive, brooding female protagonists of Gupta's Bildungsroman-like novels.

Such dislocated, fractured sensibilities play a crucial role in all of Gupta's novels, especially in her early work, as in the novels *Memories of Rain*, and *The Glassblower's Breath*. Modernist aesthetics celebrate the ordinary with a mode of articulation that is far from ordinary, that which Attridge identifi es as "its willed interference with the transparency of discourse", and this arguably heightens the dichotomy between the familiar and the alien. This 'alienness' of discourse is striking in Gupta's fiction, in a profound sense of the aesthetic craft, an Empsonian ambiguity and a complexity of prose, richly figurative, full of myth and the heavy shadows of memory, a brooding interiority of consciousness. Modernist fiction is sometimes considered to move between two poles – the extreme subjectivity of Lawrence and Woolf on one hand, and the clinical detachment of Joyce's artist paring his fingernails on the other. Gupta seems heavily tilted to the direction of the subjective, an inclination which goes with the relative lack of humour in her fiction. A figure like, for instance, Malik Solanka of Rushdie's novel *Fury*, Cambridge academic-turned maker of Little Brain dolls, protagonists of his popular TV programme on the history of philosophy, seems unlikely in her world. Gupta seems neither capable of, neither inclined towards that kind of mockingly self-ironic gesture that is so representative of postmodernism.

But even this foregrounding of subjectivity, intense and liberated within the fictional paradigms, remains true to the construction of alterity, mainly in the location of the Indian woman, as with the characters of Niharika in *A Sin of Colour* and the nameless female protagonists of *Memories of Rain* and *The Glassblower's Breath*. Attridge's claim of the potential relation of modernist aesthetics and the ethics of alterity becomes especially relevant with the dynamics of style and subject in Gupta's fiction, but what is perhaps more intriguing is the way an essentially modernist foregrounding of subjectivity seems to constitute an ethical awareness of the 'Other' *through* such subjectivity rather than *against* it. Take, for instance, the passage where the narrator-protagonist of *Memories of Rain*, a Bengali girl from a middle class Calcutta family, appears before her brother's English friend, Anthony, whom she is later to marry – and the way her own appearance, distanced and de-subjectified, is refracted through her own consciousness: "...and she was summoned to take out to her brother and his white friend a kerosene light. And so she appeared to him a second time, lantern-lit, in the damp darkness, a phantom of beauty, and his eyes roamed for a time after she had disappeared inside, the ghost of light that her presence had left, there beside him, in the rain-swollen dark" (2).

Shashi Deshpande's female protagonists are perhaps even more memorable in their finely individualized etching and in the subsequent dialectic of subjectivity and 'otherness' their location within the fictional matrices inevitably create. She employs the interiority, the figurativeness and a sense of a Dedalusian "stasis' to apprehend the intricate and elaborate fabric of the Indian extended family and especially the place of the woman in this traditional structure. In two of her finest novels, *Roots and Shadows* (1982) and *That Long Silence* (1988), she positions two unforgettable Indian women, Indu and Jaya respectively, within the matrix of the traditional, large extended family, though in very different locations with respect to individual achievement, personal freedom and power. But in both cases, the family looms large as a powerful and a paradoxical structure, replete in equal amounts with love, caring, pettiness, rivalry, patriarchal dominance, the play of materialism and idealism, ambition and its curtailment – rooted in specific cultural and geographical spaces that deeply shape their texture – Bangalore in the first instance and Bombay in the second.

It is interesting how the very modernist motifs of a self-conscious preoccupation with literature and creativity, especially in their juxtaposition with the more commercial forms of journalistic writing, something which both protagonists, both writers, actually perceive as commercial and vulgarized genres that they have to take recourse to against themselves for the sake of more secure and stable financial rewards, sacrificing, as it were, their aesthetic integrity in the process.

Indu is a successful journalist (and a less successful fiction writer) who returns to visit her father's family – a family she had alienated by an unconventional marriage to a man of another caste – following the death of her grandmother, the matriarch of the family, to find that the deceased has left her very substantial properties entirely to her, and to counter and immerse herself in the complex socio-psychological entanglements that follow.

Jaya, less successful and less empowered than Indu, is a failed writer who churns out the occasional women's column in a popular daily, tries to reconcile herself with the intricacies of womanhood in her social context and the claustrophobic shadows of her past as her husband, a civil servant, is troubled by allegations of professional malpractice. Both novels are distinctly modernist in their narrative modes, abandoning linear narration for endless digressions, fragmented interior monologues, movements back and forth in time following the course of the protagonists' memories and brooding minds, in a manner strongly reminiscent of Julia Kristeva's 'semiotic' discourse challenging epistemological certitudes of dominant patriarchal orders. Both are unselfconsciously 'Indian' in a cultural sense, providing no contextual annotations of relations, notions, customs and rituals that hardly translate beyond their immediate cultures, much less the whole of India; nor do either protagonist feel compelled to provide any background information for the reader to grasp a coherent chronology of events in the middle of the lyrical, trancelike stream of consciousness, unapologetic introductions of personal dreams and nightmares, disjointed threads of family narratives, through which the novels are narrated. In fact, though both novels have signifi cant movements and reversals at the level of concrete action, the narration rarely gives a feel of such movements; much of these movements are in fact recapitulations of events and patterns of the past, and even events of the present follow the protagonists' intense, rambling brooding on their implications. They are also deep celebration of the subjective, in its psychological intensity and the overarching point of view of the narrator-protagonist – a subjectivity that is distinctively modernist, unlike its depthless decentredness in postmodernist fiction following its critique in poststructuralist thought. However, the characters and the narration of Indu and Jaya are also distinctly different in a way that cannot be done justice to in the limited space here, but both novels are united in their use of a distinctly modernist mode to foreground a subjectivity that is simultaneously intense and liberated within the fictional paradigms and true to its construction as the silent 'Other' ("the weight of that long silence of the other half of the world," Deshpande quotes Elizabeth Robins in the epigraph) in the context of its socio-political reality.

The relevance of the critique and subsequent postmodernist decentering of subjectivity in the context of certain non-Western cultures has in fact been questioned by postcolonial writers like Amit Chaudhuri, who claims that notions of the self, realism, authenticity etc do not often have the same position in much of such traditional cultures as they have had in models of Western reason, be it logocentricism dating back to the Greeks or the Cogito of the Enlightenment, positions that have been of late, uneasy and suspect, and this is ambiguity often gets neglected in postcolonial fictions that work from within a postmodernist space. Also worth remembering here is the celebration of subjectivity in

Black American women's fiction, as an instance where a modernist foregrounding of subjectivity has been integral to the formation of a minority discourse that challenges hegemony of Eurocentricism through the very act. Such fictions as Deshpande's and Gupta's, in this sense, offer us what Jessica Berman, describing a similar dynamic between ethics and aesthetics, subjectivity and otherness in Virginia Woolf, calls "ethical folds" – "...the ethics of Woolf's writings rest in the folds between ontology and epistemology, between an intimate ethics of eros and a recognition of the public responsibility to respond to the face of the other". Such a fold, Berman indicates, is arrived at through a negotiation between Levinasian conceptions of the other as "infinitely foreign" and feminist configuration of ethical relations with the other through intimacy, in a more "personal sphere" that is the unique hallmark of a tradition of modernism which, I'd like to argue, also informs the location and sensibilities of the female protagonists of both Deshpande and Gupta.

In many ways both Deshpande's and Gupta's fictions reflect the elitism of high modernism, Gupta's probably in a more obvious way than Deshpande's, in her stylistic aesthetics, but also in her subject matter. Many of her characters are academics, scientists, writers and philosophers, preoccupied in a contemplation of their work with a solemnity and a kind of lost idealism that clearly sets itself as different as the deliberate playful irreverence of much postmodernist fi ction. Her world is often one where the old British Empire has directly given way to the feudal aristocrats of Bengal, as the Roy family in *A Sin of Colour*, who comes to own the house Mandalay, built by a British officer, or the son of the family, Debendranath Roy, who goes to Oxford as a student, an example of the privileged upper-middle class of India who has access to the best of the cultural and intellectual traditions of both the old Empire and his native country.

The academic career of his niece Niharika bears striking correspondence to that of Gupta herself, who studied at Princeton and Imperial College, London, before becoming a reader in Zoology at Oxford. The privileged nature of the author's career, educated at some of the best institutions of the Western world, is of course, fairly typical of a large cross-section of Indian-English writers who usually hail from the educated, urban middle and upper-middle class, a fact which often, though not always finds reflection in the worlds they create. This draws attention to the fact that the assessment of the colonial and postcolonial phenomenon of Indian- English writing as a discourse situated on the margins of the canon is a considerably complicated one.

While postcolonial Anglophone writing can be seen as existing on the periphery of the English canon in its Euro-American incarnation, the fact that its authors are more often than not part of the most privileged, articulate and empowered sections of the postcolonial communities invariably complicate such locations, reminding us that the issue of 'class' is a potentially important one here. The relation of Indian-English writing with modernism, or for that matter, postmodernism, will have to take into account the not only the historical position of their authors with respect to the former Empire and global canons, but also their places within the respective colonial or postcolonial societies. Attridge's argument about the modalities of 'otherness' that modernism is so sensitive to, therefore, cannot be uncomplicatedly applied to the ethical location of postcolonial writing, even if such locations happen to be on the periphery of Euro-American canons. Inasmuch as the protagonists of such fiction are subject to an 'othered' status in western societies, such a claim is true, but what I'd like to emphasize as the nodal point in modernism's relation to alterity, especially with relation to these two writers, is its celebration of the ordinary.

In fact, one needs to be vigilant in a too easy identification of women's writing with such modalities as that of alterity, the personal sphere or, at a different level, with the "inner domain" of national culture as those I've hinted throughout this essay as contributing to the dimensions of rich modernist aesthetics, as easy conclusions about such paradigms can always lead to false gender-based essentialisms, even as they hold rich ethical, political and aesthetic possibilities if perceived sensitively. Indeed, Partha Chatterjee points out that these numerous binaries operating within nationalist discourse of nineteenth century India, as that of the inner/outer, spiritual/material, home/ world, feminine/ masculine, helped to confine this discourse within such essentialisms and merely erected a new patriarchy as a hegemonic construct. Even as the inner sphere of home and the family continues to be important in these novels by Deshpande and Gupta, neither of the lives of their female protagonists are circumscribed within the domestic confines of home, and their aesthetic and professional endeavours, admittedly of varying range and intensity, make such binaries as home/world collapse, and hint at the intricate ways the public and private interact and infl uence each other. Even as they are aware of their "othered" status in a patriarchal society, their educational and professional qualifications, their place within the middle class considerably complicate such statuses. Significant components of such lives, operative within the undefined liminal spaces of the inner and the outer domains is, therefore, less the stuff of minority history than the material of "subaltern pasts," as another Subaltern historiographer, Dipesh Chakraborty, has put it. In *Provincializing Europe*, Chakraborty speaks of those irrational moments of history which cannot be integrated within the dominant, rational, teleological and historicist narratives, those which "...are marginalized not because of any conscious intentions but because they represent moments or points at which the archive the historian mines develops a degree of intractability with respect to the aims of professional history" (Chakraborty 101). Subaltern pasts can equally belong to the privileged or the marginalized populace, and as an example of the former Chakraborty describes superstitious rituals prevalent among the upper class brahmins, rituals which have been either left out of historicist narratives or have been rationalized and secularized to be made part of such narratives. To modify Attridge, therefore, I'd like to argue that modernist discourse such as Deshpande's and Gupta's are not only significant ways of apprehending the 'other,' but an important way of chronicling 'subaltern pasts' of the marginal and humdrum moments of daily life, which are neither quite the same as the narratives of the 'other' or the disempowered, nor the goings on in the "inner domain," though admittedly they have undeniable relationships with both and perhaps also overlap with their spheres. Such subaltern pasts are neither male nor female in character, just as they are neither specifically related to the lives of the privileged or the marginalized. That this narration of "subaltern pasts" through this sensitive modernist aesthetics has been predominantly done by women writers like Shashi Deshpande and Sunetra Gupta, however, is hardly coincidental. Within this feminist tradition of postcolonial modernist fiction, I'd like to argue, lie the unique power of its epiphanies, its ineluctable modality of otherness.

Works Cited

Berman, Jessica (2002) "Ethical Folds". Paper delivered at Modernist Studies Association Conference, Madison, WI.

Chakrabarty, Dipesh (2000) *Provincializing Europe*. Princeton: Princeton UP.

Chatterjee, Partha (1993) *The Nation and Its Fragments*. Princeton: Princeton UP.

Chaudhuri, Amit (2001) *The Picador Book of Modern Indian Literature*. London: Picador.

Derrida, Jacques (1977) *Of Grammatology*. Trans. Gayatri Chakravarty Spivak. Baltimore: Johns Hopkins UP.

Deshpande, Shashi (1983) *Roots and Shadows*. Hyderababd: Sangam Books.

_______ (1988) *That Long Silence*. London: Virago Press.

Jameson, Fredric (1986) "Third World Literature in the Era of Multinational Capital". *Social Text*, Fall 1986, pp. 65-88.

Gupta, Sunetra (1992) *Memories of Rain*. London: Phoenix House.

_______ (1993) *The Glassblower's Breath*. New York: Grove Press.

_______ (1999) *A Sin of Colour*. London: Phoenix House.

Lal, P. (1996) *The Alien Insiders*. Calcutta: Writers' Workshop.

Rao, Raja (1977) *Kanthapura*. Westport, Conn.: Greenwood Press.

2

Imagery of Goddess in Gita Mehta's *A River Sutra*: A Feminist Approach

— Madhuri Bite

The Narmada River, with its banks flooded with religious activity, is the setting for Gita Mehta's *A River Sutra*. Mehta centres her story on a guesthouse manager, who feeling that he is rather pious in his religious beliefs, is confronted with many stories of other people's experience. The manager, throughout the course of the novel, written in English for a broad audience, undertakes a spiritual journey that does not end where he wishes. These stories make the manager question his own religious beliefs. The imagery surfaces in different forms, such as a young girl. Through unfolding the manager's religious doubts, the Goddess emerges as a symbol as a form of cultural analysis. Also, feminist critiques of power struggles and religious symbolism as a form of agency within literature will be discussed.

River, Story and Imagery

The Goddess imagery of *A River Sutra* is complex and permeates the tale. The story is centred on the banks of the Narmada River, a holy site in India, which many people claim to be a manifestation of the Goddess. Many rivers in India are imbued with this aspect. Anne Feldhaus discusses the numerous religious meanings of rivers in Water and Womanhood. Within her study she identifies festivals and worship, such as iconography devoted to rivers in India (1995, 51-53).

The Narmada River is the first introduction of Goddess imagery within the novel, and the river is very significant to the manager. The manager perceives himself to be a very devout believer in his own faith but has tremendous curiosity about the religious experiences of those around him. Every morning he meditates looking at the river, which is very holy to him and has become a cornerstone of his faith. To the Hindus, the river is considered, and is worshipped, as the daughter of Lord Shiva. People, who have searched for the solace of the river or to study it, tell stories to the manager. All of these stories begin to shape the man's character and make him question himself to the point of doubt. Stories of desire perplex the manager as he learns of the story of a young man, Nitin Bose, who is consumed by passions for one woman who ultimately takes his soul.

The manager is asked to care of Bose by the man's father, who is a friend of the manager. He is perplexed by the man's state. He is crazed and delusional, though he manages to give the manager an account of what has happened to him (Mehta 109-120). Though the job Nitin Bose has taken on a tea plantation is well paid, the location takes him far from friends and the city life that he once enjoyed. Nitin Bose has grown weary of the consuming lifestyle he has become accustomed to, of drinking and womanizing. He feels empty and expresses the need for solitude (Mehta 110-125).

Amid these feelings of weariness about his own situation the beginning of many nightly visits by a young girl occur. She first appears nameless but beautiful, and he enjoys many nights of carnal pleasure with her. His doubt disappears as he is consumed by lust for her. Bose becomes happier and no longer has trouble with his work or late night thoughts of uncertainty. He likens her to the Goddess, for her beauty and his own desire to make more of their nightly sexual liaisons. He romanticizes their relationship, especially centring himself on his own experience, such as how she has bewitched him. She tells him her name is

Rima along with folklore from her village. These stories fascinate him, though he does not take them seriously, or as a means of communication. He feels that she told him these stories for his own amusement alone (Mehta 124-125).

Upon receiving a new assignment away from the plantation he is deeply saddened about leaving his temptress. When he tells her of his news she immediately becomes renounced of her Goddess status. She cries and begs to be taken with him. Becoming an ordinary girl, Bose feels that she has even lost some of her beauty, which had for some time been the centre of his thoughts. The Goddess is transformed into an ordinary plantation worker, with her own problems, such as the desire to marry him. He leaves and is saddened by his unproblematic ability and his own need to leave her (Mehta 126-130). However, he has slight feelings of shame about the way he left her, without a farewell. He returns to the plantation in the hopes of reaching a resolution with the woman and relieving his own guilt. But she does not return to see him that night.

His feelings toward her as a Goddess temptress fades, and he feels that there exists some dignity in the way she is handling the situation, showing he still has feelings of awe about her. He relates her behaviour "...which seemed so elegant in someone of her origins." (Mehta 132). The next night is felt by the villagers of the plantation to be an unholy night. Bose is told to take care as his soul can be taken if he leaves the safety of his house. Though many times in the story he tries to reconcile his own religious background with his modernity, he does not believe in the superstitions of the villagers. His purpose is to meet the woman and then go on with his life (Mehta 132-137).

It is on this night that he hears a woman calling his name outside. Ignoring the tribal taboo on leaving his bedroom, he quickly follows the voice into the woods. He runs fast after the voice until he hears a loud sound, as if two coconut halves have been placed together quickly and he falls to the ground. He hears the same voice of the woman he has wronged, but he cannot understand what she says (Mehta 132-137). "There was a noise of something being clapped over something else, like two books slapped together. As I heard that sound I felt the air being sucked out of my lungs." (Mehta 133). Rima has taken his soul and leaves him feeling empty. He returns to his room and quickly writes down his experience, so as to explain himself before madness hits him. He then searches the countryside in the hope of finding a cure for his madness (Mehta 143-148). He learns of Narmada's ability to help people who believe in the Goddess, which brings him to the manager. This touches upon the holiness of the river (Feldhaus 1995, 160-165). Upon reading the account, the manager is confounded. He does not believe, as do the tribal communities around him, that a person can be healed in such a way.

However, upon journeying out to the countryside Bose returns with his sanity intact and thanks the manager for being so understanding. He leaves the manager with doubt about his own assumptions, for he cannot believe the change that has come over Bose. Confused, he does not know what to believe. However his experiences with Nitin Bose are set aside when he reconciles his feelings toward the situation. He dismisses the event as ridiculous. His faith is never reinforced by the others' experiences with the Goddess; he is only repelled by their lack of self-control. In his case he negates his story as nonsense, not believing that a shrine to the Goddess on the river will save him, though his own religious beliefs are centred on the holiness of the river (Mehta 143-148).

Quickly after the manger's experiences with Bose he meets a young girl at a local spiritual area. He is taken aback by her ugliness, especially by his lack of control of his own disgust. He has prided himself in having more control over his own emotions. He is fascinated by her and provokes her to tell him her story (Mehta 201- 203).

The woman was raised in the family of a famous musician. Upon realizing that her ugliness has set her apart from society, her father, who has never taken a student, teaches his daughter. She excels as a musician. Later her father is propositioned by a young man to teach him. The father acquiesces, only if the man marries his daughter. He agrees without meeting her but is soon repelled by her ugliness (Mehta 203-225). The daughter is wounded by her father's designs. She has fallen in love with the musician upon first sight, but because of her ugliness she feels unworthy of his love. Despite her dejected feelings she begins to practise with him and her father daily. They find solace in each other from her father's callousness as a teacher. She has always felt the spirituality attached to the music she plays and soon passes these feelings of reverence to the student. In return she believes that he might have fallen in love with her (Mehta 220-225).

At a festival to Shiva, the famous musician plays for an assembled audience. However, this year he lets his two students play to fulfil his vow of offering his daughter to music as a bride. The young man and she play together, and she feels bliss. She feels as if they have transformed into Parvati and Shiva. This symbolism shows how she has accepted in her heart that he actually would want to marry her and that they would be happy. It also characterizes the feelings of spirituality that she possesses for her music. Released from his own vow of making her a bride to music, the musician frees the man of his vow to marry his daughter.

The girl is heartbroken. Though she feels their connection within the music as a conjoined couple, her own feelings of ineptitude, due to her outward appearance, surfaces Nevertheless the man stops saying that he would return and make her his bride (Mehta 225). However, this is not to be. He declines their marriage as soon as his lessons are finished. The daughter no longer wishes to play, for her heart has been broken, and she feels as if her father has not protected her. She has been transformed into a longing Parvati. She longs to be a wife, like Parvati, and to find love but feels cursed for she has been denied it. The manager is troubled by this story for he feels such pity for the girl, and she cannot find a solution to her feelings (Mehta 226-228). Though his faith has been repeatedly called into question throughout the other stories the musician affects him seriously. He is unsure of feelings, despite the fact that he knows these feelings are negative. He goes to a friend to try to explain his melancholy and find a reprieve (Mehta 228).

In the hope of showing his friend a more merciful side of life, Tariq Mia begins to tell the manager of Naga Baba. The importance of the relationship of the Narmada River with the people who surround the banks is demonstrated through the story of Naga Baba and his disciple Uma. Having arrived at a whorehouse for alms on the night of Shiva, Naga Baba, an ascetic and worshipper of Shiva, finds Uma enslaved there at a very young age. Feeling pity for the girl he instructs the Madame to give her to him, which she does out of fear. Naga Baba proceeds to raise Uma, whom he names in honour of the Goddess, and teaches her songs of Shiva. He becomes her guardian and raises her in accordance with his ascetic lifestyle. He teaches her how to read and write. At night he sings to her songs of the Narmada, which would serve her later in life (Mehta 255-257).

Toward the end of the story the reader discovers the Goddess imagery has woven itself together to symbolize the characteristics of Uma and the Narmada. It is said that the Narmada was created as an act of Shiva's penance. Uma too is given this meaning for Naga Baba by a temple priest who tells the story. She is given as a form of penance by the head of the whorehouse to Naga Baba, so as not to incur his wrath. Both Uma and the Narmada are intertwined, due to Uma's religious connection to the river. She becomes the embodiment of the Goddess for her faith and her dedication to the river and its traditions. Her songs and religious reverence of the river begin to symbolize the nature of the river to those who worship the Narmada. Mehta uses Uma and the Narmada as symbolism for each other. They are both given attributes of the Goddess, through names, stories and the amount of worship that they engender. Though Uma is a personification of the Goddess, the Goddess is always a living force within the novel, as the Narmada. Just as Shiva bore the weight of his penance by creating the Narmada, so does Uma bear the weight of transmitting this religious purpose (Mehta 257-258). They become a part of each other. This is symbolized with Uma's immersion into the Narmada on her first night with Naga Baba. "Suddenly he gripped her arms and lowered her into the water. 'The Narmada claims all girls as hers. Tonight you become a daughter of the Narmada'" (Mehta 254). This event shows the power of the Goddess as a religious entity. She has the power to affiliate other females to herself, and is perceived as having the agency to do so.

Though Uma represents Naga Baba's "fruits of austerity", she also begins to generate her own holiness. With the songs of tribute she has learned about the Narmada she becomes a wandering minister at its banks when Naga Baba moves on to other stages of his journey to enlightenment (Mehta 257-258). The manager is left with renewed faith in his position. The austere lifestyle of Naga Baba makes him feel rejuvenated. He soon begins to have an obsession with Uma. He feels that his spirituality would be restored if he could hear her songs of the Narmada. Uma has begun to personify the Goddess to the overseer (Mehta 260). At the same time an archeologist and his crew overrun the bungalow that the overseer manages. They are doing a study of the spiritual history of the Narmada.

Having attached his ego to the holy Narmada the overseer feels overjoyed by their enthusiasm for the river. He also begins to enjoy their company, realizing that his solitude has left him lonely. He asks the archaeologist if he has heard of the minstrels who live on the banks of the Narmada. He said he has. The overseer asks him to notify him of their location so he can hear them sing (Mehta 206-261). The following day a minstrel appears singing in praise of the Narmada. This makes the manager overjoyous, and he feels his faith completely renewed by this holy experience. It seems as if the Goddess of the river has come to life in her song, and the manager knows in his heart that he was wrong to doubt his choice in life which is to devote himself to his worship of the river (Mehta 277-280).

Ripped from his renewed feelings of holiness he hears the archaeologist refer to the singer as Uma. From their familiarity he begins to doubt again. He asks the archeologist if he is Naga Baba, to which he replies positively. This shatters the overseer for Naga Baba's austerity has begun to be a cornerstone of his renewed faith. The overseer begins flooding him with questions. Naga Baba's answers infuriates the overseer. He tells him that he decided to leave has meditation, but he cannot give him details. The archeologist tells him that everyone's experiences are different and that he is only sure of his own experiences in life when the overseer asks him what is to become of him. Quickly, the archaeologist leaves the overseer dejected and in perpetual doubt (Mehta 281-282).

Uma and Naga Baba have replaced the pillars of his faith, especially through Uma's representation of the Goddess. Their respect for the river, which the hotel overseer shares, helps him identify with them. Upon hearing their faith is not what he has imagined, he is once again cast into doubt, which has been growing since the beginning of the novel. In the end he is left with his faith close to destruction. However his lack of conviction in his own faith of the river and the Goddess seems to be the result of his lack of spirituality. He needs other people very much, though he is slowly trying to become a renunciate. As is the goal of most householding men in Indian society, they plan to devote their later life to religious reflection and seclusion. However, his goal as a renunciate is marred by his need to have his faith constantly renewed. Without others around him this will not happen. Mehta uses the overseer to show the frailty of people's spirituality and how lack of inner faith can destroy hopes of worship and austerity (Mehta 269-282).

In the end the Goddess is the driving force throughout the novel, mentioned in many forms. The manager bases his life around other people's perceptions of the Goddess and spirituality. With his faith shattered what will become of him? The end of the novel offers no insight into his future but leaves the reader with the knowledge that people still worship the river and the Goddess, as the overseen sits dejected by the river, which is affecting his spirituality once again (Mehta 277-282).

Equally important in the discussion of *A River Sutra* is the strong female attributes given to certain characters in the story. The river is personified as female and a source of immense spiritual power. This power affects everyone in the story (Feldhaus 1995, 51-53). The characters of Rima and Uma both defy perceptions of femininity, while simultaneously encapsulating gender roles. In many ways Rima is shown as a feminist character. She is a tribal woman. Due to this she can be regarded by a caste-conscious Hindu to be outside of civilization. Therefore she is not controlled by patriarchal norms. She takes control of her own sexuality, initiating sex, which, as R.P. Sharma suggests, is anti-ethical to the traditional way women are portrayed in Indian literature (138-139). Subsequently she is not punished for taking control of her own sexual desires. Instead she is revered and given Goddess-like qualities. She is even worshiped by her sexual partner. She uses her sexuality as a means of getting what she desires, instead of being ashamed of it or trying to conform to traditional modes, as a wife and mother. When scorned she does not lie down and accept her abuse. She resorts to stealing his soul, returning to her Goddess status by her ability to control Bose (Clinton 100-104). This is symbolized by her supernatural powers that are accentuated by her ability to use them to get what she desires.

She displays this power as Bose finds her on his return to the plantation. "'You will never leave me now, no matter how far you go,' she said triumphantly, waving her trophy in front of me. It was a coconut... Picking up her lantern she disappeared into the jungle" (Mehta 134). On the other hand Uma, though forced to become unchaste at a very young age, is revered for her holiness and is also attributed with Goddess features. Her faith in the river and her ability to transcend gender roles due to this holiness personifies her as part of the power of the river. She becomes a very powerful symbol who can make her own destiny. She is not looked down upon for her past as a child prostitute, and she is revered (Feldhaus 42-47).

Uma's role as a prostitute can be viewed differently through a feminist lens. Shalini Shah states that femininity is directly affected by how women's sexuality is socially perceived (57-58). Though Uma is given a forced sexuality as a child prostitute she is quickly removed from that environment and placed within a genderless relationship with an aesthetic. Her prostitution makes her polluted, so she is set apart from society. This further enables her to enter a religious life with Naga Baba. Thus her forced sexuality can become her liberation from societal cruelties placed on her due to her gender (54-58). Again both characters use their abject status to achieve a new identity. The identity they gain is set apart from normative roles of gender division, such as women relegated to the home as protector (Bow 42). This identity is perceived through a religious viewpoint. This viewpoint uses the image of the Goddess to show the metamorphosis of the characters as well as other characters in the story.

Criticisms

Many authors have written about Mehta's works. Her work in *A River Sutra* is held by many to bring an Indian perspective closer to other countries. Merle Rubin states in his works that there is something for everyone, including every religion (10). C.N. Ramachandran and A. G. Kahn compare this novel to *The*

Canterbury Tales remarking how each tale goes against others, but how each is meant to teach the reader something, in this case about religion (1-15). Marlene Fisher feels that it is a good book for everyone to read due to its dealings with various religions (214). In the end the criticisms denote that the religious nature of the books enhances the readers' experience and knowledge.

Conclusion

In conclusion the use of Goddess imagery with *A River Sutra* is used as a cultural agent and as a form of analysis. The spiritual journey of the manager emerges as filled with an urgency and doubt. He however continues to be imbued with many visions of the Goddess that he cannot resolve with his growing lack of faith. He reaches this impasse through other people's lives, their narratives to him. The Narmada, the main focus of the Goddess within the story, is the centre where many different forms of religious expression can be scrutinized and called into question. Mehta's characters, through the Goddess imagery attached to them, such as Uma and Rima, are given a certain agency that can be looked at through a feminist lens. Uma and Rima become powerful characters that transcend normative modes of behaviour. When this behaviour is changed they are themed with the Goddess imagery, such as the power to entice and beauty. Due to these factors the Goddess imagery within this story helps to illustrate the religious discovery of the manager.

Works Cited

Bow, Leslie. Betrayal and Other acts of Subversion: Feminism, Sexual Politics, *Asian American Women Literature*. Princeton: Princeton University Press, 2001.

Feldhaus, Anne. *Water and Womanhood: Religious Meanings of Rivers in Maharashtra*. Oxford: Oxford University Press, 1995.

_______ (Ed.). *Images of Women in Maharashtrian Literature and Religion*. New York, State University of New York Press, 1996.

Fisher, Marlene. Review of A River Sutra by Gita Mehta. *World Literature Today* 68, no. 1, 1994: 214.

Mehta, Gita. *A River Sutra.* New York: Vintage Books, 1993.

Ramachandra, C.N. and A.G. Kahn. "Gita Mehta's A River Sutra: Two Views." *Literary Criterion* 29, no. 3 (1994): 1-15.

Rubin, Merle. A Review of *A River Sutra* by Gita Mehta. *Christian Science Monitor* 85, no. 152, July 1993:10.

Seely, Clinton B. (Ed.). *Women Politics, and Literature in Bengal.* Michigan, Asian Studies Center, Michigan State University, 1981.

Shah, Shalini. *The Making of Womanhood: Gender Relations in the Mahabharata.* New Delhi: Manohar Publishers, 1995.

Sharma, R.P. *Woman in Hindu Literature.* New Delhi: Gyan Publishing House, 1995.

3

An Ecocritical Reading of Amitav Ghosh's *The Hungry Tide*

— Sophia Jaychandran

The Hungry Tide by Amita Ghosh narrates a very contemporary story of adventure and improbable love, identity and history, set in one of the most beguiling regions on the earth. Off the easternmost coast of India, in the Bay of Bengal, lies the colossal network of infinitesimal islands known as the Sundarbans. For settlers here, life is awfully hazardous as attacks by deadly tigers are common. Apart from that, turbulence and expulsion are a matter of relentless fear. Without warning, at any time, tidal floods rise and surge over the land, leaving devastation in their wake.

In this place of vengeful beauty, the lives of three people from different worlds collide. Piyali Roy is a young marine biologist, of Indian descent but stubbornly American, in search of a rare, endangered river dolphin, *Orcaella brevirostris.* Her journey commences on an ominous note as she is thrown from a boat into crocodile-infested waters. A young, illiterate fisherman, Fokir rescues her in the nick of time. Although they have no language between them for communication, both Piya and Fokir are impressively drawn to each other, sharing a mystifying impulse for the ways of the sea. Piya connects with Fokir to help with her research and finds a translator in Kanai Dutt, a businessman from Delhi whose idealistic aunt Nilima and uncle Nirmal are longtime settlers in the Sundarbans. As the three of them embark onto the convoluted backwaters, they are drawn unawares into the mysterious undercurrents of this remote world, where political mayhem demands a personal toll that is every bit as forceful as the devastating tide.

Already an international success, *The Hungry Tide* published in the year 2004 is a prophetic novel of remarkable insight, beauty and humanity.

Ecocriticism has emerged as a contemporary trend in the world of literary criticism. It is a form of literary criticism based on an ecological perspective. Ecocriticism investigates the relation between humans and the natural world in literature. The ways in which environmental issues, cultural issues concerning the environment and attitudes towards nature are presented and analyzed. One of the main goals in ecocriticism is to study how individuals in society behave and react in relation to nature and ecological aspects. This form of criticism has gained a lot of attention during recent years (approximately since 2000) due to higher social emphasis on environmental destruction and increased technology. It is hence a fresh way of analyzing and interpreting literary texts, which brings new dimensions to the field literary criticism. The approach in which environmental issues relate to cultural, and the way in which attitudes towards nature are presented and analyzed is the heart of eco criticism.

Greg Garrard has this to say:

> ......environmental problems require analysis in cultural as well as scientific terms, because they are outcome of an interaction between ecological knowledge of nature and its cultural inflection. This will involve inter-disciplinary scholarship that draws on literary and cultural theory, philosophy, sociology, psychology and environmental history, as well as ecology. The study of rhetoric supplies us with a model of a cultural reading practice tied to moral and political concerns and one which is alert to both the real or literal and the figural or constructed interpretations of 'nature' and the 'environment'. Breaking these monolithic concepts into key structuring metaphors, or tropes, enables attention to be paid to

> the thematic, historical and geographical particularities of environmental discourse, and reveals that any environmental tropes susceptible to appropriation and deployment in the service of a variety of potentially conflicting interests. Ecocriticism makes it possible to analyze critically the tropes brought into play in environmental debate, and, more tentatively, to predict which will have a desired effect on a specific audience at a given historical juncture.
>
> (Garrard 14)

The paper investigates how unrefined environmental preservation policies, ignoring the material reality of a landscape are disadvantageous to the socially and economically backward classes like indigenous people, forest dwellers, tribals and nomads. The most glaring question that Ghosh poses throughout the novel is the concern of environment and the impoverished people.

Kusum's narration evinces ecological concerns:

> Saar,' she said, wiping her face, 'the worst part was not the hunger or the thirst. It was to sit here, helpless, and listen to the policemen making their announcements, hearing them say that our lives, our existence, was worth less than dirt or dust. This island has to be saved for its trees, it has to be saved for its animals, it is a part of a reserve forest, it belongs to a project to save tigers, which is paid for by people from all around the world. Every day, sitting here, with hunger gnawing at our bellies, we would listen to these words, over and over again. Who are these people, I wondered, who love animals so much that they are willing to kill us for them? Do they know what is being done in their names? Where do they live, these people, do they have children, do they have mothers, fathers? As I thought of these things, it seemed to that this whole world has become a place of animals, and our fault, our crime, was that we were just human beings, trying to live as human beings always have, from the water and the soil. No human being could think this is a crime unless they have forgotten that this is how humans have always lived – by fishing, by clearing land and by planting the soil.
>
> (Ghosh 261-262)

These lines enhance the fictional and factual roots of the discord in *The Hungry Tide*. As the novel focuses on the socioenvironmental politics of the environmental conservation drive instituted by the state, it also gives voice to the challenging claims of human and non-human species for survival. Issues of mutual intrusion and the politics therein are fictionalized to bring to light the disturbed conscience of many a post-colonial conventional ethic. In locating the novel in this interstitial space of struggle between species conservation and the dispossession of the indigenous poor, in the midst of an unpredictable and hazardous setting as the Sundarbans, the conflict pitting man against nature and man against man plays out with unmitigated power and force.

Glen Love remarks,

> At the beginning of the third millennium and of a new century often heralded as "the century of the environment", a coherent and broadly based movement embracing literary-environmental interconnections, commonly termed as "ecocriticism" is emerging. Environmental and population pressures inevitably and increasingly support the position that any literary criticism which purports to deal with social and physical reality will encompass ecological considerations.
>
> (Love 1)

This paper brings to light the ecopolitical and ecosocial issues that the novel addresses in the milieu of the contemporary historical and social events decisive in shaping the conservation policies of the Sundarbans. The Sundarbans is the world's largest mangrove forest area, situated in the delta where the three rivers Ganges, Brahmaputra and the Meghna meet the sea. It covers an area of 10,000 square kilometres sprawling across India and Bangladesh. The Indian fraction of the Sundarbans was declared a Tiger Reserve in 1973, a National Park in 1984, World Heritage Site in 1985 and a Biosphere Reserve in 1989. It is also the habitat of the largest number of tigers living in the world. The Indian and the Bangladeshi parts of the Sundarbans together have a human population of more than seven million. In locating his account in this effervescent setting, Ghosh opens up various questions pertaining to ecological conservation – species extinction, ecological conservation, ecotourism, environmental economics, environmental policies of the state and so on.

The Sundarbans is a topography that emerges and submerges in a continuous interplay between and the sea. Islands appear and disappear in the span of a few hours with every turn of the tide, vacillating between being a safe abode or a threatening presence for its inhabitants. Stories of people drowned in the tide or fallen prey to the wild beasts of the forests, of the weird qualities of the wildlife, like the man-eating habitat of the Sundarbans tiger are all ascribed to the distinctiveness of the tide country. In this sense, both history and geography of the Sundarbans for both man and beast are infact shaped and restructured by the ebb and flow of the tide. The beauty of the Sundarbans is recorded in Nirmal's diary read by Kanai.

> There are no borders here to divide fresh water from salt, river from sea. The tides reach as far as three hundred kilometers inland and every day thousands of acres of forest disappear underwater only to re-emerge hours later. The currents are so powerful as to reshape the islands almost daily – some days the water tears away entire promontories and peninsulas; at other times it throws up new shelves and sandbanks where there none before.
>
> When the tides create new land, overnight mangroves begin to gestate, and if the conditions are right they can spread so fast as to cover a new island within a few short years. A mangrove forest is a universe unto itself, utterly unlike other woodlands or jungles. There are no towering, vine-looped trees, no ferns, no wildflowers, no chattering monkeys or cockatoos. Mangrove leaves are tough and leathery, the branched gnarled and the foliage often impassably dense. Visibility is short and the air still and fetid. At no moment can human beings have any doubt of the terrain's utter hostility to their presence, of its cunning and resourcefulness, of its determination to destroy or expel them. Every year dozens of people perish in the embrace of that dense foliage, killed by tigers, snakes and crocodiles.
>
> (Ghosh 7-8)

Nirmal's journals read by Kanai at intervals indicate the appetite for revolution. Fokir, the illiterate fisherman who saves Piya's life twice and guides Piya and Kanai through the perilous canals in search of the dolphins, is portrayed as the most deprived individual, susceptible to both the natural hazards and the oppression of an overbearing bureaucratic system. Though superstitious, he is a dependable guide. Piya and Kanai both depend on Fokir for their safety and security in the Sundarbans. The portrayal of the indigenous communities by Amitav Ghosh deserves appreciation. The indigenous communities in the Sundarbans have their own rules and beliefs governing their access and use of the forests. Cultural discourses are integral to their existence. Oral narratives in the form of myths and folklore, rituals, customs and conventions facilitate a symbiotic relationship between man and nature.

The novel does not fail to delineate the anomalous state-sponsored conservation policy for the Sundarbans that disregards the social and economic factors. The Morichjhanpi (1978-79), when the newly elected CPI (M) government of West Bengal forcibly evicted thousands of Bengali refugees who had settled on the island, forms a background for some parts of the novel. The novel explores topics like humanism and environmentalism, especially when they come into a conflict of interest with each other. Ecological issues frame a major portion of the novel. Nirmal's diary becomes a significant document that showcases the picturesque islands in its pristine form. Here is an account of the description:

> There is no prettiness here to invite the stranger in: yet, to the world at large this archipelago is known as "the Sundarban", which means, "the beautiful forest". There are some who believe the word to be derived from the name of a common species of mangrove – the *sundari* tree, *Hereteria minor*. But the word's origin is no easier to account for than its present prevalence, for in the record books of the Mughal emperors this region is named not in reference to a tree but to a tide – *bhati.*and to the inhabitants of the islands this land is known as *bhatirdesh* – the tide country – except that *bhati* is not just the "tide" but one tide in particular, the ebb-tide, the *bhata.* This is a land half-submerged at high tide: it is only in *falling*

> that the water gives birth to the forest. To look upon this strange parturition, midwived by the moon, is to know why the name "tide country" is not just right but necessary.
>
> (Ghosh 8)

The thematic concerns of the novel also revolve around an issue of global dimension. The novel forges a prominent concern about the survival of an ecologically balanced labyrinth like the Sundarbans. At the same time, the novel documents the pitiable plight of the impoverished and homeless refugees in their fertile surroundings to ensure their survival. Now, the task lies with people like Piyali, Kanai and Mashima who devote their lives to create bearable living conditions for the original people of the Sundarbans.

The plot structure reveals itself as multiple-layered depicting the various characters' relationships as they develop. Most striking is the Piyali-Fokir relationship implanted in the natural world of water and islands that is juxtaposed by local myths and legends. Both motifs are intertwined in a text that forms part of, as much as it contributes to issues of eco-literature, a new kind of writing that has evolved in recent years and has been met with increased attention by writers and readers. *The Hungry Tide* thus points towards a new direction in Indian English fiction which in the past has paid but scant attention to nature and instead has privileged topics pertinent to the urbanized middle-class of the big cities. The vast and fragile ecosystem of the mangrove forests is home to a variety of rare flora and fauna and the inferences in the novel are a testament to that.

Works Cited

Garrard, Greg. *Ecocriticism*. New York: Routledge, 2004.

Ghosh, Amitav. *The Hungry Tide.* Noida: HarperCollins Publishers Limited, 2004.

Love, Glen. A. *Practical Ecocriticism: Literature, Biology and the Environment.* Virginia: University of Virginia Press, 2003.

4

Women's Empowerment and Personal Mobility in the Novels of Shashi Deshpande and Nayantara Sahgal

— Grishma Manikrao Khobragade

Indian Independence produced radical and lasting changes in Indian social and cultural life. Besides new technology, knowledge, institutions, beliefs and values also dominated the Indian social minds. Subsequently, many cultural practices changed slowly and they started acting as a barrier to successful social adjustment.

Contemporary Indian English novels portray images of protagonists confined to rigid tradition and orthodoxy. The novels produced after independence show that the Western culture has been partly assimilated by Indians. Post-Independence Indian society also witnessed a new social and economic empowerment of women coming into existence. It was also to see the emergence of new patterns of class structure and the formation of new communities, i.e., educated women community according to the changing patterns of life.

Up to the end of the eighteenth century, England was an agricultural country. England was subsequently on the way to industrialization and there was a lot of improvement in the methods of production. The population of the towns increased with the migrants from villages thronging the towns in search of job opportunities. It resulted in the creation of a new social order – labour class and capitalist.

India too had a similar developmental phase. Although some of the class barriers have broken down in this country, it is a mistake to think that India is classless society. Social change takes many forms and each change in the structure and function of a society has effects on other aspects of the society. Thus urbanization and industrialization have affected the patterns of social class as well as those of living and working condition. The increase in population in this period, the improvement in working conditions and the growth of trade unions has all changed pattern of social behaviour.

The present study makes an attempt to read certain selected novels of Shashi Deshpande and Nayantara Sahagal with the objective of locating the class and community structures embedded in them. It also tries to detect the class interest of the perspective that travels along her narratives as the point of view. The study is based on the hypothesis that novelist's novels reveal her views and opinions on empowerment of women community and personal mobility. The basic methodology used in the study is those of analytical study wherein fiction is considered as valuable social document and by analyzing fiction, social structures too are analyzed. The scope of this study is the possibility of using the same parameters in analyzing the works of various other Indian English novelists and in making the study of literature an interdisciplinary exercise.

Shashi Deshpande's fiction focuses on a real-life situation of society. Her description of person of one class assimilating into another class is a realistic picture of modern urban society and cross-cultural social realities. She acknowledges that higher class and lower class or male or female gender can come together and they are closely interdependent. She has presented a variety of such images in *The Dark Holds No Terrors (*1980*).*

This novel is about the homecoming of Saru, the protagonist. In this novel, Saru, a successful married doctor, rejects her husband, Manohar. She returns to her father's home after 15 years. By doing so, she tries the gap between herself and her father.

This novel is also concerned with the suffering of the modern educated Indian woman who is in search of her individuality. Saru, who is such a woman, also tries to fight from the constraints of caste-based traditional social system.

Sarita is a successful, well settled doctor. Her husband Manohar is an English teacher in college. She has two children. But she is not happy with her married life. Saru had left her parents in a fit of anger to get married to her lover. The novel opens with Saru returning after 15 years to her father's house. She had decided never to return but she has to change her mind with her mother's death. This homecoming gives her a chance to think about her past. The novel explores the various dimension of middle class family life and the liability which controls a woman's conduct and responsibility.

Saru is the narrator of the novel. She remembers her childhood experiences and her stay in her father's home gives Saru an opportunity to re-assess her relationship with her father, her dead mother, her dead brother, Dhruva and her children Renu and Abhi. She finds that Father lives along with Madhav. She tries to understand herself and others by redefining her relations. This makes her mentally strong to face realities. The darkness no longer holds any terror and Saru is highly self-determined and she discards traditional rules. She rejects her mother to become a doctor; she rejects caste to marry outside; and defies social limitation by using Boozie, her friend, to advance her career. These moves are possible for her because she is economically independent and it gives her courage to take an action against social system. Saru wants to become self-sufficient and her every effort in life is towards this goal. When Saru earns Manu's love, she feels that it is her great achievement. However, she is not a passive woman. However, she always tries to prove her individuality as a doctor. While Manu is anxious, Saru is aware of the facts of life. She observes: "And yet we stayed physically apart It's my painful middle-class inhibitions, I told myself, making marriage the open sesame of all enjoyment for me."(40)

Saru is interested in improving her financial and social status. She does not like to live a life of common person. When she realizes the inequality of success between herself and her husband is the cause of domestic squabbles. She marries him only when she thinks that he would consider her to be equal. She is also self-centered. She always tries to build up her self-image, so much so that she forces him to surrender his ego before her. She nullifies Manu's existence and makes him a cipher. She thinks that all the men are weak and inferior. Her profession makes her conscious of her self sufficient status and she learns to command the others.

Saru has a very gracious and receptive but very cautious personality. She lacks confidence as a middle class woman. She knows her limitations and abilities. She is ready to overcome strict traditional, social limitations and accept new modern vision wherein all are equal. She develops a sense of self-image and cultivates self-confidence. She understands herself without exaggeration and without underestimation. The manner in which she behaves, communicates and relates with others, reflects her personality and upbringing. Society, education, peer group interaction, mental and every physical characteristic add to her personality, sometimes positively, sometimes negatively. Her behaviour is not only governed by base instincts, but by higher motives or values. She rejects her father's home and her search leads her to realize the potential in human life. She wants to be free person and wants to prove her independent identity in society. She says:

> "My life is my own..." Somehow, she felt as if she had found it now, the connecting link. It means you are not just a strutting, grimacing puppet, standing futilely on the stage for a brief while between areas of darkness. If I have been a puppet, it is because I made myself one. I have been clinging to tenuous shadow of a marriage whose substance has long since disintegrated because I have been afraid of proving my mother right. (220)

Saru's love for power can be acknowledged with her relationship with every character in the novel. She thinks that she may be responsible for all happenings. She says: "The helplessness of trying to go back into that time, that state of mind, trying to be definite about what I did and why."(184)

She celebrates her children's birthday party and games. When Saru goes away to her father's house, she remembers the need of her children. Yet, Saru is in favour of family planning. She says: "One boy and one girl. A family the right size. The right kind. Like the ads. A happy family. Healthy, happy, smiling and in colour" (20). Saru is also realistic. She believes that. Family planning is connected to liberation, empowerment of women, and with social and gender equality.

Saru makes efforts to raise her dignity and image in society. She realizes that her basic drive is the greed for money. Saru resorts to hard work and makes effective use of her skill to earn money. She recalls her frugal life:

> It is a marvel how we managed to live. Manu's salary, never very much, barely covered our expenses. And for two years I was earning nothing. At first it didn't matter that I was out of all the things that were so much a part of student life—the parties, the eating out, the movies, casual trips. (92)

Saru who has a healthy personality approaches situations with a rational attitude, accepting them. She knows that success comes only with hard work and strives for long-term gains rather than immediate pleasure. She accepts her drawbacks and improves those in which she is the strongest. She lives in the present, and does not turn back to the past. Saru is self-governed and is independent in her thoughts and action. She keeps her emotions under control and doses not harm herself. She is able to meet frustrations without conflicts. She also develops tolerance towards stress, anxiety, depression, pain and emotional disturbance.

Saru also sets realistic goals. She acquires the knowledge, skill and qualification to reach her goals. She is well organized and consistent. She also makes the best use of their time and effort to achieve her dream. She remembers:

> A year later I was his Registrar. In less than two year I passed my MD. Four years later I was an Assistant Honorary at a suburban hospital. (92)

At the end, she realizes that she has broken her past life and peaceful harmony. She is isolated in her own house. She always feels insecure, alone. She feels herself as homeless.

Saru plays different role at different times – one a successful doctor in a white coat by day and a trapped animal by night. She always depressed in her mind, even though she is a doctor, in the eyes of her husband, she is just a slave. When she has been ill-treated and victimized by her husband, she wants to escape from her house. This is her difficult time when she has to face the inner crisis and conflict. She says:

> a+b they told us in mathematics is equal to b+a.But here a+b was not, definitely not equal to b+a. It became a monstrously unbalanced equation, lopsided, unequal, and impossible. But is that the only reason, or would it have happened in any case, What happened to us later, he being what he is and I being what I am? I have a feeling I will never know the answer to that one. (42)

Saru represents a middle class girl in a modern Indian social structure. She has been trapped in a conflict between traditional ideas and new. She is brought up in a traditional family. However, her education has changed her attitude towards life. She becomes rebellious towards mindless orthodoxy. However, Saru is self-centred person. In her world, there are only her two children, her home, her practice, and her patients. Her circle of interest is very limited. Manu, her husband is out of her circle. She is responsible for her own critical situation. Saru is very professional. She tells Manu:

> You want clothes, good food, lots of books and magazines, movie and plays, the best cigarettes. And do you get. All that without money? (152)

Saru gives preference to her job not for her family. She is first a doctor, then a wife or mother in her image. But because of her profession, she is motivated and has the courage to face her husband. Manu has to face the reality of his failure. Saru tells: "I was too busy, I was too tired, I was too exhilarated with the dignity and importance that my status as a doctor seemed to have given me. (42)

People visit Saru's house for different purposes, which creates a gap between her and her husband Manu. She remembers a leisure time spend in the company of her friend. For her friend, "the only one she knew there treacherously deserted her for others, cousins and closer friend."(47). She had attached herself to one group or another, hoping to be taken for one of them. Groups often develop because the individual members have one or more common characteristics. The members of the group interact and influence each other in collective pursuit of a common goal. The behaviour of each member of a group is influenced by the behaviour of others of the group. Social alliances extend outside the work situation: they can be based on similar age, gender, hobbies, religious or political affiliations. The only time she did belong to a group was when they all gathered together for a meal, a ritual. And then, when it was over, "the crowd dissolved into people who had nothing to do with her, shattering the semblance of belonging, of togetherness." (47)

Saru realizes that her superiority complex is the root cause of her predicament and suffering. At the end of the novel, she receives a letter from Manu. He decides to visit and to get her back home. He tries to compromise and even she is ready to go back. She asks her father, "Baba, if Manu comes tell him to wait. I'll be back as soon as I can" (221). This decision shows that she is psychologically prepared to admit the reality of her life. She emerges as a new different woman who can control herself and ready to surrender before her ego and her negative idea. Saru represents a middle class working person in post-Independence period. She revolts against customs and traditions. She is ready to understand a life outside the family and faces the critical life. She fights to make her free from social tradition and use her womanhood to show her identity and realize her self-image.

Saru is a career-oriented woman whose income and profession status is greater than her husband. Meenakshi Bharat observes:

> This is a gendered imbalance that sits in opposition to the socially prescribed ' right' balance in which the scales of married life are, under ideal conditions, weighted equally by material provision at one end-the male end- emotional provision at the other end- the female end. If the roles are reversed, surely the scales remain balanced; but mathematical equations tend to operate in the field of the ideal, unaffected by the less than ideal conditions of social reality.

Saru is presented an emerging female character. The novel starts with her visiting her father's home after a gap of 15 years. Now she is a well-known reputed established doctor and mother of two children. When she reaches father's house, she gets a cold reception. "She is confused, helpless and almost miserable." (15)

Shashi Deshpande believes that society will not change because men will never give anything to women. It is a desirable social duty of women that they should come forward and bring certain change in themselves to face the ground reality. It is observed that no one comes forward to make other free. Meenakshi Bharati observes:

> I think consumerism is good in one way. You see a TV, you see all those things, and you say I want to have that. And how do you get that if you don't work and your husband alone is earning? You know, my servant who has been working with me for many years, whatever she wants she buys with her own money. She does not wait for her husband to buy it. Therefore, consumerism is going to be good in one way. Because if people want the goods, they'll need their own money. To earn the money they want to

> take up a job. Once you take up a job you become a independent person.

After intercaste marriage with Manu, they live in the room in the chawl and start their married life. But she is not satisfied in this environment and she tries to mobilize her life towards her destination to live in a flat. In the novel, *The Dark Holds No Terrors*, the society presented is in transition. The women who are financially independent have always a choice to enjoy their life with pride.

Shashi Deshpande's Saru, the protagonist, finds her position as a married woman and therefore she has certain limitations. But at the end of the story, the novelist has shown her character at two levels. She is sentimental and emotional: however, she is intellectual. She has to keep on struggling her own battle alone, redefine, and rediscover her life. Vijayalakshmi Sheshadri rightly states:

> This becomes crucial to the characterization of Sarita, who is presented as a woman with tremendous possibilities of movement, which match her desire for new places. In the terminology applied by black feminist critics, she could be described as an 'assimilated heroine' who has gained control over her life, a woman who apparently has combined career and marriage successfully.

Shashi Deshpande depicts a character that is in search of identity. Her characters accept the confined mobility in life. Therefore, Saru compromises with the crucial situation and proves herself as an educated woman. Saru makes her journey to her father's house after 15 years to find her existence. This displacement forces her to think. She is in a dilemma but she controls her life. The status of working woman facilitates her to face the basic needs it adds a new dimension to female mobility. Saru gains her mobility through education.

Saru represents a middle class woman in a present society. She revolts against traditions because of her education but at the end of novel she compromises with the ground reality. Her problem is the problem of educated class. Her job draws her away from her family and from her husband. Deshpande says:

> She knew now it was her middle –class upbringing and ideas that had made her regard an unemployed husband as a nightmare, a horrible humiliation.... when he had managed to get a lecturer's job in a private college. With her hospital pay and his salary, they would manage .But he had not been convinced. (152)

Saru realizes that there is lack of communication with her own children. Jasbir Jain writes about the dilemma of a professional woman who is caught between her family and job:

> Sarita cannot forget her children,or the sick needing her expert attention;and so she decides to face her home again.

However, Saru is neither a committed mother nor a thorough professional. Deshpande observes: "She was not a wife, not a mother, not a professional woman whom others looked up to. She was the wronged child again, the unloved daughter, the scapegoat." (182)

Economic betterment enables peoples to have better living, make the efficient worker and earn more income, more educated, more information and knowledgeable and more courageous to oppose economic and social exploitation. She proves these points. Being educated, Saru is financially independent; her financial position brings security to her. She thinks that it was easier in the past that woman had no other choice. She a model to Manu but later he becomes a cruel man and starts insulting her. every time. She maintains her position in society by acquiring higher education and better quality life. She recalls:

> It was marvel how we managed to live. Manu's salary, never very much, barely covered our expenses. And for two years, was earning nothing. At first it didn't matter that I was out of all the things that were so much a part of student life-the parties the eating out,

> the movies, casual trips...we told each other, would change once I had my degree. (92)

Deshpande's women characters are stronger than they are in real life. She reveals a community of women in their humbleness, nervousness and chaos as observed in a transitional era. Sarbjit K.Sandhu explains the nature of the new class of Deshpande's women, as pinpointed by him:

> The educated women demand more sexual freedom and independence but are not very sure about what they should do with the same, which leads them to a bitter confusion, anxiety and tension.

Deshpande's women characters are not historical or aristocratic but they are common social members. They face reality of their lives and finds individuality. They also define themselves.

Nayantara Sahgal may be called a feminist novelist as she started her literary movement and became popular in India. Her women characters, unlike stereotype women, are intelligent, perceptive, free and expressive, and search for justice, identity and equality with men. These women characters are not satisfied with economic liberty and security. They are strivers and aspirers toward freedom, integrity and a considerate world. The unique virtue of these women characters are a quality of heart and mind. Simrit in *A Day in Shadow*, Rose and Sonali in *Rich Like Us* announce the 'modern woman' in no uncertain terms.

Women characters in the novels of Nayantara Sahgal acquire the strength of the traditional set of values, and rebel against the existing moral codes and social norms which deny the freedom that nourishes the individual self, and paves the way for the realization of one's own creative skills and true potential. These women, being conscious of their emotional and existential needs, refuse to end up as the suffering, and sacrificing lot. They attempt for a change of social order that starves them of individual fulfilment. They long for a sociable atmosphere for self-expression and supportive to self-fulfilment. They try to establish a new social order with changed values where they can be their true selves and where there is no need for hypocrisy. They believe that individual worth is not to be judged by such patriarchal norms as chastity of body but by purity of heart.

One of the early novels of Sahgal, *The Day in Shadow* depicts, the existential, emotional, and materialist struggles of a woman in Indian society when she chooses to dissolve a marriage 17 years old. Simrit finds it impossible to carry on her marital relationship with her husband Som. Once she realizes the lack of loving partnership, intensity, depth, and commitment in their relationship, it is the clash of personalities that prompts their separation. Som's male ego is offended at the surfacing of individuality in Simirit and deliberately plans the "consent terms" to cripple her economically. Simrit feels humiliated. She feels herself to have been reduced just to a beast of burden, an "over-loaded donkey... with its back breaking, and no one doing anything about it, not because they can't see it, but because it's a donkey and loads are for donkeys." (p.56) and "may be she had always been an animal, only a nice, obedient, domestic one, sitting on a cushion, doing as she was old. And in return she had been fed and sheltered" (p.57)

The suffering which Simrit undergoes at this point, after her divorce, she is a representative of the predicament of any woman. Nayantara Sahgal confesses that:

> In this book, I tried to figure out something that had happened to me- the shattering experience of divorce. I wanted to show how even in a free country like ours, where women are equal citizens; a woman can be criminally exploited without creating a ripple.

Simrit's efforts to fight against the callous world and against the laws which see no reason and the insensitive neglect of her children, powerfully portray the existential struggle of an individual against the hostile surroundings. With her strength of mind to overcome depression and dejection. She represents a "liberated" woman who has the courage to break a long and suitable relationship when it turns out to be meaningless and false. She finds a kindred soul in Raj in whose friendship she hopes to realize her ambition to live a truer life without any pretence.

In her more recent novel, *Rich Like Us,* Sahgal tries to make the narrative look more than merely a story of a woman by referring to Hinduism and Christianity and contemporary political scene. In the present patriarchal society, man being not only a master of his life dictates woman's destiny as well. Ram, married with a newborn child in India, is found free to court Rose in England. Only when he is assured of her deep love for him, he announces that he is already married. He later goes to the extent of marrying, Rose even as Mona, her first wife, is in the same house. Mona, for him is meant for looking after his son and house while Rose is to shower love and attention on him. When he meets Marcella, he rejects Rose as he had rejected Mona earlier. More than anything else, their identical suffering unites Mona and Rose.

The women characters in this novel are depicted as being more aware of the injustice meted out to them by man but habit makes them willing victims in this world of exploitation and injustice. The need for "sisterhood" or "sister solidarity" figures in Sahgal's novels as one of the means to cope with male aggression. Mona in her depression gets welded to Rose and they become 'sisters". After the death of Mona, who leaves her two children under the supervision of Rose, Rose banks upon Sonali for solace and help.

All the characters of Sahgal ranging from Simrit, Saroj, Rose to Sonali give a new meaning to the identity of women by charting out crucial courses of their life's journeys. They give an idea as to how a woman can empower herself by being true to herself, her identity and her individuality. Their successful journeys are all indicative of one fact, that is, the first step to empowerment of the individual is to be one's own self by safeguarding one's personal freedom and self-respect which automatically takes care of the other aspects of the individual's life in any society.

Shashi Despande's novel *The Dark Holds No Terrors* and Nayantara Sahgal's novel reveal women empowerment and personal mobility. The protagonists in both the novels represent the middle class and they show urge for upward social mobility and interest in better education. Rose the protagonist in *Rich Like Us* and Saru, the protagonist in *The Dark Hold No Terrors* represent this middle class. They also represent the community of educated, employed urban women who have their financial, independence and better freedom of choice. Shashi Deshpande makes such the focal character of her narratives, and juxtaposes other characters with them to show how higher social class male gender and urban society afford certain privileges in Indian society.

Further, Deshpande also makes a micro-segmentation of Indian society by bringing the variables such as caste, gender and geographical location which makes subtle differences within a class. She also helps reader to look largely into the lives of Indian women, both employed and unemployed women. Deshpande and Sahgal also look at various social institutions such marriage, education and religion and their influences on women class. They imply that women of better education and financial freedom, though are still victims of patriarchal bias, are less oppressed as compare to the less fortunate women.

However, Shashi Deshpande and Nayantara Sahagal focus the middle class women. Though they depict men and women of lower economic strata, they merely provide a contrast to the main characters who are invariably picked from the middle class or upper middle classes. In their novels, women of all class are marginalized though the degree of marginalization differs from person to person.

Deshpande also propels her characters across the divides of the communities. Most of her characters are at once the members of many communities. Saru, for instance, has a childhood spent in a rural community and her later life spent in an urban community. Similarly she changes her status form an unemployed girl to a professional woman with the help of education.

The novels of Shashi Despande and Nayantara Sahgal also bring to light the specific behavioural pattern of people belonging to different class and community. She indicates in *The Dark Holds No Terrors* that certain social and individual behaviours are common to classes and communities. Marginalization of female, for instance, is seen in all classes and communities. Religious belief is another factor which cuts across classes and communities.

Thus *Rich Like Us* and *The Dark Holds No Terrors* bring out the subtle implications of women empowerment and their mobility in Indian society. These novels analyze the basic fabric of the Indian society. In this respect, Shashi Deshpande and Nayantara Sahgal's novels have distinct Indianness. One can also say that they have both used the class of women and their empowerment of Indian society effectively in their novels, in the naturalistic tradition to locate their characters and to study the causes of their problems.

Works Cited

Bharucha, Nilufer E Vilas Sarang,. *Indian-English Fiction 1980-90: An Assessment* New Delhi: B. R. Publishing Corporation, 1994.

Bose, Pradip Kumar. *Classes In A Rural Society A Sociological Study of Some Bengal Villages.* New Delhi: Ajanta Publications, 1984,

Das, Bijay Kumar. *Post modern Indian English Literature.* New Delhi: Atlantic Publishers and Distributors, 2003.

Dawan, R.K. *Indian Women Novelists,* Set-3:Vol.4, New Delhi: Prestige Book, 1995; Deshpande Shashi, *The Dark Holds No Terrors.* New Delhi: Penguin, 1990.

Jain, Jasbir. *Gendered Realities, Human Spaces the Writing of Shashi Deshpande.* New Delhi: Rawat Publication, 2003.

_______ & Amin, Amina (ed). *Margins of Erasure Purdah in the Sub continental Novel in English,* New Delhi: Sterling Publishers Pvt Ltd, 1995.

_______, *Gendered Realities, Human Spaces the Writing of Shashi Deshpande.* New Delhi: Rawat Publication, 2003. p-50.

Kirpal, Viney (ed). *The New Indian Novel in English: A Study of the 1980s.* New Delhi: Allied Publishers Ltd., 1990.

Menakshi Bharat, *Desert in Bloom, and Contemporary Indian Women's Fiction in English.* Delhi: Pencraft International, 2004. p-63.

Naik, M.K. and Shyamala A. Narayan. *Indian English Literature 1980-2000, a Critical Survey.* Delhi: Pencraft International, 2001.

Nayantara Sahgal, *Rich like Us.*

_______, *The Day in Shadow*

Pathak, R.S. Ed. *The Fiction of Shashi Deshpande.* New Delhi: Creative Books, 1997.

Pier, Paolo Piciucco. *A Companion to Indian Fiction in English.* New Delhi; Atlantic Publishers and Distributors, 2004.

Prasad, Amarnath. *New Light On Indian Women Novelists in English* New Delhi; Sarup & Sons, 2003.

Ray, Mohit K and Kundu Rama. *Studies in Women Writers in English, Vol-2,* New Delhi: Atlantic, 1990.

Sandhu, Sarbjit K. *The Image of Woman in the Novels of Shashi Deshpande.* New Delhi: Prestige Books, 1991.

Sebastine, Mrinalini. *The Novels of Shashi Deshpande in Post-Colonial Argumenst.* New Delhi: Prestige Books, 1997.

Sheshadri, Vijayalakshmi *The New Woman in Indian-English Women Writers since the 1970s.* Delhi: B.R. Publishing Corporation; 1995.

Shrivasta, Ramesh K. *Symbolism in Indian Fiction in English.* New Delhi: ABS Publication, 2003.

Singh, Pramod Kumar (Ed*). Indian Fiction in English.* New Delhi: Atlantic Publishers and Distributors, 2001.

Singh, R. A. and K. Kumar. *Critical Studies on Indian Writing in English.* Jaipur: Book Enclave, 2003.

Sree, Prasanna. *Woman in The Novels of Shashi Deshpande: A Study.* New Delhi: Sarup and Sons, 2003.

Suneel, Seema *Man-Woman Relationship in Indian Fiction.* New Delhi: Prestige Books, 1995.

5

Individuality and Space in Salman Rushdie's Fiction: A Postmodern Perspective

— Mohamed Hamoud Kassim Al-Mahfedi
& Abdulmonim Ali Ben Ali

Literature transcends the everyday world because its producers are above political motivations. This is a very important idea because it tells the relationship between literature and culture. It tells that literature has no meaning without the cultural, ideological and political situation. Literature reflects the ideological and cultural forces. In other words, the literary text is infused with the cultural and historical context. Of these cultural and ideological issues are power, class, and culture and gender. These elements affect the role of the individual and his position in society. The individual struggles in the limits of these concepts. The individual is also determined by these forces, his identity and his destiny. The question that is posed in this paper is: to what extent are these elements productive or destructive to the individual and how does Rushdie navigate the individual's position in a postmodern space of cultural hybridity?

The postmodern scenario compels a writer to search for alternatives, to negotiate a circumstance and readdress history. Reality is eclipsed by the fact that the reality is nothing but a fake one. The real is sunk in the illusive hyperreal. Therefore, geographical space is summoned and the position of the individual is restructured not in the form of closed cycles of conceptualization, but in a form of alternative versions of histories and realties. Plurality has replaced singularity and democracy takes the place of the unjust determinism.

In the works of Rushdie, there is nothing like a clear-cut between postcolonialism and postmodernism. Such binary thinking is much left behind for the benefit of a humanist perspective. His characters are searching for a position beyond the socio-historical tradition. On the one hand, reality is false and painful, and exclusive and aggressive on the other. In his addressing of the reality of postcolonial individual, Rushdie has developed certain narrative techniques which combine mythical thought and new historical presentation by way of which the individual becomes the central theme throughout his fictional oeuvre. The freedom of the individual is located within the freedom of the collective nation from the shackles of the tradition. In order to move freely in his treatment of his subject, Rushdie, like many other postimperial and postmodern writers and critics, adheres to secular interpretation of history and culture. He has done this through various technical and narratological devices such as irony, allusion, fantasy, juxtaposition, intertextuality, paratextuality, metatextuality, hypertextuality and archtextuality.

The most obvious postmodern element in Rushdie's novels is the use of "imagined geographies" as a spatial common denominator in the postmodern writings. Through creating an imagined space, the postmodern writer critiques the existing social system governed by certain conventional codes which downtrodden the individual and abuse his freedom. Reality becomes painful and much more complex and that a single view of it is incomplete, exclusionary and totalitarian. As a result, writers reflect on this fact by providing a fictional representation which is polyphonic, plural and multidimensional. Rushdie in this is not an exception. His novels are transnational world of individuals, rather than nations, inhabiting a timeless space of localities.

What is more interesting in Rushdie's novels is his

history. Rushdie is undoubtedly a postcolonial writer who mostly engages in the concepts of nation and national history, but he is nonetheless a much celebrated writer who advocates the cosmopolitan vision of "glocal" identity in which the artificial national borders are blurred. History for him is a changing process characterized by plurality and dynamism. Historical truth is not final. History is made by individuals–men and women—and collective memory is another form of hegemony. By doing so, Rushdie has established for himself a fictional approach to human individuality in which the sense of exile and alienation are not an exterior effect so much as an innate human reactions to loneliness and separation. Narration like regeneration is a symbolic act of life against deadly silence and segregation.

History of the nation in Rushdie's novels is narrated and unfolded through the life of the individual. The national history is composed of individual events which are themselves occasioned relatively with relation to other events. Therefore, we cannot separate the colonial history of a nation from its postcolonial or pre-colonial era. Is it a result or an effect that makes this historical fact? This is a type question that Rushdie's fiction attempts to rehearse. Human history is like a running text which composes within itself the past as well as the contemporary sources. It is also subject to various interpretations, readings and views. It has no beginning, middle or end. It is also open for addition and elision, writing and re-writing.

Another interesting point which shows Rushdie the postmodern is his insistence on new possibilities and the creation of new spaces. Rushdie seems to search for new social order and realties. This world is no more real it is a fake place of forged realities. This is explained in his fabulous representation of historical and mythical realities. The space for Rushdie is an instrumental element in his representation of the postcolonial situation. This world is hybrid and complex, and its common relations are intermingled. It cannot be represented in clear-cut boundaries.

What characterized the postmodern trend is its "paradigmic turn" as far-reaching ruptures in the critical thinking. The postmodern era is characterized by methodological pluralism and theoretical syncretism. Therefore, it is strictly impossible to identify all-comprehensive paradigms or epistemes shared by every "community", let alone whole "cultures". "Turns", in this context, are rather to be understood as processes of differentiation and specialization, as shifts in critical perspective and attention. (Michael C 65)

The spatial turn is one of the most recently proclaimed turns within the human and social sciences. At its most basic, the phrase "spatial turn" refers to "an increased attention to the spatial side of the historical world", as German historian Karl Schlogel put it (Qtd. in C. Michael 66). Writing from the perspective of his own discipline, Schlogel characterizes the spatial turn as an attempt to end the one-sided historicist emphasis on time and to investigate how history literally takes place – how space and time are inextricably linked.

This raises the question of how space is "produced" in the course of history. This strain of spatial criticism can be described as a social constructivist re-conceptualization of the category of "space" itself. Initiated by the French Marxist philosopher, Henri Lefebvre, the concept of "space has now become something more than the theatre, the disinterested stage or setting, of action . . . its role is less and less neutral, more and more active, both as instrument and as goal, as means and as end" (Lefebvre 410–411) . Perhaps this is what Foucault means when he writes:

> We are in the epoch of simultaneity: We are in the epoch of juxtaposition, the epoch of the near and far, of the side-by-side, of the dispersed. We are at a moment, I believe, when our experience of the world is less that of a long life developing through time than that of a network that connects points and intersects with its own skein. (Foucault 22)

According to Edward W. Soja, the "'epoch of space' is nothing but a distinctively postmodern and critical human geography" (11).

Rushdie's novels revolve around two strands or visions of human space: political domain and humane domain. Whereas the former refers to the political ideology and human collectivity, the latter deals with the humanistic urgency and human individual. In the politically charged space, the individual and human history along with it is subjected to the force of the dominant structures. Its movements are determined by the desire and the ideology of those structural forces. Hence, the human subject is never free from the impositions of the socio-political codes. He acts as an agent rather than a free individual subject. Rushdie's conceptualization of space is through the interventions of historical and cultural tropes such as national and social norms. To break with the traditional concepts of national identity to that of cultural identity needs to break away with the determining factors of religion, convention, and nation. History is seen as a dynamic process of social and political realities. Rushdie himself is an epitome of this cultural product. To be an Indian in the strict sense of conventiality is to emphasize the prochality of one's identity, and then the fossilization of one's space.

The political strand of space conceives human history as constituted by the permanent roar of battles. Politics in this way functions both as a historical discourse whose instrumental uses must be interrogated, as well as a present reality that gives us a way of analyzing, and intervening in, the political present. Or, as Foucault writes, historical knowledge "becomes an element of the struggle; it is both a description of struggles and a weapon in the struggle. History gave us the idea that we are at war; and we wage war through history." (Foucault 172)

Terms such as "clash of civilization", "permanent war" and "cultural dichotomy" become concepts that incited critical speculations on the importance of geo-cultural space. Thus, more attention has been paid to the spatial paradigm in the scholarly as well as artistic or fictional works. This venture is characterized by a rhetorical address which shows how various individuals see their positions with broader political realities. This, of course, navigates those questions and interventions regarding the politics of space in providing a critical voice on contemporary concerns of the oppressed individuals and minorities.

It is the manipulation of the gaze which made the permissible possible, the comprehensible attainable and the political humane that Rushdie excels most and makes him the postmodern. Moreover, it is this seemingly indeterminate human geography of unallocated cultures with which Rushdie is fervently concerned. He has domesticated the human space and ironically reflected on the spatial issue of the individual within a broader cycle of cosmopolitan space. To put it differently, the geo-cultural space of the individual is discussed in terms of spots of socio-political tensions in which history and geography are rehearsed, recalled and juxtaposed with the new existential realties. The complex interrelationships of the individual acquire a third dimension of temporality with the emergence of the third interval of space in addition to time and place. Therefore, one is here and there in time and place connected by the space. These complex sets of relationships should be addressed not within a culturally closed set of concepts like nation and territory, though artificially they are, but within a pluralistic and alternative versions of possible realities. This cannot be done without giving voice to the individual imaginary over the collective memory.

Rushdie's achievement as a postmodern writer is that he ordered the chaos of his existence into a highly patterned art. Because he, like so many of his characters, lived life at the extreme, he was more acutely conscious of community. Driven back on his individuality, he accepted its burdens and its uncompromisingly pessimistic vision of reality. He has to create the movement of his characters, a movement of gesture of defiance against the cruel joke played on him by history when it offered him only a stunted, incomplete legacy of national identity, dissipated in an obscure and chaotic world. Rushdie has viewed the world as a huge knitting machine that has evolved itself out of interrelated histories and territories. His approach to this world is inscribed by a weird mixture of irony and critique. This particular urgency is conveyed by the lengths of fantasy in order to make a point.

If we approach the concepts of territory, home, lands, nation, etc., from the postcolonial perspective, the notion of space becomes problematic for two aspects. First, we have to take into account the initial approach the colonist made towards the new unknown territories, and the transformations they forced upon the lands in order to make them *sound/feel/look* familiar to them. The second is the postcolonial repercussion of counter-approach of territories that resulted in *imaginary lands.* Edward Said describes this twofold process as follows:

> Imperialism after all is an act of geographical violence through which virtually every space in the world is explored, charted, and finally brought under control. For the native, the history of colonial servitude is inaugurated by loss of the locality to the outsider; its geographical identity must thereafter be searched for and somehow restored .Because of the presence of the colonizing outsider, the land is recoverable at first only through imagination. (77)

In line with this thought of recoverability, Rushdie's job seems to be the representation of individual's position through the use of fantasy. His characters are floating between the world of reality and hyper-reality or fantasy.This blurring of the dividing line between the real and hyper-real and the disassociation of locality and individuality is a celebrated technique of Rushdie's postmodernism. His method is based on analyzing history in relation to the individual. He exposes the problems of the individual and his suffering under the collective and repressive history. Rushdie's individuals are not bound by time and place.

They are floating subjects moving between temporality and spatiality to timelessness and simultaneity. It is a pickling history, the cancellation of time that Rushdie evokes in his fiction. It was a *terra nullis* lacking all traces of history. (Boehmer 186)

Space, gender and politics are the tri through which Rushdie has mostly been realized as a postmodern writer. His characters are moving ones, and they are haunted by the quest for a new world. In *Grimus*, for instance, the central character, Flapping Eagle, breaks the stagnation of life in Axona searching for the home of vitality and communication. Rushdie's approach to spatiality is through the Flapping Eagle a symbol of freedom, hybridity multiculturalism and transnationalism. He is a national without nation, a floating subject, an insider and outsider and cosmopolitan citizen.

Adding to his symbolic significance as a product of cultural hybridity, Flapping Eagle is described as one who combines all the contradictory qualities. The novelist highlights the contradiction in the Eagle's personality as an unstable character. The instability of Eagle's character is also related to the idea of 'unstable identity'. His identity is made of different cultures and is a process of cultural assimilation. "Several times he changed the name he gave to people. His face was such, his skin was such" (Rushdie, *Grimus* 32). This tells that he is a seeking man of truth, and that truth has not a fixed shape. Similarly, history does not have one fixed version.

There is nothing like a fixed idea such as identity, history etc. in the postmodern thought as everything tends to change and metamorphose. The citation quoted above tells that the major character is looking for his identity, freedom and history. He is "looking for a suitable voice to speak in" (32). He is looking for a new language and new culture where he can find himself. To him, history is made of many voices and spoken by many languages. For this, Flapping Eagle wants to relocate his position, formulate his identity and regain a new history of new ideals which can express his entity.

Rushdie has reflected on the concept of individuality in a subtle way that he juxtaposes two worlds of human experience. The individual needs not be a man or a woman. It may be a hermaphrodite bird as is the Flapping Eagle in Rushdie's *Grimus*. This genderless bird is treated in Axona as a stranger simply because he has different features of race, colour and attitudes. The traditional system in Axona does not accept the 'difference' in race, opinion and attitude. It introduces itself as a system of prejudice. "For three reasons: first, my confused sex; second the circumstances of my birth; and third, my pigmentation. To be a hermaphrodite among the Axona is to be bad medicine. A monster." (18)

Rushdie's *Grimus* is a tale of man's identity and his travelling over history. Man searches for new realities over history. He searches for himself in the sands of times. He is also a time-traveller who narrates the human experiences and their longings for new universes. The technique of fantasy supports this theme—the yearning of humanity for immortality and freedom. The protagonist is a free non-conformist subject who travels across the limit of time and place to his new place in Calf Island. Through the myth of alchemy, Rushdie shows that the individual is a free spirit featured in a transformational process of fluidity and transparency that resists the temporality and stasis. In his critical essay *Imaginary Homelands* (1981), Rushdie writes, "It may be that writers in my position, exiles or emigrants or expatriates, are haunted by some sense of loss, some urge to reclaim." He adds, "[- - -] and I suppose somewhat Proustion ambition to unlock the gates of lost time so that the past reappeared as it actually had been, unaffected by the distortions of memory, so that my India was just that: 'my' India, a version and no more than one version of all the hundreds millions of possible versions. I tried to make it as imaginatively true as I could, but imaginative truth is simultaneously honourable and suspect". He also argues that "the past is a country, from which we have all emigrated, that its loss is part of our common humanity" and that " re-describing a world is the necessary first step towards changing it ... And the novel is one way of denying the official, politicians, version of truth." (9-14)

Rushdie uses three main techniques in writing about individuality and historical truth: memory, fantasy and myth. By memory he recalls the past and brings it back; by fantasy he enriches realism, and uses myth to criticize the historical realities. These techniques are methods of meaning. Truths given by history are incomplete. The novelist has a deep yearning for perfect meanings of lives. The purpose of fiction, says Rushdie, "is telling truth" (Grass 73). His job is to complete what is incomplete and open what is thought to be closed. He also regards history as a closed one. His fictions deal with history as an imaginary idea away from the confines of space and time. The ultimate purpose is also to have meanings for the present situation. He creates from what had happened in the past meanings for the present social and political reality. For him, memory is a curious tryst with history.

Rushdie's *Shame* celebrates sexuality as a naturally predominating human force. Yet, this human force is dealt with through socio-political pretentions and counter-force against the domination of patriarchy. There is a shift from the humane to the political to the humane once again. This artistic purview is a deliberate act which combines within itself celebration and revolt. There is a reworking of woman's position in the society against the history that marginalized her. At the same time, there is a common human denominator that is the sexual force that asserts the individual urge across the border of constructed social codes. As a fantasy of painful penetration and mutilation, human society becomes great knitting machines that "knit you in and knit you out."

Sexuality has been redefined by Rushdie as an expression of individuality that has been repressed by the official social codes. This is suggested through Rushdie's indirect critique of "shame".

This feminist strand is directed toward the metamorphosis of Shakil girls, Chunni, Munnee, and Bunny from submissively idle figures to socio-politically engaged individuals. This new position of the woman is contrasted with the traditional view of woman under the patriarchally-governed society. Rushdie's society is a secular world where "shame" is looked at as a form of social repression of individuality and as an exclusionary tool based on religiously identifying principles. Secular identity is identified by Rushdie in relation to cultural space not to nation, religion or ethnicity.

Moreover, Rushdie's *Shame* can be described as a journey of self-realization or individual's re-positioning. Sufiya Zinobia, for example, eventually realizes that her identity should not be gained from what others define, but what she herself is, regardless of others' viewing gaze. She represents what Dey Pradip Kumar describes as "floating upwards" from history, from society, from one's time (107).

If *The Satanic Verses* functionally welcomes a multitude of subject positions, all of which occupy a sanctioned portion of narrative space, *Shame* operates within a poetics of self-removal. Its ostensible hero, Omar Khayyam Shakil, is described as a "peripheral man," one who mostly lacks the agency to propel the plot meaningfully. Distancing the reader from this putative protagonist is the novel's intrusive narrator, who at once underscores the shamefulness of Pakistani politics and argues quite defensively for his right to do so, despite his non-native status. Indeed, the narrator overtly locates himself within a specific set of national frames— "I am an emigrant from one country (India) and a newcomer into (England, where I live, and Pakistan, to which my family moved against my will)"—and *points* to these multiple sites as the factors that legitimate his views: " We [*mohajirs*, immigrants]have performed the act of which all men anciently dream ... we have flown" .This process of "floating upwards", hints the narrator, enables an uncontaminated critique of the nation. (Rushdie, *Shame* 85, 91).

The theme of dislocation is a postmodern idea in which an individual's position remains unstable and struggles to establish his new shelter. The individual subject in such instance is stripped off his past and history. The subject is represented to us as one who has no belonging or a specific fixed position. The subject is dislocated and has no home or shelter. This is the general category of the individual in *Shame.* Scott D. Walker observes:

> Unlike *The Satanic Verses,* the narrative structure of *Shame* emphasizes the theme of unbelonging without suggesting the compensatory plenitude of subject positions many postcolonial theorists claim for the migrant1. Instead of figuring dislocation within a particular context, this fractured narrative displays unbelonging as generic category. The novel refuses to assimilate, as it were. (78)

For the purpose of establishing the individual narrative and individual view of history, Rushdie relies on the individual's own memory to recreate a new reality. What is meant by new reality and new historical truth is, briefly, multiplicity of reality, and the creation of many possible views of life because life is not confined to one particular, official view. For example, the central character in *Midnight's Children,* Saleem draws attention to the role of memory in the process of constructing reality by pointing to memory's selecting certain events:

> "I told you the truth," I say yet again. "Memory's truth, because memory has its own special kind, it selects, eliminates, alters, exaggerates, minimizes, glorifies, and vilifies also; but in the end it creates its own reality, its heterogeneous but usually coherent version of events; and no sane human being ever trusts someone else's version more than his own." (211)

Midnight's Children also emphasizes another aspect of individuality which Rushdie struggles for throughout his literary career, that is, history is an individual event rather than a collective memory, and that what is received by us is only one version among many possible versions.

A careful reading of Rushdie's essays, interviews, documents and novels have always pointed to the dangers of monolithic narrative. His novels reveal that he is always on the side of heterogeneity and variety, and his impulse is to always be inclusive of past and present, old and new, religious and secular. His attempt, in short, is always to deconstruct the binary. "The problem of otherzing individuals and communities arises because of a binary perspective that insists on dividing the world into East/ West, Knowledge/Ignorance, Subject/Object, White/Black, Secular- Christian/Fundamentalist- Muslim" (Hassumani 98). Rushdie denies in his novels the behaviour of mastery and hierarchy over others because it is a sort of categorization of the colonial discourse. This kind of categorization results in suppressed and repressed acts against the individuals who try to establish their free society and their own perspective.

The alternative realities of art and myth-making are used by Rushdie as a reaction against the political narrative. '"Life, history, is always narrative," Rushdie has always maintained. Rushdie also points out that "religious or political leaders who present it as a system of binaries are actively creating a myth and then selling it as "reality". He says, "It is a writer's job to counter such myth-making by offering one's own version of "reality" which may be contrary to the status quo's". (99).

Further, *Haroun and the Sea of Stories* is a celebration of cultural diversity and human creativity against the political repression and human rigidity. The novel was set up against the backdrop of Khomeini's *fatwa* which kills human communication and individual freedom. Rushdie's narrator (Haroun) is a reminiscence of the Khalif, Haroun Khalifa.Haroun Al-Rashid supported the freedom of speech and recognized the cultural differences in the Islamic state, which was a flourishing state and a centre of civilization. The most celebrated of all Muslims Caliphs was Haroun-al-Rashid, which means, in English, Aaron the Just. Haroun is also the hero in Arabian *Nights*, a famous book, which contains many curious and wonderful tales in it.

Basic to his advocacy of the individual, Rushdie privileges the concepts of secularism, pluralism and fragmentary history. His technical strategy is to re-write a fragmentary secular history as a resisting version against the official collective and nationalistic version. This idea also applies to all his novels. He creates his new myths of multi-views and pluralistic free secular society as a counter-myth to the fundamental and religious forms of reality. In *Midnight's Children*, he relies on the rhetoric discourse to create a new shape of life.

Haroun and the Sea of Stories continues Rushdie's effort to imagine a heterogeneous space where neither Chup (East) nor Gup (West) is privileged and where the project of reality-making is attempted on a register that is outside the earlier "speech/ silence" hierarchial structure. It is important to note that Rushdie attempts to disrupt the binary opposition "Gup/Chup"by revealing it to be a cultural construct. The text ends up by privileging notions of "equality," "fairness," and "free speech" which are the defining elements of existence. Ultimately, Rushdie's point in *Haroun and the Sea of Stories* is that "this system of binaries is a construct and that as long as dividing boundaries exist to prevent intermingling, everyone who buys into their need is complicit in the inevitably resulting violence" (Hassumani 101).

By focusing exclusively on newness and novelty, the Guppees have foregrounded the present moment to the exclusion of the past, or their "roots". The ideal space in Rushdie is always a heterogeneous one in which the past commingles with the present to create a "new" moment in time. Rushdie pushes himself out to the Sea of Stories on his fictional boat by choosing to imagine a reality that is obviously more enabling than the one Khattam-Shud attempted to thrust upon him. By constructing a "happy ending" for Haroun, Rushdie asserts his imaginative will over the forces that seek to shut him down, and once again he chooses a life of heterogeneity, hodgepodge, and mélange where "reality" and " fiction" intermingle to create a new moment of hope for a writer who must remain in hiding (112). *Haroun and the Sea of Stories*, in fact, is largely about oppositions between fantasy and reality, between child and adult, between good and bad – Rushdie is being careful to suggest that there can be "dialogue" and "crossover" between categories: the various political and cultural categories. On several levels, therefore, he has created in *Haroun and the Sea of Stories* a complex allegory that emphasizes the importance of exchange between different cultural groupings. "Rushdie has extended the reach of the traditional fable by making intertextuality serve an additional allegorical function". (Teverson 460)

Haroun and the Sea of Stories is a metaphor of individuality and free speech. The story, according to this interpretation, is not just a metaphor for free speech and free narrations. It also offers a model for an ideal concept of nationhood that permits unlimited interaction and exchanged between cultural interests. Rushdie's vision is to "wage war on totality" (qtd.in Teverson 460). His aim is to imagine a form for the nation, if nation is understood not as a unified and holistic entity defined by the exclusion of "others" but as a fluid, provisional entity defined by its capacity to incorporate difference and variation. In the light of this interpretation, we can re-read the conflict between the Guppees and Khattam-Shud not as the battle between absolute free speech and censorship, but as the collision between conceptions of nationhood identified by Homi Bhabha. Khattam-Shud represents the Bhabha's theory of pedagogical fundamentalist ideal of a nation that exists as an essentialized entity independent of any actual manifestation of national life and that defines itself by its opposition and difference. Khattam-Shud demands a nation that can be homogenized according to some re-established blue-print. On this basis, it is now possible to suggest that Rushdie's call for freedom of narration in *Haroun and the Sea of Stories* cannot be reduced so easily to a facile, liberal plea for freedom of speech. The demand for free interaction of stories in the story sea is linked to the demand for the freedom of individuals, groups, minorities, to be a part of the nation with which they are affiliated. It is also a reinforcement of the rights of individuals, groups, minorities, to be a part of the nation and not to be excluded from the nation.

In his re-conception of society as a complex and multiform body of competing discourses, Rushdie has moved a fair distance from the vision of society prompted by Farid Ud-Din Attar in "The Conference of the Birds". "Rushdie's hoopoe is a postmodern bird, whose quest leads toward a celebration of diversity, and who has, appropriately, a mechanical, computerized brain; Attar's hoopoe is a spiritual entity whose quest leads in the opposite direction toward the absolute eradication of difference" (464). We have then two different systems of believe concerning the concept of individual and nation.

In *The Moor's Last Sigh* Rushdie describes the journey of Moraes Zogoiby, a half Christian, half Jewish narrator living in India. Born into a country divided along Hindu Muslim lines and occupied by Christian Westeners. The novel narrates the Moor's struggle to forge an identity takes him from Bombay to Spain, as religious clashes and cultural conflicts. The novel mainly deals with the contemporary context, the exclusion of others in the name of religion. Located within a postmodern condition, the novel celebrates multiculturalism and global identity in a productively free human society. It acknowledges the free individual and heterogeneity against the imposed homogeneous culture. It can be also read as a novel of cultural multiplicity, and political protest against singularity.

The narrator, Moraes Zogoiby, called the Moor is the central character of the novel. Rushdie makes a parallel between the Moor and Boabdil, the last Moorish king who was conquered by Christian forces and was forced to submit Spain to the Christians. The purpose of this parallel is a kind of admonition against the dangers of fundamentalism and rigid definition of self. This parallelism is a sort of criticism against the rigid forms of nation-state and religious identity in the present of India. This is the use of history and its relation to the realist political situations in India. Rushdie connects the past history of Spain to the present history of India. The parallelism serves the purpose of criticism. He attacks the religious intolerance and bigotry. He undoubtedly attacks all kinds of religious intolerance, whether Spanish or Indian. But he also highlights the problems with blind multiculturalism, suggesting that dissolution of self-identity to pursue tolerance and peace is unrealistic at best. Centred on multiculturalism and pluralism in the face of singularity and rigidity, he treats history from a view of myth and fiction in this novel. He uses the historical story of tolerance in Andalusia, the myth of Islamic tolerance as a material for his story in order to attack and criticize the intolerance and bigotry.

In fact, Rushdie criticizes blind pluralism and chauvinistic singularity. He hints at the constraints of pluralism through the demise of Uma, the Moor's lover. Uma believes in "multiple selves" (Rushdie, *The Moor's Last Sigh* 272) and she embodies her thought in her drawings and works of arts. But Uma is a con artist, creating various persons among different company. Uma pits the Moor against a ghostly con that breaks the Zogoibys apart. Aurora is a classical artist who only believes in 'blind nationalism'. The Moor attacks "the pluralist Uma, with her multiple selves, her highly commitment to the infinite malleability of the real, her modernistically provisional sense of truth, who had turned out to be the bad egg" (272). Through her actions, Rushdie condemns the fraudulent human beings that blind pluralism can produce. Uma is a destructive model of plurality. What Rushdie hints at here is that both blind plurality and rigid singularity are devastating to humanity. According to him, truth lies in free individuality and cultural identity.

In this particular juncture, Rushdie attempts a theoretical conceptualization of the concepts of identity and nation by invoking historical realities and repositioning of the individual contemporary context. Which identity do we seek: the individual self identity or the national identity? His general mission is that the social and political life should be based on both views: singularity and plurality, the individual self and the nation. His concern in *The Moor's Last Sigh* is not only the general struggle for living in a world where one finds oneself an exile and a hybrid, but also the specific struggle of certain art from this position of cultural dislocation and disunity. The form of art in the novel allegorizes the relationship and debatable concepts of hybridity, identity and nationalism. By drawing on a parallelism between the old Spain and modern India, he condemns the religious bigotry and 'blind nationalism' of the present India, and invokes the cultural hybridity and tolerance in the past Andalusia.

In these important cultural issues, Rushdie reveals a spatial turn in the formation of one's identity free from the shackles of religion, nation and zonality. The Moor's grandfather, for example, dreams of an independent India which could he "above religious because secular, above class because socialist above caste because enlightened, above hatred because loving". (Rushdie, *The Moor's Last Sigh* 51)

More interestingly, Rushdie does not have heroes. His central characters are common peoples suffering from the fragmented psyche and searching for reconciliatory resolution for their crises. These crises are the result of certain historical forces such as past memories and conventional norms. In other words, the forces of the "old" are battling with the "new". Rushdie's intervention, as a postmodern writer, lies in-between—hybridity and multiplicity. Read this way, *Midnight's Children* can be analyzed as a postmodern hybrid form of identity. Its community is a blend of diverse cultural identities and fragmented entities sharing a common human space. More precisely, he has given space for the individual self that crosses the boundaries of time and place, and nation and culture. Nothing is fixed, certain, or absolute, and that historical truth is incomplete. By this it is meant that he wants to liberate history from the imposed views which even cannot be justified or examined by concrete evidence. So, his job becomes to re-write and question all that is given as absolute truths.

The form of art and paintings function as a symbolism in *The Moor's Last Sigh.* They symbolize the confusion of identity and its position in the cultural reality. This sort of art tells the tale of the narrator and his quest of harmony and peace in the world. The Moor himself is also an artist, and his tale is not only a multigenerational family saga, but a portrait of artist. Yet he does write his own story, and the first-person novel is the evidence of his artistic success. How exactly does he overcome his multiple handicaps, writing with a bad left hand? The meaning of this symbolism is that an art is a medium by which we can express ourselves and our history. Art is the medium through which we express our identity and that it is part of our entity.

In reading *The Moor's Last Sigh* as a novel of an artist's development, one must recognize that writing and art are signs and symbols of identity expression. It is the real power which permits us to narrate and unfold our story and history. Through art we express our thought and ideas. The mission of Rushdie is that as this man has a power to write or paint, he can express his identity, he can preserve his identity and history.

Framed within the dialectics of human geo-cultural space, *The Moor's Last Sigh* records confusing concepts of ambivalence of identity. Every character tries to define India and nationalism from his own thought and position. *The Moor's Last Sigh* is a novel which searches for meanings that can be grasped from the issues concerning the individual identity and the impact of collective nationalism. The form of art plays as a symbolism that connects the different cultural thoughts and the language that expresses the thought of each of the main characters. Rushdie deals with the issue of artists in relation to the political force. Living in a hybrid cultural world who cannot afford becoming part of it, he compares himself to his projected hero, Moor. Between these two positions of identity—the historical past and the political present—lies a postmodern utopian self that defies any form of definition.

The Moor's Last Sigh is not just a story of an exile, of a travelling man, but about "how stories travel, what mouths they end up in". How exactly does a Christian story about Martin Luther in Wittenberg end up in the mouth of a Hindu woman in India? Why does a Christian Indian artist paint her greatest series about an Iberian Muslim? Why does a secular Muslim from Bombay find the need to allude to Rabindranath Tagore, Rudyard Kipling, the *Ramayana*, the *Thousand and one Nights,* James Joyce, Lewis Carroll, John Ford, etc. Rushdie connects the present cultural and political crisis of the artists to the old ones that happened to pioneering world artists. The purpose of this is to connect the problems of these greatest artists to the problems of the contemporary ones. The novel connects the past to the present. *The Moor's Last Sigh,* therefore, not only offers a tale of the artist's development but also gives us a tale about that tale, a story about what happens to stories when they are exiled. This is actually a central trope in the hands of Rushdie. In her paintings, She creates a fictional location, an imaginary homeland, where the Moor will no longer be considered a freak. First, she calls this land Mooristan, then, she changes to Palimpstine. Aurora describes Palimpstine as a "[P]lace where worlds collide, flow in and out of one another, and washofy away . . . one universe one dimension, one country, one dream" (Rushdie, *The Moor's Last Sigh* 226)

Rushdie always invites his characters and heroes, and necessarily his readers, to develop a consciousness of history. The consciousness of history involves a sense of the timeless as well as of the temporal together. This makes an individual conscious of his own place in time as well as of his among his contemporaries. He does not minimize the value of the past. He says, "What you were forever who you are". He writes further in *Shame*, "Men who deny their past become incapable of thinking them real" (144).To recreate the past, implies a desire to percept the past in relation to present.

If we read Rushdie's novels altogether, we will actually find a postmodern condition and a trajectory of utopian imaginary homelands. In fact, his novels taken as a whole provide an artistic representation of the individual and his identity in the transnational and multicultural world of overlapping territories and entwined histories. If *Midnight's Children* is about "the squandered mandate" the *Moor's Last Sigh* is about a "lost world". However, the two novels deal with the idea of history in the sense that there is a relationship between the individual and history or, in other words, the individual and the great forces of history.

In the two novels Rushdie recognizes the significance of the elemental power operating upon the destiny of a nation and the individuals. Right from the beginning, Saleem in *Midnight's Children* is conscious of his historical centrality. At the outset, he reminds his readers of his being "mysteriously handcuffed to history", his destiny being "indissolubly chained" to those of his country (Rushdie, *Midnight's Children* 3). On the other hand, *The Moor's Last Sigh* is a novel about how to think beyond memories and vestiges. In this sense, Moor lives and experiences the bitterness of loss, frustration and disillusionment. Then, it is a matter of how to transform this experience of loss and destruction into fleeting moments of commonality and openness. Moraes says in *The Moor's Last Sigh*: "I found for the first time in my short-long life, the feeling of normality, of being *nothing special*, the sense of being among kindred spirits, among people –like me, that is defining quality of home" (305).

Rushdie's emphasis on history as a construct connects him to poststruturalist and postmodern theory. The brief idea of this theory is that history is made of many complex factors so that any representation of history is expected to reflect all these factors and historical conditions. The notion of textuality is related to the nation of "the worlding of a world on a supposedly uniscribed territory" (qtd. in Hassumani 134). This is the most important feature in his novels. His method is not to "reverse" the binary concepts, but to "resolve" them and compromise them. His ultimate aim is to celebrate all possibilities and versions or patterns of reality. His ultimate aim is to have many alternative versions and perspectives of history. He represents history as text in which he imagines the possible ways of life.

Rushdie's *Midnight's Children* can be seen as a re-reading of his own identity and a recovering of his past in Bombay. It can be then taken as a tantamount to Wordsworth's subjective revisiting of Tintern Abbey, a second re-evaluation of his constructed identity through experience. Likewise, with his reconstruction of the city in *The Moor's Last Sigh*, Rushdie's reliance on memory becomes a personal and political necessity. It is also a novel about reconstructing the history in Coachin, the native place of the hero and Spain. This technique is to recreate history and connect the hybridity of India to that in Spain. The setting of the novel is Coatchin, Southern India which is described as a place of hybridity. It is the stop of the present from which Rushdie travels to the past. Bombay and Coachin are two mythical cities of world hybridity and cultural tolerance. The two cities are chosen by him to translate his both real and mythical project of a postmodern multicultural state which encompasses all diversities and ethnic cultural groups. He subverts the myth of the nation by the myth of hybridity. Beyond this, the idea of *Bharat Mata* or "Mother India", the myth of the nation as a nurturing form is itself explored in its different manifestations. Indira Gandhi identified herself with the nation for political purposes as her election slogan – 'India is Indira and Indira is India? – testifies. Rushdie seems to criticize and allegorize this nationalistic thought." (Cundy111)

Aurora's art assumes the same symbolic status within the text as did Rani Harappa's embroidered shawls in *Shame*. Aurora, like

Rushdie beyond her, is obsessed with the "mythic-romantic mode in which history, family, politics and fantasy jostle each other". Aurora is obsessed with the romantic idea of nation, the imagined nation. She translates in her paintings the romantic ideas of her own world; she creates the tension between the realism and fantasy. It is again a recurrence of a theme within *Midnight's Children* and much of Rushdie's fictional and non-fictional writing, the question of the best way of depicting 'reality' (113). His message is that a society cannot be "one thing". There should be various approaches and ideas to include all differences and cultural fragmentations.

Apart from *Horoun and the Sea of Stories*, one could mention such fairy tale transformations as the coherent use of the utopian qualities of the genre in *Midnight's Children, The Satanic Verses, The Moor's Last Sigh, and Fury*, and the deployment of female fairy-tale heroines as vehicles for Rushdie's involvement with feminist discourses as in *Shame* and *Grimus.* Hence, Rushdie emerges as a storyteller who is "implicated in processes of cultural formation, of recycling (fairy-tale) frames used to make sense of culture" (Deszcz 29). In this sense, the various instances of his intervention in the commonly accepted framework of the fairy tale reveal his artistic and ideological positions of an another engaged in what Benjamin R.Barber defined as "a war within civilization, a struggle that expresses the ambivalence within each culture as it faces a global, networked, material future and wonders whether cultural and national autonomy can be retained; the ambivalence within each individual juggling the obvious benefits of modernity within its equally obvious costs" (qtd. in Deszcz 29). Enthralling tales usually stem from actual struggles over power and hopes to stamp out social conflict by changing dominant social structures. Such struggles and hopes often play themselves out in utopian worlds that take the form of fairy-tales. Rushdie values the fairy tale category not just as a literary category, but also as a strategy of life. In short, he uses fairy-tale as a device of creation and invention of new cultural worlds. This technique translates his project of multiculturalism.

Rushdie's fictions are subversively potent narrative acts that intervene in and disrupt obsolete notions of nation and nationalism, culture and identity. However, his continuing analysis of postimperial and neoimperial attitudes and the extension of this analysis into the territory of globalization and multinational celebrity places him as a significant postmodern voice. His novel *The Satanic Verses* employs a narrative of global mobility, in which the protagonist must reject the place of his birth in order to discover the true value in what he has forsaken. Chamcha's "comparative cosmopolitanism" structures the text plot of personal development. His journey is the catalyst that inspires him to rediscover his Indian roots. The novel offers a question about the relationship between postcolonialism and globalization.

Rushdie, as a postmodern writer, tries to offer new views and arguments about what are thought to be essentialist concepts. Sabrina Hassumani argues, "Rushdie is a political writer who deploys poststructuralist strategies to problematize essential myths such as 'identity', 'nationalism', and 'religion' that are based on binary oppositions such as US/Them, East/West and secular/religions" (16). By this is meant that Rushdie's approach is to deconstruct these issues and question their authenticity. His approach is based on analyzing these concepts and exploring new meanings out of his analysis. He "problematizes" those issues and tries to subvert and deconstruct the idea of their validity in order to create his new terms instead of the traditional and classic ones. This approach is based on the fact that a postmodernist thought has to doubt all the 'essential myths' and authorized codes.

Generally, a postmodern writer is concerned with drawing all 'new maps' of realities. For example, "the nation-state" has no more become an ideal fact and this by itself intersects with the nation of cultural differences. Singularity cannot claim the entire truth of society. Also, the idea of "territorial sovereignty" has no validity in the postmodernist thought. As he privileges the multiple versions of history, Rushdie intimately acknowledges the postmodern cultural expression of the subcontinent. His fictional oeuvre discusses the idea of postmodern and cultural identity. His novels generally deal with how identity is perceived in the postmodern thought as they asserted 'incredulity towards' all 'master-narratives'.

One important thing is that Rushdie does not believe in the master narrative and thus he subjects it into examination and analysis. It is a master narrative because it speaks from a position of power and superiority. So, his novels came as a response to the superior narrative that stems from the idea of the centre metropolitan and marginal periphery. The most significant aspect of grand tales of postmodernism is fragmentation and indifference, and this is actually the main concern of Rushdie. His subject is imagined, neither only stable, alienated nor wholly fragmented. It is sometimes a mixture of all such aspects. In the very special case of Rushdie, however, the supposed gap between postmodernism and postcolonialism is quite easily bridged. For this matter, he enjoys the status of being a cosmopolitan writer who combines within his art the grand postmodern scope, on the one hand and, the postcolonial thought, on the other. To say it differently, however, the discourses of postcolonialism and postmodernism, in the hands of Rushdie, need not necessarily to be read as strictly opposed to each other. The two approaches deconstruct the great narratives of modern cultures in the West.

The postmodern theories of subjectivity are re-connected to the novels of Salman Rushdie though inter-connected categories of fragmentation, mutability and identity verses alterity. These three aspects of identity-formation are, in fact, alluded to in the following central passage from Rushdie's oeuvre:

> O eternal opposition of inside and outside! Because, a human being, inside himself, is anything but a whole, anything but

> homogenous; all kinds of everywhichthing (sic) are jumbled up inside him, and he is one person one minute and another the next. (*Midnight's Children* 236-37)

Fragmentation of personal selves is a recurring theme in Rushdie's novels. Physical fragmentation, for example, is particularly significant as a central metaphor for psychic fragmentation in *Midnight's Children.* Apart from Adam Sinai's "fragmented" views of his future bride through the perforated sheet at the outset of the novel and the symbolic "hole" inside of him. There is further textual evidence regarding Saleem Sinai's bodily mutilation. The physical mutilations thus point towards Saleem's split identity and his schizophrenia. Rushdie's narrator deliberately implants in the tale. Saleem's psychic split is formally emphasized by his continually speaking of himself in first and third person. Thus, he is presented, interestingly, as having a double perspective which makes him a seemingly omniscient and limited first-person narrator at the same time. The simple connection between the subject (Saleem) and the object (pickle jar) is an instance which symbolizes the cultural identity. There is thus a simple relationship between the individual and his objects of living. Such a pickle object constitutes the cultural personality. Furthermore, Saleem's psychological fragmentation is symbolized by the famous pickling of his life in jars, each jar of pickles. A similar metaphor for identity:

> Sometimes, in the pickles' version of history, Saleem appears to have known too little; at other times, too much... yes, I should revise and revise, improve and improve...In the spice bases, I reconcile myself to the inevitable distortions of the pickling process. To pickle is to give immortality...One day, perhaps, the world may taste the pickles of history" (*Midnight's Children* 460-61)

Also, we find Saleem speaking in the novel, "No, that won't do, I shall have to write the future as I have written the past, to set it down with the absolute certainty of a prophet. But the future cannot be preserved in a jar; one jar must remain empty..." (462)

The formation of the self in a larger context connects the question of how a migrant who is moving between different nations and cultures is able to form his or her personal identity. This also refers to Bhabha's theory of hybridity and alterity, conceptualizing a 'third space' that is used to "deconstruct" the boundaries between the self and other. The central idea here is that there is what is termed as 'the third space', which means the result of relationship between the self and others (Bhabha, *The Location of Culture* 37). The self-identity has its own entity and fragmented self. The self is one independent identity. In this sense, identity, fragmentary in shape, achieves its positionality through a dialogical process with the general concepts of nation and culturality. Identity is therefore sought by the individual outside his individual self and his genealogy, with the articulation of the body and history, whereby the result is a patchwork figure. "In the *Moor's Last Sigh*, Rushdie gives us the twentieth century speeded up into the reading space of the time it takes each reader to read the novel. Moor's body reflects this speeding up process, and as Foucault said, the body is imprinted by history and the process of history destroys the body" (qtd. in Wallhead 80).

It becomes obvious that Rushdie defends the fragmented identities and subaltern views throughout his fictional and non-fictional works. This is also another point which explains why Rushdie problematises the concept of history. Rushdie's primary concern in dealing with history is to reveal that what is called as "momentous events" should be discussed and conveyed only through their relation to the position of the individuals and minor elements in society. For this reason, we see Rushdie intermingling personal histories of fictional characters with the general and public events. Rushdie traces the individual in relation to the cultural and ideological forces. He does this simply because his main subject in writing is the individual and the fragmented individual. He does this because Rushdie not only introduces himself as a postcolonial novelist who defends the cultural differences but also as a postmodern writer whose main business is to subvert and destroy the traditional foundations of historical forces. Rushdie says:

> Our identity is at once plural and partial. Sometimes we feel that we straddle two cultures; at other times, that we fall between two stools. But however, ambiguous and shifting this ground may be, it is not an infertile territory for a writer to occupy. If literature is in part the business of finding new angles at which to enter reality, then once again our distance, our long geographical perspective, may provide us with such angles (*Imaginary Homelands* 15).

Michael Hensen reveals that Rushdie's novels suggest that an individual can never restrain from being influenced by cultural identity (173) Moraes speaks about "a self without walls" (*The Moor's Last Sigh* 288) and finally even draws the parallel between fourteenth–century multi-ethic *Granada* and its *Alhambra* and the "need for flowing together, for putting an end to frontiers, for the dropping of the boundaries of the self" (433).

The major characters of Rushdie, especially the Moor in *The Moor's Last Sigh,* seek a 'third space' of reality, a history without walls or boundaries. The Moor seeks a space of humanity, fraternity and tolerance. He seeks a safe home without frontiers. He searches for a hybrid identity without any religious or cultural boundaries because self-identity is a product of society, culture and religion. What Rushdie wants to convey is that identity is not a fixed thing but a process of construction. By imagination, the writer suggests that there should be a large cultural space of imagination for the individual. In a PBS interview with Charlie Rose, Rushdie states that "the character of Aurora, the painter, embodies some of his own ideas, and that the kind of painter she is, is a little bit the kind of writer I would like to be . . . she tries to put the world on her canvas." (qtd. in Hassumani 116). Rushdie's impulse for inclusiveness is, what leads to his notion of hybridity. Significantly, the notion of utopian homecoming is particularly relevant to his writing, which turns around the difficult task of redefining home for one's modified self, torn between the emotional poles of indigenousness and cultural acceptance, cultural banishment and the longing for total assimilation. Moreover, he does not simply emphasize the need to create optional versions of the world, but importantly he advocates the active struggle against reality: "unreality is the only weapon with which reality can be mashed, so that it may be subsequently reconstructed" (*Imaginary Homelands* 122). It would be also true that Rushdie does not struggle against the current social systems. But rather he suggests new other possible versions of social life. The social structure that he wants to reconstruct is one that allows all shapes of variety and individuality. Through telling stories about imaginary realms and creatures freely entering the "painfully established" and systematized world order Rushdie wants to establish a new imaginary world without cultural pains.

Works Cited

Bhabha, Homi K. *The Location of Culture.* London and New York: Routledge, 1994.

Boehmer, Elleke. *Colonial and Postcolonial Literature. Migrant Metaphors.* 2nd ed. New York: Oxford University Press, 2005.

Cundy, Catherine. *Salman Rushdie.* Manchester: Manchester UP. 1996.

Deszcz, Jusyana. "Salman Rushdie's Magical Kingdom: *The Moor's Last Sigh* and Fairy-Tale Utopia." *Marvels &Tales: Journal of Fairy-Tale Studies.* 18.1 (2004): 28-52.

Dey, Pradip Kumar. "*Shame* and *Midnight's Children*: A Postcolonial Critique". *Salman Rushdie: Critical Essays.* Ed. Ray Mohit K. and Rama Kundu. Vol.1. NewDelhi: Atlantic, 2006.

Eagleton, Terry, Fredric Jameson, Edward W. Said. *Nationalism, Colonialism, and Literature.* Minneapolis and London: University of Minnesota Press, 1990.

Foucault, M. "Of Other Spaces." Trans. Jay Miskowiec. *Diacritics* 16.1. (1986): 22–27.

_______. *"Society Must Be Defended": Lectures at the Collège de France, 1975–1976.* Trans. David Macey. New York: Picador, 2003.

Frank, Michael C. "Imaginative Geography as a Travelling Concept." *European Journal of English Studies.* 13. 1. (2009): 61-77. < *http://dx.doi.org/10.1080/13825570802708188*> Accessed: 27 February 2011.

Grass, Gunter. "Fictions Are Lies That Tell the Truth: Salman Rushdie and Gunter Grass: In Conversation." *Conversation with Salman Rushdie*. Ed. Michael Reder. Jackson: University Press of Missisipi, 2000.

Haffenden, John. "Salman Rushdie." *Conversations with Salman Rushdie*. Ed.Michael Reder. Jackson: UP Mississippi, 2000.

Hansen, Michael. "Old Stable Ego of the Character: The Politics of Identity in Rushdie's Fiction." *Salman Rushdie: New Critical Insights*. Vol.2. Ed. Rajeshwar Mittapalli and Joel Kuortti. New Delhi: Atlantic, 2003. 164-176.

Hassumani, Sabrina. *Salman Rushdie: A Postmodern Reading of His Major Works*. London: Fairleigh Dickinson University Press, 2002.

Lefebvre, Henri. *The Production of Space*. Trans. Donald Nicholson-Smith. [1974]. Cambridge, MA and Oxford: Blackwell, 1991.

Rushdie, Salman. *Grimus*. 1975. Delhi: Vintage, 1996.

_______. *Midnight's Children*. 1981. Delhi: Vintage, 1995.

_______. *Shame*. 1983. Delhi: Vintage, 1995. cited in parenthesis.

_______. *Haroun and the Sea of Stories*. 1990. New Delhi: Granta Books, 1991.

_______. *Imaginary Homelands: Essays and Criticism 1981-1991*. London: Granta Books, 1991.

_______. *The Moor's Last Sigh*. 1995. London: Vintage, 1996.

Soja, Edward W. *Postmodern Geographies: The Reassertion of Space in Critical Social Theory*. London and New York: Verso, 1989.

Teverson, Andrew S. "Fairy Tale Politics: Free Speech and Multiculturalism in *Haroun and the Sea of Stories*." *Twentieth-Century Literature*. 47.4 (Winter 2001): 444-466.

Wallhead, Celia M. "The Subversive Sub-text of Spice in Salman Rushdie's *The Moor's Last Sigh*." *Salman Rushdie: New Critical Insights*. Vol.2. Ed. Rajeshwar Mittapalli and Joel. Kuortti. New Delhi: Atlantic, 2003.65-89.

Walker, Scott D. *Broken Mirrors: The Question of Migrancy in South Asian Fiction in English*. Ph.D Diss. Faculty of the University of Carolina, 2003. Chapel Hill: Umi, 2003.

6

Interpreting Anita Desai's *In Custody* in the Light of Susan Sontag's Critical Essay *Against Interpretation*

— Kirti B. Vitthani

To the question of the purpose of literature, R. A. Scott-James rightly quotes Dryden:

> Dryden is more direct. Delight is the chief, if not the only, end of poesy.
>
> (Scott-James, 2000, 141)

The literary scholars have elucidated theories and concepts which try to make their explanation about the question 'Why do we read literature?' Plato, Aristotle, Phillip Sidney and many others gave their views and opinions on the aim and purpose of literature. The present paper discusses *In Custody* by Anita Desai and Susan Sontag's theory of interpreting any work of art comparatively. In the beginning of the paper, there is a brief discussion of the essay *Against Interpretation* by Susan Sontag and her theory of interpretation. The paper attempts a correlation between the theory and the novel with examples and arguments. There are many inter-links between these two pieces of writings. There are common issues and thoughts in both the works which raise many questions to the topic in question 'how to read literature'. Both of them mostly discuss the function of poetry and its survival from time to time. If we compare both – the novel and the essay—we can find both of them go parallel. Susan Sontag, in her essay, discusses her views about interpretation of art in general and literature in particular. She has compared many arts and the interpretation of the old and the modern. *Against Interpretation* is an essay that makes the interpreter of art aware about the misunderstandings and assumptions about art. She discusses interpretation not in the broadest sense. But by making it narrow, she calls it an act of defending, understanding, or to pick out certain codes and rules on the work of art of particular elements.

Anita Desai insightfully narrates the aesthetics of art versus modern tools of comprehension. The novel mainly concentrates on Urdu poet Nur and the lover of his poetry Deven. Deven undertakes the project and a task to interview the poet and make him known to the outer world. He has a noble cause in his mind but he cannot manage with the situation since he is the man belonging to the category which believes in pleasure giving quality of art and literature. As Urdu language and the poet himself are dying, it causes lots of problems to Deven to accomplish his task. In doing so, he is searching for a way to satisfy his own self for Urdu poetry as he is a great lover of it. He faces bitter reality and gets frustrated when he finds his childhood hero and a great poet Nur in his worst condition. He cannot understand the co-relation between the poet and his poetry. Even he realises that he lives a doubled life. He teaches Hindi at a college and loves Urdu which splits his personality apart. Finally he decides to be the guardian of the dying poetry of Nur. He feels the beauty of the poetry from within and goes beyond the criticism of literature which we might call aesthetics.

Though Anita Desai stated once that "her novels are no reflection of Indian society, politics or character", her novels deal with issues which have great relevance to modern times. Her novels are not only the social documents but they are also really great works of art. She herself says, "Writing is to me a process of discovering the truth – the truth that is nine-tenth of the iceberg that lies submerged beneath the one-tenth of visible portion we call reality. Writing is my way of plunging to the depths and exploring this underlying truth. All my writing is an effort to discover, to underline and convey the true significance of things."

In Anita Desai's *In Custody,* one can easily find a dexterous use of symbols, feminist approach, and an attempt to depict the truth of human life. *In Custody* describes the life of an ordinary man, called Deven Sharma, a lecturer of Hindi at a small college in a small town. A timid, ordinary man leads his life of mediocrity with empty dreams. Through this character, Anita Desai deals with the issue which has great relevance to modern materialistic world where money seems to be the only goal worth aspiring for. What is the place of art in such a world forms the theme of this novel. We can find the chain of happenings, one leading to the other, which bring the protagonist on the verge of ruin.

Susan Sontag in her essay emphasizes on the outer beauty, the pleasure one gets while reading literature. She believes that it is harmful to analyze literature from the scientific approach or else the work of art is destroyed.

> Today is such a time, when the project of interpretation is largely reactionary, stifling. Like the fumes of the automobile and of heavy industry which befoul the urban atmosphere, the effusion of interpretations of art today poisons our sensibilities. In a culture whose already classical dilemma is the hypertrophy of the intellect at the expense of energy and sensual capability, interpretation is the revenge of the intellect upon art.
>
> (Sontag, 2001, 07)

Deven is a (sort of) lover of Urdu poetry, like his father, and considers himself to be failure in life, with one aspiration in life. The novel is about his journey, in which he becomes something from nothing. He remains passive in the most part of action of the novel. He is given the idea to take aninterview of a great Urdu poet, Nur, and prepare an article upon him by his friend Murad. Suddenly he remembers his childhood days when his father and mother used to recite Nur's Urdu poetry to him. He could enjoy the poetry much then and still remembers them. Now, too, he can memorize some lines from him and we find him reciting them whenever he feels so. Since childhood, he has developed and continued his interest in Nur's poetry. Nur becomes his holy hero though he never met him before. This shows the effect of art – work of art – on the reader, that art has the power of its own to attract the people in its own way. The poetry of Nur had been never explained to Deven, yet he enjoys them. But as soon as he takes the project to record the poetry, what he finds is only scribbles and scraps. It is a very strong example relevant to the above statement by Sontag. When he delivers the completed project to the authority of his college, and plays the tape, it is almost nothing. All his hard work and labour is a big zero.

> It was a big fiasco. There was no other word for it. Disbelievingly, Deven had the first tape removed, the second tried and then the third and the fourth. The cardboard carton that held them seemed bottomless, there were so many… When the tapes could be induced to produce sound, there seemed to be nothing to listen to – long intervals of crackling and sputtering interspersed with a sudden blare of horns from the street, the shrieking of nest-building birds, loud explosions of laughter and incoherent joviality, drunken voices bawling, singing, stopping short. Where was Nur? Occasionally his voice wandered in like some lost mendicant off a crowded street, offering a few lines of verse in a faint, foundering voice, then breaking off…"
>
> (Desai, 1984, 173)

Interpretation sometimes becomes an intellectual revenge upon art. As we find in the novel, the central idea of Deven's – rather Murad's project – is to introduce Nur and his outdated, old poetry to the outer world. But when Nur's first wife demands money for the project, Deven drops his mission. He has no more interest in Nur's poetry now. He suddenly forgets his hero and the power of his poetry. In a way, he is trying to make it a materialistic issue. But once he gets money from his college, he once again starts his mission, fighting against many problems, domestic as well as social. Nur's 'The World' which is so marvellous in Deven's past memories has now faded and becomes this world – the world in which Sarla and Manu are also living, the world of his college and so on. His personality is torn among so many worlds in which he is living. It contributes to the loss of the aesthetic values of his imaginative world – the world of Nur's poetry.

One more example we can find in the novel is that we can call the same kind of revenge. Deven goes very near with some assumptions and some prejudices in his mind. Now, he wants to criticize Nur's poetry with his intellectual mind. But he finds at the end that his intellectual analysis of the poetry kills the real glamour of the poetry. Even the process is quite time consuming. It requires much money as well as energy, simultaneously less sensuousness. There was a time when he did not know Nur very closely; he was very excited by even one thought. Though he was teaching Hindi, he was a fan of Urdu poetry. But when he is himself too close to Nur's life, he suddenly is no more sensitive.

When Deven asks Nur to recite poetry of some particular period, Nur becomes very angry. His anger expresses his sad and disillusioned state of mind. It is Nur whose poetry fascinated Deven to accept the project in the beginning, and it is the same Nur who evaporates all the belief of Deven about the relationship of the author and his creations. Nur argues about the evergreen effect of poetry and poet. They cannot be confined to a limited space.

> The effect was disastrous. Nur, in the act of reaching out for a drink, froze. 'Poetry?' he shot at Deven, harshly. 'Poetry of the period? Do you think a poet can be ground between stones, and bled, in order to produce poetry – for *you*? You think you can switch on that mincing machine, and I will instantly produce for you length of raw, red minced meat that you can carry off to your professors to eat?'
>
> (Desai, 1984, 156)

When Deven visits Nur, he realises that he has made a mistake. His prior assumptions do not help him. He finds that Nur is not the sublime genius, not the holy hero of Deven's imaginings, but an old man with an old man's problems and weaknesses. This shows no connection between the art and the artists. Poetry gives him pleasure when he is away from it but poetry itself creates so many problems when he tries to go deep into. What he has imagined fades away when even Murad gets less interested in the same project. He undertakes the assignment to enjoy Nur's poetry completely. And for this reason he enters the world of the author to interpret his poetry more precisely. But he finds that his sense of pleasure-giving quality of Urdu poetry is collapsing. Not only Urdu poetry and Nur are degrading from their higher degree but also the whole tradition of aesthetic is descending because of the interference of modern techniques to literature. He tries to relate his past memories of pleasure to the modern ways of interpretation. It is the perfect example where one can find parallelism between the idea of interpretation and its harmfulness.

The history of interpreting art is nothing but only defence. In the novel, *In Custody*, we find that everybody defends himself with one or another reason. Murad always finds excuses to make Deven ready to work for his journal. Deven also finds excuses to save his project and himself. He always seems to tell that for this mistake he is not responsible. After the recording is finished, when he comes to know that it is good for nothing, he blames the boy Chiku, the technical assistant, and Jain the shopkeeper. He is not ready to accept the truth that Nur and his poetry stay in totally opposite direction.

Deven unconsciously reveals the hollowness of his project. Nur himself and his life poison the beauty of his poetry that prevailed in the beginning. According to Sontag, interpretation is the act of mind which picks out some elements, rules and codes of interpretation (deriving limited meaning of the text). That is what Deven continuously tries to find out from the poetry of Nur through him. He plays the role of an observer, whenever he meets

Nur and tries to find out or to know the reasons why Nur's poetry is so much effective and why it is so different from his life. He is so alienated from the real situation that he misleadingly falls into the wrong track. He tries to store the beautiful poetry into a scientific device. But in doing so, the aesthetic power completely collapses.

> The room in which the poet lay resting, like a great bolster laid on a flat low wooden divan, was in semi darkness. Not only were the bamboo screens hanging in every doorway let down to keep out the sun that beat upon the top floor of the building most fiercely, but the walls were lined with dark green tiles that added to the shadowy gloom. The few pieces of furniture – single armchair with elongated arms that seemed designed for some earlier, larger species of man, a small gate-legged table, piled with very shabby books, a revolving bookcase with more of them, several solid cushions and bolsters cast upon the cotton mats on the floor—were like objects carved out of this murkiness, heavy and palpable with gloom.
>
> (Desai, 1984, 40)

The semi-darkness is very symbolic here. It is the real beauty of poetry which lies within as darkness. The poet lives in the room where minimum light falls. Sun light is a symbol for criticism which by nature is interested in inward rather than outward beauty. It tries to dig out the innermost part of the rhetoric and by doing so accesses the fact lying within. Consciously or unconsciously it extinguishes the pleasure one should get by feeling it.

> 'Urdu poetry?' he finally sighed, turning a little to one side, towards Deven although not actually addressing himself to a person, merely to a direction, it seemed. 'How can there be Urdu poetry when there is no Urdu language left? It is dead, finished. The defeat of the Moghuls by British threw a noose over its head, and the defeat of British by the Hindi-wallahs tightened it. So now you see its corpse lying here, waiting to be buried.' He tapped his chest with one finger.
>
> (Desai, 1984, 42)

The dying condition of the poet and poetry points out toward the horrible nature of criticism and interpretations. The colonial and post-colonial elements and effects are revealed here in the voice of Nur. Other things like pigeons, the darkness of the house, silence are also very important which give a little more idea about the poet's life. Nobody in the novel can understand why Nur takes so much care of pigeons. But he himself makes it clear that his poetry lives with pigeons and will die with them. Even Deven takes the voice of pigeons as a disturbance for him in his work whereas pigeons are the very soul of Nur and his poetry.

The interpretation of any work of art keeps on changing by time and its demands. The same thing happens in the novel. In his childhood, Deven had one particular idea about Nur's poetry but by and by he starts to understand it. And finally he decides to go to the bottom of the poetry but what he finds is disastrous. For going into the inner depth of the poetry, he has perhaps selected wrong way to go to Nur. He should have concentrated upon the poetry itself and tried to judge it by itself. Finally when he realises his mistake, he reconciles with the situation and gets ready to answer anything, to face any difficulty. What Nur feels for his poetry is entirely different from what Deven experts. And these both may be different from the true one.

By interpreting any text, the interpreter claims to make it easy to understand it. For example, Murad indirectly forces Deven to take an interview of Nur and let him be popular and alive in the world. Deven takes it as a golden opportunity of making Nur his hero alive by his own strength. But in doing so, we find that the recording he has prepared after the interview is as meaningless as his own and Nur's life. Still he claims that it should be kept in a library for others to know Nur. And finally we find him as a guardian of Nur's poetry which is within himself. It shows that he has the sense of poetry. It is not complete realization but a disillusionment of a common lover of literature.

Susan Sontag says in her essay:

> The modern style of interpretation excavates, destroys, digs 'behind' the text to find a sub-text which is the true one. To interpret is to impoverish, to deplete the world – in order to set up a shadow world of 'meanings'. It is to turn 'the world' into 'this world'. ('This world'! As if there were any other.)
>
> (Sontag, 2001, 07)

Nur's personal life, Deven's role in the novel, the author's biography, the historical background of the novel etc. are considered as complements to make the text comprehensible. But in doing so the beauty of the text gets disguised. When we dig the earth, we get the real true soil – true knowledge—but by deforming the same. When we relate it to any art, it harms the real charm of art. In doing so, the aesthetic power of art will be destroyed. A post-mortem of a body will destroy the beauty of it. The same thing Deven wants to do with the Urdu poetry. By taking an interview of the great Urdu poet, he wants to know about the past. But when he gets closer and nearer, he finds only raw material that is absolutely in a mess. After a hot discussion on the survival of Urdu versus Hindi, Nur gets upset and cannot digest his food. He vomits. This nausea is very symbolic here. The substance which Deven looks for as it comes out of the mouth of Nur suggests inner reality. Whenever anyone tries to interpret or to analyze the poetry, he will find some undigested/ indigestible substance like Nur's vomit. Deven is asked to clean the vomit of Nur with old papers which he does. When he is standing in the veranda with the papers in his hand:

> The papers between his fingers oozed and stank. He stared at them in repulsion, not quite certain how he came to be holding them... He clutched them tightly in order to overcome his own repulsion and then did what every instinct in him told him to do – raced down the veranda, hurled himself down the stairs, broke through the door into the lane, and there dropped the parcel into the gutter, and fled. He was at the end of the lane, at the corner where the

> street light blazed with normality, before it occurred to him that those papers he had thrown away might have been inscribed with Nur's Poetry.
>
> (Desai, 1984, 61-62)

Today it is believed that art should be judged by itself, without its author, culture, history and so on. But Deven is trying to relate poetry with the poet's past and present, which makes him somewhat biased, taking away from the real pleasure of art. Without any prejudice, if one judges art, one may have innumerable dimensions, but still the merit of work of art lies somewhere else.

Deven wants to make poetry easy to understand and to keep it alive with his project of his recording. He wants to make poetry somewhat popular in the modern age, and that is why he is struggling throughout the novel. But at the end he fails to do so. He understands the poetry to some extent and gets success at some extent but not entirely. It is interesting to note that he skips some part in recording from the original. If we consider the whole recording as art, it gives a hint that he is trying to find out the contents to make it easy to understand, to make it acceptable so that every common person can understand it. But it is felt that the whole activity of making art understandable that Deven is doing seems to be for himself and not for the others. All critics are doing the same! And finally the real art is replaced by its content – that we call criticism. As R. J. Rees rightly comments on the production of 'books about books' – criticism:

> The habit of reading too many 'books about books' is one which the students of literature should do his best to avoid. The production of such books is now almost a major industry; and for everyone reputable poet or novelist or dramatist there are probably a hundred research students, lecturers, professors or critics, all busily interpreting the *real* writers, and of course writing books about each other's books... In our time they deal with wider variety of subjects... being literary criticism of the kind which serves to

> divert our attention from the real works of literature we ought to be studying and enjoying.
>
> (Rees, 1973, 17)

Sometimes we can find that Nur's poetry is transferred to his second wife and to Deven. It is important to note that after this transfer, it becomes an art of re-writing the text by somebody else. Unconsciously Deven becomes a critic of Nur's poetry and by giving another voice to it, he is in reality altering the text. On the last day of recording, when poetry was recited by some another person, Deven loses his own interest that was there in the beginning. It is a nice example to quote which shows the destruction of the original art. Art is transferred from its originality and the claim is made to make it intelligible and manageable. But in doing so the original beauty is ruined.

The novel also points a finger towards the extinction of arts and humanities departments in the universities. When Deven goes for the fund for his project of recording of Nur's poetry, he depicts the status of humanities departments.

> Not being sure either what the status of Urdu department was, he could not predict how the proposal would be met. He was perfectly aware that funds were being made readily available to the science departments, that the sciences were the rajas of the empire with the humanities pushed to the dustier and ore neglected corner where they languished. If any of the humanities departments received any attention, it was usually economics and political science. The languages were not considered departments worthy of any attention of the financial kind beyond the meager funds allocated to the library.
>
> (Desai, 1984, 102)

Sometimes in the novel, Deven tries to separate the poet and his poetry as in the episode of vomiting. It is impossible to sift them. They are like body and soul. The interview is taken in brothel that shows again the importance of an art, not its meaning – history, time and place. The place of interview is arranged by

Nur's first wife who does not know anything about poetry and only interested in money. She receives the same as Murad is interested in the article.

We should receive art as it is instead of making its post-mortem. The beauty of art lies within art itself. It does not lie in the life of a poet or its interpretation of the interpreter or in the mind of the reader. There is no interpretation, all are misinterpretations. So many interpretations can be possible or made possible of any art. Even the title seems problematic because of its meanings. It has positive and negative interpretations. Instead of doing its scientific analysis, we should enjoy it from the very soul. At the end of the novel, we can find that Deven accepted Nur's poetry from within. He got courage to face any difficulties in being the custodian of his hero's poetry. Instead of our mind, we should try to appreciate poetry with our heart. Art appeals to the heart rather than the mind.

Criticism of art should be transparent so as to understand the art. To interpret does not mean to find just plenty of elements or contents – criticism but it also means the need to—understand the art. It is the first step. Further, one requires more attention from the heart to see more, to feel more and to hear more. Our senses should be very powerful and attentive if we really want to enjoy art. Then and only then can we have enough courage to keep art in our custody – guardianship. Otherwise it becomes imprisonment as happens to Deven in the novel.

While returning:

> ... he tried to return to his old idolatry of the poet, his awe of him, his devotion when it had still been pure, and his gratitude for his poetry and friendship, that strange, unexpected, unimaginable friendship that had brought him so much pain.
>
> That friendship still existed, even if there had been a muddle, a misunderstanding. He had imagined he was taking Nur's poetry into safe custody, and not realized that if he was to be custodian of Nur's genius, then Nur would become his custodian and place

> him in custody too. This alliance could be considered an unendurable burden – or else a shining honour."
>
> (Desai, 1984, 203)

The spiritual relation that continues even after the death of the great poet gives the gist of the real aesthetic which literature always acquires.

Works Cited

Desai, Anita. *In Custody*. England: Penguin Books Ltd. 1985. Print *http://biography.jrank.org/pages/4264/Desai-Anita.html*, Accessed on 22/03/2011

Kohli, Devindra and Mellanie Maria Just. *Anita Desai: Critical Perspective.* New Delhi: Pencraft International. 2008. Print

Rees, R. J. *English Literature: An Introduction for Foreign Readers.* New Delhi: MacMillan India Ltd. 2000. Print

Scott-James. R. A. *The Making of Literature.* New Delhi: Allied Publishers Limited. 2000. Print

Sontag, Susan. *Against Interpretation and Other Essays.* New York: Picador USA. 2001. Print

7

Postmodern Diasporic Sensibility: Rereading Jhumpa Lahiri's Oeuvre

— Pinaki Roy

It has long been debated whether Indian-English writers of the diaspora can be included in the list of the Indo-Anglian litterateurs. More specifically, the point of scepticism is whether the oeuvres of Bharati Mukherjee, Salman Rushdie, Amitav Ghosh, Rohinton Mistry or Kiran Desai can be, on terms of conceptual and productive excellence, compared to or contrasted with those of Raja Rao, Rasipuram Krishnaswami Narayan, Mulk Raj Anand, Anita Desai, Kamala Markandaya or Nayantara Sahgal.

Interestingly, Uma Parameswaran prioritises the Indian English writers of the diaspora for being more consciously efficient because, first of all, they have to adjust themselves to the new country of immigration; second, they have to balance their senses of their self-identity and ethno-cultural community against the demands for objective writings, and finally, nostalgia for homeland always remains a powerfully distracting force to be reckoned with (12). She writes, "[...] [O]ne needs to look between the lines of Diaspora writings to analyse the presence of various factors such as western readers' neo imperialism, western publishers' marketability requirements, the liminality of the Diasporic world, authors' psychological hang-ups about their original homelands, [...] and [...] anglomania [...]".

The only novel and two short-story collections of Jhumpa Lahiri, born 'Nilanjana Sudeshna' in London on 11 July 1967, exhibit the presence of almost all the factors demarcated by Parameswaran, and yet, in the twenty-first century, they are being hailed as being among the more important contributions to the fast and ever-expanding realms of Indian Writings in English *(I.W.E.)*.

Writing about Jhumpa Lahiri's first collection of short-stories, *Interpreter of Maladies: Stories of Bengal, Boston and Beyond* (1999), which was awarded the 2000 Pulitzer Prize for Fiction, C.V.B.T. Sundari comments, "Jhumpa Lahiri represents the school of postmodern feminism where the focus is on understanding the role of women in the society and striving for their betterment as a whole, which is in sharp contrast to the rebellious modern feminism which was very popular in 60s and 70s. Hence, not very surprisingly, her stories are woven around women characters with myriad temperaments which are as varied as the collection of species in any Indian kitchen" (169).

Lahiri, other than being identifiably a feminist, poignantly but artistically presents the disillusionment and despair that the people of Indian origin, particularly those with relatives or ancestors in Bengal, face while adjusting to the Western culture and ethos in neo-imperialist or colonising countries like the United states of America and the United Kingdom. Her own experiences, enlisted below, perceptibly influenced her constructing the unforgettable and mostly-female characters that contribute to the readability of her novel and short-story collections: *Interpreter of Maladies, The Namesake* (2003), and *Unaccustomed Earth* (2008). *Unaccustomed Earth*, a collection of five short-stories and an episode "Hema and Kaushik", won, respectively in 2008 and 2009, the Frank O' Connor International Short Story Award and Asian American Literary Award. In 1999, she won O' Henry Award for Short Story and P.E.N./Hemingway Award for Best Fiction Debut of the Year for her Interpreter of Maladies.

This essay aims to focus limitedly on Lahiri's oeuvre. Prior to this, it needs a brief discussion on whether twentieth and twenty-first century Indian writers in English can be termed as postmodernists. Geoffrey Lord writes that the role of multicultural authors in the advancement of literary postmodernism, particularly that in English, in the present century is becoming complex but substantial. The boundaries of 'English' have spread – subsuming works from all over the English-speaking world – and so have that of English postmodernism (Lord 50-6). Authors of Indian origin writing in English, including those belonging to the diaspora, are, in this context, normally identified as postmodernists. In the introduction to *Indian English Literature: A Postcolonial Response*, Kumar and Ojha reread the connection to postmodernism and postcolonial responses like Indo-Anglian literature (7-8), just like Sobha Chattopadhyay juxtaposes postmodernism and the postcoloniality of Indian English writings (119-20). In addition, Ghosh-Schellhorn and Alexander, in their 'Introduction' to *Peripheral Centres, Central Peripheries* (5), and Ellen Dengel-Janic in "South Asia" (147-8) have tried to show the connection between postmodernism and Indian English writings of the diaspora. In such contexts, Lahiri may be identified as a postmodernist writer of the Indian diaspora.

However, readers of her short-stories and novel also need to refer to some of the biographical facts from the litterateur's life for a deeper understanding of the psychological constructs of her essentially Indian and mostly Bengali characters like Shobha and Shukumar ("A Temporary Matter"), Mr. Pirzada ("When Mr. Pirzada came to Dine"), Ashoke Ganguli and Ashima Bhaduri (*The Namesake*), Ruma and her father ("Unaccustomed Earth"), or Pranab Chakraborty ("Hell-Heaven"). Many of her characters have emerged out of the author's personal acquaintances and experiences. To exemplify, Jhumpa Lahiri's father is confessedly the basis for the protagonist-narrator of "The Third and Final Continent".[1] The train accident, an important episode in *The Namesake* which forever binds Ashoke Ganguli to Nikolai

Gogol, actually occurred in 1961 in which one of the cousins of Jhumpa's father was almost-fatally injured.[2] Haldar of "The Treatment of Bibi Haldar" was actually a young and impoverished spinster whom the author met during her several visits to her uncle's Kolkata residence.[3] In her writings, the Bengali immigrants are always found cautious not to forget their Bengali roots and often pay visits to Kolkata – sentiments which the writer's mother herself nursed.[4] In *The Namesake*, Ashima Bhaduri shrinks one of her husband's sweaters in a washing machine (Lahiri, *The Namesake* 10): an incident undoubtedly drawn on the confusion Lahiri's mother had with the Laundromat after migrating to the United States.[5] Phani Bhushan Sanyal, Jhumpa's maternal grandfather, was a painter, just like Nikhil Ganguli's in the 2003 novel.[6]

Jhumpa Lahiri, who is presently a member of the U.S. President's Committee on the Arts and Humanities, was born in London to the U.K.-immigrated Bengalis, Amar Lahiri and Tia Sanyal, a teacher. The Lahiris migrated to the United States of America in 1970, and the future Indo-Anglian writer grew up in Kingston, where Amar Lahiri found employment as a librarian with the University of Rhode Island. At the future-litterateur's Kingston kindergarten school, one of her teachers deducted her first names 'Nilanjana' and 'Sudeshna' and opted for the pet name 'Jhumpa' because it was easy to pronounce. In "Diasporic Crisis of Dual Identity n Jhumpa Lahiri's *The Namesake*", Sujata Rana quotes the novelist to show how the first names and surnames are important in identity formations of individuals, and yet they cannot choose them (180). Lahiri used this 'embarrassing experience of having a pet-name as the first name' to depict the ambivalence exhibited by Nikhil 'Gogol' Ganguli in *The Namesake*.[7] She competed her schooling from South Kingstown High School, Washington County, and received her graduate degree in 1989 from Barnard College, New York. She thereafter took three masters degrees – in English, Creative Writing, and Comparative Literature – from Boston University, Boston, also obtaining a doctorate in Renaissance Studies. In 1997-98, she was a fellow at Provincetown's Fine Arts Work Centre, and in 2001 married the Guatemalan-Greek-American journalist, Alberto Vourvoulias-Bush, with whom and her two children Octavio (born in 2002) and Noor (born 2005), she presently lives in Brooklyn, New York. In her infancy, Noor Vourvoulias-Bush was shown having her first meal (as Sonia Ganguli as a child) by Mira Nair in her film-adaptation of *The Namesake*, which premiered in 2006.

During Precious Williams's interview with Lahiri, the Indo-Anglian author recounts how the short stories and articles she has had been writing since 1977 used to be rejected by publishers.[8] Almost frustrated, she began to prepare for teaching at a university or college. However, during her studentship at *Boston University*, she once again began to pursue seriously her dreams of becoming a published author, writing 'enough' essays to win a seven-month writing fellowship in Provincetown, Massachusetts. In 1998, three of her short stories including "A Temporary Matter" (which were later to be included in *The Interpreter of Maladies*) were published in *The New Yorker* to rave reviews. In the following year, Houghton Mifflin Harcourt, Boston, published *Interpreter of Maladies*, which was immediately chosen as *The New Yorker*'s 'Best Debut of the Year' and went on Oprah Winfrey's *Top Ten Books' List.* The stories, dealing with Indian-Americans caught between the cultures of their homeland and their newly-adopted country, have been described by Katrak as unitedly reflecting the trauma of self-transformation through immigration (5-6), and, to reiterate, won in 2002 the Pulitzer Prize for Fiction.

Interpreter of Maladies is a collection of nine short stories – "A Temporary Matter" (pp. 1-22 in Harper Collins's edition), "When Mr. Pirzada Came to Dine" (pp. 23-42), "Interpreter of Maladies" (pp. 43-69), "A Real Durwan" (pp. 70-82), "Sexy" (pp. 83-110), "Mrs. Sen's" (pp. 111-135), "This Blessed House" (pp. 136-157), "The Treatment of Bibi Haldar" (pp. 158-172), and

"The Third and Final Continent" (pp. 173-198). In "A Temporary Matter", Shoba and Shukumar are two U.S.-immigrated Bengali couple that are having serious problems with their marriage – which are not comprehended by the husband himself. Their still-born son has had further estranged the couple, and while Shoba gets more and more self-absorbed and negligent to her household chores, Shukumar blames her without attempting to understand her sentiments. When the electric-supply department of their U.S. town decide to repair the fledging lines, shutting off supply for one hour between eight and nine in evening for five consecutive days, the husband and wife decide to pass the time confessing their dark secrets to each other. This serves to bring them together temporarily: "His heart quickened. All day Shukumar had looked forward to the lights going out" (Lahiri, *Interpreter* 15).

Finally, Shoba manages to tell her husband in darkness that she has had found a separate apartment on Beacon Hill and the story-telling concludes with obvious signs of an irreparable breakdown of marriage: "It was nobody's fault, she continued. They'd been through enough. She needed some time alone. [...] It sickened Shukumar, knowing that she had spent these past evenings preparing for a life without him. He was relieved and yet he was sickened" (ibid. 21). Nicole Smith thus reads the story: "Unfortunately, the power outage is a 'temporary matter' and something that is not a great life event, and thus it cannot trump all of the little things that have been a signalling a problem with the couple's marriage. 'A Temporary Matter' by Jhumpa Lahiri has shown that is the little things in life that form and define all of the major events in our lives and it will take more than something temporary to solve these problems or shed light on the truth. Although it may seem as though the couple's problems do not come to light until the temporary matter of the power outage, the whole story, comprised of small, seemingly insignificant memories or thoughts are just as important as the confessions of not being in love the same way".[9] It needs mentioned that "A

Temporary Matter" was dramatised and staged by the performers of *Expressions* in Hyderabad in July 2010.

"When Mr. Pirzada Came to Dine" is narrated by Lilia, an Indo-American girl, settled in New England, who, just like the narrators of Amitav Ghosh's *The Shadow Lines* (1988) and Bapsi Sidhwa's *Ice-Candy Man* (1991), exhibits perplexity at how the 1971-war between India and Pakistan occurring thousands of kilometres away from the United States of America changes the relationship between the former-Dacca-resident Mr. Pirzada and her parents who have had initially preferred dining or watching television with the U.S.-settled South Asian about whom they know so little. Earlier, the child-narrator thought that Mr. Pirzada was Indian just like them, but her father tells her, "Mr. Pirzada won't be coming today. More importantly, Mr. Pirzada is no longer considered Indian. [...] Not since Partition. [...] One moment we were free and then we were sliced up" (Lahiri, *Interpreter* 25). Lilia mentions, "For many, the idea of eating in the other's company was still unthinkable" (ibid.), which makes no sense to her because "Mr. Pirzada and [her] parents spoke the same language, laughed at the same jokes, looked more or less the same" (ibid.). An anonymous reviewer of the short-story comments, "It is amazing how we consider ourselves different sometimes. Whether it is our value in society, our goals and our dreams, and sometimes even the food we eat. Lahiri shows us what the common ground is through Lilia's eyes. It is our reasons and our concerns about the people we love that should bring us together. Only then can we find a familiar ground".[10]

In "The Interpreter of Maladies", Mr. Kapasi acts as a guide to the New-Jersey-settled couple – the Dass – who are visiting Orissa with their three children Ronny, Bobby, and Tina. When Mina Das finds Mr. Kapasi's job as an interpreter of Gujarati patients' problems at a physician's chamber 'romantic' and one of a 'big responsibility' (Lahiri, *Interpreter* 50-1), he begins to take a romantic interest in the young woman. She responds by confiding in him the secret that her son Bobby is not of Raj Das but born out of an adulterous affair with one of her husband's friends (ibid. 64). Mina Das had expected no comments or judgement from Mr. Kapasi but he soon reveals his disappointment in her and points out her guilt, which angers her and she abruptly ends the guide's fancied bond of attachment. Anurima Banerjee writes, "In the end, the guide is stymied by the psychological nature of [...] [Mina Das's] particular ailment, unable to answer her disillusion and depression with any hope of consolation. His inability to deliver a prognosis paralyses them both, and their brief connection is severed. While he is adequate to the task of translating illnesses of the body, he has failed as an interpreter of maladies afflicting the soul. All of Lahiri's stories are infused with this characteristic imprint of melancholy" (37).

"A Real Durwan" is probably the most pathetic and poignant of all the collections in *Interpreter of Maladies*. A critique of globalisation that began seriously affecting the common Indians' life in late-twentieth century, rendering millions homeless and alienating individuals even within the same society, the story concerns with how Boori Maa, an emaciated sexagenarian from Kolkata, is thrown out from an old brick building under whose staircase she has had been granted temporary residence by the occupants in exchange for floor-sweeping and 'surveillance'. The old woman is initially taken care of by the Dalals, who leave for a visit to Shimla promising to bring a real woollen blanket for the destitute (Lahiri, *Interpreter* 79).

When in their absence, one of the building's sinks installed by them is stolen, Boori Maa is suspected of informing 'robbers' and accused of 'neglecting surveillance duties', following which she is expelled from the house and a search for a salaried caretaker is initiated. Nayar writes abut how the notions of belonging or home and the resulting dilemmas of dislocation or preoccupations present themselves in a subtle manner even in "A Real Durwan": "Boori Ma [...] sweeper of the stairwell in an old Calcutta building, stays but does not belong. Lahiri brings out the pathos of her situation with gentle sympathy. Graphically brought alive, Boori Ma, with her mite-infested quilt, broom and skeleton keys (of closets left behind in Pakistan) tied along with her life savings to the free end of her sari, loved to chronicle the easier times, she had or did not have. Twice a day, she would enumerate details of her plight and losses suffered since her deportation to Calcutta after Partition. An outsider, she narrates what is sceptically viewed as fictional account of her days spent in clover'.[11] Haldar, the 29-year-old 'protagonist' of "The Treatment of Bibi Haldar", finds herself in a disposition not very unlike that of Boori Maa, perceptively because she also belongs to one of the lower economic strata of Indian society. Katherine Wcislo writes, "[The] [...] epileptic woman in Kolkata with few relations remains in the grudging care of her cousin and his wife while attempting to find herself a husband and a cure for her ailments. While it remains consistent with Lahiri's overall theme of isolation, she says herself that 'the story is basically about the town's involvement' in Bibi's search for a husband and her own sense of happiness [...]. Community solidifies the identity of Bibi Haldar because she has no real family. Through the communal device, Lahiri identifies the accentuated isolation of this character in her native city even when surrounded by the same people that have always surrounded her".[12]

"Sexy" recounts the affair of (most probably an American woman) Miranda, with a married Indian man, Dev. Unable to identify his precise nationality and having succumbed to the charms of the exotic older man (Lahiri, *Interpreter* 88), Miranda both prizes and despises the epithet Dev has had whispered to her while visiting the Mapparium at the Christian Science Plaza, Boston (ibid. 91). The story concludes with the non-Indian woman's remembrance of her own status as an adulterous intruder when an eight-year-old-boy, Rohin, who she tries to baby-sit, repeats precisely Dev's line: "You are sexy" (ibid. 107). This shocks her into ending the adulterous liaison immediately.

"Mrs. Sen's" catches the university professor's Indian wife in a dilemma over adjusting herself to the life in the United States. To the eleven-year-old Eliot, whom she looks after following the boy's school-hours, she narrates stories about her previous life in Kolkata, crafting her own separate identity in the process. A significant part of the plot revolves around the Indian woman's tradition of purchasing fish from a local seafood market (ibid. 123-4). Such purchases remind Eliot's elder acquaintance of her home. However, she needs to learn driving to reach the seafood market, but she has hot been able to master the skill. Towards the conclusion of the story, Mrs. Sen attempts to drive to the market without her husband, and ends up in a minor automobile accident. The Indian woman's nostalgia tires Eliot who is relived to be taken away from her. Champeon writes, "[...] [T]he suspicion that Mrs. Sen and Eliot are more than just accidental companions is confirmed [at the end of the story]. Eliot is the product of an advanced stage of social dysfunction, which Mrs. Sen is encountering for the first time. Each has only one other, barely present family member, whom each cannot leave because of emotional dependence created by a void – 'the gray waves' receding from the shore".[13]

"This Blessed House" catches the newly-married Twinkle and Sanjeev coming at terms with their newly-purchased Hartford house, which seems to have had been owned by fanatic Christians. While Sanjeev's wife is delighted to discover in various parts of the house numerous religious symbols and token related to Christianity and wants to display them especially during a forthcoming housewarming party, the husband is uncomfortable because of his remembrance of their Hindu origin. Ironically describing Twinkle's obsession, Lahiri writes, "The weekend before the party, they were raking the lawn when he heard Twinkle shriek. He ran to her, clutching his rake, worried that she had discovered a dead animal, or a snake. [...] When he reached her, she had collapsed on the grass, dissolved in nearly silent laughter. Behind an overgrown forsythia bush was a plaster

Virgin Mary as tall as their waists [...]. Twinkle grabbed the hem of her T-shirt and began wiping away the dirt staining the statue's brow" (Lahiri, *Interpreter* 145-6). On the party-day, the guests praise Twinkle but Sanjeev feels irritated by her naïveté. The story concludes with the disgruntled husband meekly carrying downstairs a large bust of Jesus Christ discovered in the attic. The Indian Hindu Sanjeev may have finally been pressurised into accepting the Western socio-cultural norms, or his action can be reread as his surrendering for the final time to the demands of a marriage he looks forward to end.

The final story in *Interpreter of Maladies* "The Third and Final Continent" deals with how a young immigrant to the 1960s' Massachusetts, who is also the narrator, adjusts to his new American home and new bride. The heroine of the story is perceptively the hundred-and-three-year-old Mrs. Croft, who manages to help the young narrator feel less lonely even after the non-consummation of his marriage. She shows him qualities in his wife that he had not noticed and provides him with a model for his future life. As Wcislo writes, "At the end of the story, Lahiri introduces the idea of loss of cultural identification through passing generations by mentioning the college aged child of the couple. They bring him home to 'eat rice with his hands and speak Bengali' which are 'things [they] sometimes worry he will no longer do after [they] die' [...]. Lahiri presents a couple whose only remaining connection with the country of their origin has a definitive death with their own end because the assimilation of their son into American culture leaves no room for their own cultural orientation".[14]

Lahiri's only novel until 2011, *The Namesake*, was released by *Houghton Mifflin* in a 291-page-format in September 2003. Alternating between Kolkata and New York, the novel, like Lahiri's short stories, explores the different experiences of the Ganguli family members caught between the conflicting cultures of the United States and India.

At the beginning of the novel, Ashoke Ganguli, an engineering student of the Massachusetts Institute of Technology, departs from Kolkata with his newly-married wife, Ashima Bhaduri, and begins to reside at the Central Square of Cambridge, Massachusetts. As the pregnant Bhaduri lie in a Massachusetts hospital for delivering her first child, she realises the extent of her isolation from the country of her birth. At the hospital, she overcomes linguistic barriers to communicate with the gynaecologist, Ashley, and delivers a male child, but she learns that she and Ganguli would not be allowed to leave the hospital until they found a legal name for their chid.

The Gangulis cannot wait for a letter from Ashima's Kolkata grandmother naming the child, and Ashoke christens him 'Gogol'. It is the surname of the M.I.T.-student's favourite author and he was saved by clutching at and slowly waving a Nikolai Gogol-collection while lying in open with broken back following a fatal train accident.

As Gogol grows up, gradually experiencing the ethno-cultural differences among the Americans and the Indian migrants, he starts hating his own name. Ashoke Ganguli feels that he is too young to understand the significance of his name, and together with Bhaduri, names him 'Nikhil'. At college, Gogol uses his official, public name 'Nikhil'. By the time the Yale- and thereafter M.I.T.-educated Gogol is inordinately delayed while returning home by train, an unbridgeable distance has been created between him and his parents. He has begun dating American girls and emulating everything American. Returning home with his son, a concerned Ashoke Ganguli narrates to him the true significance of his name, which makes Gogol changing his own name.

According to Julia Hanna, "No obvious plot line drives *The Namesake*; its movement is managed through matter-of-fact leaps in time that cover a dozen years in straightforward summary. The book also advances through the women who serve as signposts along the road of Gogol's search for identity".[15] While Ashoke Ganguli expires following a massive heart attack working on a project at Ohio, Gogol befriends Maxine Ratliff, an American girl, and accepted as a prospective son-in-law by her financially-privileged, New-York-based parents. However, after his father's death, he moves away from Maxine, and devotes his time to his mother and sister, Sonali. Soon, Ashima introduces him to Moushumi Mazoomdar, the daughter of one of her Bengali friends. They eventually marry, but the relation ends when Mazoomdar begins a sexual affair with Dimitri, one of her earlier acquaintances. At conclusion of the novel, Ashima sells her American house, intending to return back to India. Sonali is poised to marry an American, Benjamin, leaving Gogol all alone, who, nevertheless, finds comfort in his father's memories and the Russian author's stories. Kakutani, in her review of the novel, writes, "Although Lahiri's portraits of the women in Gogol's life are somewhat sketchy, [...] she narrates the story of her hero's coming of age with enormous sympathy and aplomb, while cutting back and forth to fill in the lives of his parents, as they settle into the modest satisfactions of middle age. She uses her unerring eye for detail to annotate their emotional lives. [...] In chronicling more than three decades in the Gangulis' lives, Lahiri has not only given us a wonderfully intimate and knowing family portrait, she has also taken the haunting chamber music of her first collection of stories and reorchestrated its themes of exile and identity to create a symphonic work, a debut novel that is as assured and eloquent as the work of a longtime master of the craft".[16]

C.J. Gillen has compared Lahiri's *The Namesake* to the paintings of Jan Vermeer. The critic is fascinated with the fact that like the seventeenth century-painter, the Indo-Anglian novelist has chosen a limited canvas for an excellent story: "Her tale is modest in proportions, the story of a first-generation Bengali-American boy and his family and their lives in the interstices between the land and culture of their heritage and the social ecology of their life in the U.S.A. Reports from the front lines of twenty-and-thirty-something Americans of South Asian descent indicate that Lahiri's representation is spot on in its particulars – the family and community gatherings watching television with other kids and 'eating watered-down curry off paper plates' while parents converse loudly 'in the Bengali the children do not speak among themselves', the trips 'home' to a strange country, the every-other-Saturday Bengali lessons taught in a friend's house from 'hand sewn primers brought back by their teacher from Kolkata, intended for five-year-olds, printed, Gogol cannot help noticing, on paper that resembles the folded toilet paper he uses at school' – all carefully chosen details that bring the reader right into the settings along with her characters".[17]

Lahiri's second collection of short-stories, *Unaccustomed Earth*, is formed of "Unaccustomed Earth" (pp. 3-59, in the Random House India-edition), "Hell-Heaven" (pp. 60-83), "A Choice of Accommodations" (pp. 84-127), "Only Goodness" (pp. 128-173), "Nobody's Business" (pp. 174-219), and the second section, "Hema and Kaushik", comprising of "Once in a Lifetime" (pp. 223-251), "Year's End" (pp. 252-293), and "Going Ashore" (pp. 294-333). The collection, which takes its name from a passage in Nathaniel Hawthorne's "The Custom-House" (1850), has thus been reviewed by Liesl Schillinger, 'It is easy to forget, given the sensitivities that have been awakened in the U.S.A. since 9/11, thrusting lifelong citizens under suspicion for having foreign-sounding names and subjecting visitors to the indignity of being fingerprinted, that America was conceived in a spirit of openness, as a land where people could build new identities, grounded in the present and the future, not the past. This dream, despite current fears, has in great part been made real. And the fact that America is still a place where the rest of the world comes to reinvent itself – accepting with excitement and anxiety the necessity of leaving behind the constrictions and comforts of distant customs – is the underlying theme of Jhumpa Lahiri's sensitive new collection of stories [...]. Lahiri [...] shows that the place to which you feel the strongest attachment is not necessarily the country you are tied to by blood or birth: it is the place that allows you to become yourself. This place, she quietly indicates, may not lie on any map".[18]

In the title-story of Lahiri's 2008-collection, Ruma and her son Akash, who live in Seattle with Adam, are visited by Ruma's father, a retiree and widower, from Kolkata. When the old man arrives, he is already feeling liberated in the company of Meenakshi Bagchi, a Long Island-woman whom he has befriended. Both the father and his daughter converse limitedly throughout the story – both know that they have moved away from their own cultures and are scared to acknowledge it. About Ruma's father's harmless but secret relationship, Lahiri writes, "That night after dinner he showed his videos. [...] Most of the videos were captured through the window of the tour bus, as a guide explained things about the monuments they were passing. He has always been careful to keep Mrs. Bagchi out of the frame, but as he watched the video enlarged on his daughter's television, he realised that there were traces throughout [...]" (Lahiri, *Unaccustomed* 39). However, slowly Ruma becomes reattached to the elderly man about whose impeding arrival she has had been so uncomfortable – partly because she finds a reassurance in one of her unorthodox parents and partly because the old man devotes much of his time to his grandson.

Only after her father leaves the U.S.A. for India does Ruma come to learn the real cause for his arrival – meeting his newfound companion. Gebbie writes, "Lahiri knows about children. Akash is a wonderful little character, the perfect catalyst to allow his mother and his grandfather to discover things about each other that they do not want to reveal openly. There are many types of unaccustomed earth, literal and metaphorical. Ruma's garden, untended and bare, is planted by her father during his visit, with help (both hilariously and movingly) from Akash. After her father's departure, I like to think that the garden will thrive. The isolation and disempowerment of Ruma sets the theme for the collection".[19]

In "Hell-Heaven", Usha and her traditional Bengali mother, Aparna, who live in Massachusetts with Shyamal, are befriended by Pranab Chakraborty, a graduate student of the M.I.T. As a bond of love slowly develops between Chakraborty and Aparna, Usha the narrator tells how Chakraborty ('Pranabkaku') begins to date an American woman, Deborah – a fact deeply hated and jealously resented by Usha's mother. Aparna guesses that Deborah would divorce Chakraborty within a few years. The couple ultimately divorces after 23 years, but before that "Hell-Heaven" has successfully explored several complex human emotions such as loneliness, love, jealousy, and also described how people change drastically over time. To Apte, "The emotional nuances in this – and all of Lahiri's stories – for that matter, are so beautifully realised that they take your breath away. [...] In her best stories, the most touching realisations come from what is left unsaid, and here too, in Lahiri's signature style, the narrator slowly pieces together the nuggets of information leading to the stunning conclusion in the end".[20]

"A Choice of Accommodations" has as its protagonists the U.S.-settled Amit Sarkar and his American wife, Megan. The couple decides to attend Pam's wedding – Pam being the friend of Sarkar – and they travel without their children. While at the party, Megan is relaxed, the doting Sarkar fears that his children are not safe with his mother-in-law and thinks about past accidents. Readers finally learn that the husband's own childhood experiences with his parents who left him alone at Langford to return to India were the reasons for his insecurity. The sense of fear in him almost makes him jealous of his wife. His insecurities creep in different forms, not allowing him to enjoy his blessings but fear losing them. The story, interestingly, ends with a description of Sarkar and his wife enjoying sexually (Lahiri,

Unaccustomed 126-7). Schillinger so simply sums up, "A Choice of Accommodations' shows a shift in power dynamics between a Bengali-American husband and his workaholic Anglo wife during a weekend away from their kids – at the wedding of the husband's prep-school crush".[21]

"Only Goodness" concerns with a Pennsylvania-settled Bengali sister – Sudha – who feels herself to be responsible for her brother Rahul's alcoholism. Rahul's parents however, tend to overlook his faults, but he does not rectify himself, and leaves his studies at Cornell. The erratic but loving brother visits Sudha's house after her marriage with Roger, and is found sleeping while Sudha's infant son, Neel, sits unattended in cold water (Lahiri, *Unaccustomed* 169-170). Finally, Sudha expels her brother out of her house, comprehending how human beings, however perfect they may appear to be, have their own fallacies.

In "Nobody's Business", the Harvard-attended Sangeeta ('Sang') is depicted as preferring the American ways of life to her Indian remembrances. Love can never be arranged for her. Schillinger mentions, "The American graduate student at the centre of the story pines for his Bengali-American roommate, a graduate-school dropout who entertains no romantic feelings for him, spurns the polite advances of 'prospective grooms' from the global Bengali singles circuit and considers herself engaged to a selfish, foul-tempered Egyptian historian".[22]

"Nobody's Business" depicts how the unmarried and beautiful Sang, a beautiful fields telephone calls from Indian suitors who have acquired her number from the vast Cambridge Bengali network. Narrated through the eyes of her American housemate, Paul, the glamorous Indian-American is rendered pathetic by her love for a selfish man. The story does not end happily because the writer's eye is fixed on exploring the multiplicity of reality, which turns out to be painful.

Finally, in "Hema and Kaushik", Lahiri uses the second-person form of narration. The 'episode' focuses on the U.S-settled

Kaushik and Hema, who, in spite of having common roots, are leading separate ways of life. Just before entering two completely different phases of their lives, two decades after Kaushik's parents lodged with Hema's family as guests, the two characters meet and find that they were mutually tied and attracted. In "Once in a Lifetime", Hema narrates, using the second-person-mode, stories of her own and Kaushik's childhood. Their commonly-acquainted families are described as drifting apart while adjusting to new cultures. In "Year's End", Kaushik tells how he began facing a complicated relationship with his father who remarried after the death of his first wife. Kaushik's changing attitudes towards his stepmother and two stepsisters influence him to adopt the life of a wanderer. In the conclusive "Going Ashore", told by the writer herself, Kaushik and Hema – the former a successful photojournalist and the latter a college-teacher who has had an unsuccessful affair with a married man – meet in Italy and are immediately attracted to each other, though the story ends without their final reunion.

It may said in conclusion that Lahiri's novel and short stories are mostly read for their precise presentation of the sentiments and disillusionments of Indians settled especially in the United States. It is true that she presents strong female characters, but Lahiri has never have been an outright feminist. Rather, Suchitra Joshi's observations may be quoted here: "[Jhumpa Lahiri] [...] has been born, brought up, and educated in London and Boston. Her connectivity with India and Indian people is borrowed from her grandparents, books, and other N.R.I.s. [She] [...] has travelled extensively to India and has experienced the effects of colonialism as well as experienced the issues of the Diaspora as it exists. She feels strong ties to her parents' homeland as well as the United States and England" (85). While rereading her oeuvre, one must not expect radicalism or outrightly postcolonial tirades, but a sensitive and sympathetic approach to the problems usually faced by the West-migrated Indians.

Notes and References

1. Flynn, Gillian. "*Passage to India*: First-time Author Jhumpa Lahiri nabs a Pulitzer". *Entertainment Weekly.Com.* 28 April 2000. Accessed on 12 January 2011. *<http://www.ew.com/ew/article/0,,276075,00.html>*
2. "We have become part of *The Namesake*". Rediff Movies – *Rediff.com.* 12 March 2007. Accessed on 12 January 2011. *<http://www.rediff.com/movies/2007/mar/12lahiri.htm>*
3. Aguiar, Arun. "Interview with Jhumpa Lahiri". *Pif Magazine.* 1 August 1999. Accessed on 12 January 2011. *<http://www.pifmagazine.com/1999/08/interview-with-jhumpa-lahiri/#>*
4. Ibid.
5. "We have become part of *The Namesake*".
6. Ibid.
7. Minzesheimer, Robert. "For Pulitzer-winner Lahiri a Novel Approach". *U.S.A. Today* – 'Books'. 19 August 2003. Accessed on 12 January 2011. *<http://www.usatoday.com/life/books/news/2003-08-19-lahiri-books_x.htm>*
8. Williams, Precious. "Interview with Jhumpa Lahiri". 21 March 2010. Accessed on 12 January 2011. *<http://preciouswilliams.typepad.com/precious-williams-blog/2010/03/interview-jhumpa-lahiri.html#tp>*
9. Smith, Nicole. "Short Story Analysis and Theme's Summary of 'A Temporary Matter' by Jhumpa Lahiri". *Article Myriad.* 2010. Accessed on 12 January 2011. *<http://www.articlemyriad.com/temporary_matter.htm>*
10. "Short Story Essay: 'When Mr. Pirzada Came to Dine'". 25 December 2005. Accessed on 12 January 2011. *<http://echeat.net/essay.php?t=28258>*
11. Nayar, Aruti. "Jhumpa Lahiri: An Interpreter of Exiles". *The Sunday Tribune India.* 28 May 2000. Accessed on 12 January 2011. *<http://www.tribuneindia.com/2000/20000528/spectrum/main1.htm>*
12. Wcislo, Katherine. "Jhumpa Lahiri". *Emory University-Postcolonial Studies' Website.* Autumn 2001. Accessed on 12 January 2011. *<http://www.english.emory.edu/Bahri/Lahiri.html>*
13. Champeon, Kenneth. "Exiles of the World Unite: Jhumpa Lahiri's *Interpreter of Maladies*". *Things Asian-Literature.* 26 March 2001. Accessed on 12 January 2011. *<http://www.thingsasian.com/stories-photos/1508>*
14. Wcislo, Katherine. "Jhumpa Lahiri".
15. Hanna, Julia. "Second Helpings: Jhumpa Lahiri returns with a Novel". *The Boston Phoenix* 12-18 September 2003. Accessed on 12 January 2011. *<http://www.bostonphoenix.com/boston/arts/books/documents/03146771>*

16. Kakutani, Michiko. "Books of the Times – from Kolkata to Suburbia: A Family's Perplexing Journey". *The New York Times – Books*. 2 September 2003. Accessed on 12 January 2011. *<http://query.nytimes.com/gst* fullpage.html?res= *9A02E0DE1538F931A3575AC0A9659C8B63>*
17. Gillen, C.J. "*The Namesake* by Jhumpa Lahiri". *SAWNET Book Review*. 16 February 2009. Accessed on 12 January 2011. *<http://www.sawnet.org/books/reviews.php?The+Namesake>*
18. Schillinger, Liesl. "American Children". *Sunday Book Review – The New York Times*. 6 April 2008. Accessed on 12 January 2011. *<http://www.nytimes.com/2008/04/06/books/review/Schillinger3-t.html>*
19. Gebbie, Vanessa. *The Short Review – Unaccustomed Earth*. Accessed on 12 January 2011. *<http://www.theshortreview.com/reviews/JhumpaLahiriUnaccustomedEarth.htm>*
20. Apte, Poornima. "Unaccustomed Earth". *Mostly Fiction Book Reviews*. 24 April 2008. Accessed on 12 January 2011. *<http://www.mostlyfiction.com/world/lahiri.htm>*
21. Schillinger, Liesl. "American Children".
22. Ibid.

8

Salman Rushdie's *Grimus* as an Alternative History

— Abdulmonim Ali Ben Ali

> There are a million possible Earths with a million possible histories, all of which actually exist simultaneously.
>
> —(*Grimus* 53)

> As for me; I, too, like all migrants, am a fantasist. I build imaginary countries and try to impose them on the ones that exist. I, too, face the problem of history; what to retain, what to dump, how to hold on to what memory insists on relinquishing, how to deal with change.
>
> —(*Shame* 87-88)

The main contention of Salman Rushdie's *Grimus* is to offer an alternative version of history. The aim of this paper is to question the efficacy of historical truth as factual knowledge in the light of Rushdie's concept of history. This metahistorical text reveals new meanings of history in relation to the postcolonial context. Since history is a man-made activity, and since historical experience and its conclusions varied from one individual to another and from one society to another, the certainty of historical truth is invalid. What we have, then, are different forms of realities, each has its particular truth.

According to Rushdie, there are two forms of history: formal, exclusionary, totalitarian history which offers a singular view of the historical events, and polyphonically representational history which provides multiple realities and multidimensional historical truths. Whereas the former relies on the recording of "facts" and dated events, the latter is based on the representation of them. These New Historical speculations constitute the theoretical foundations of this paper.

Grimus is a history-seeking novel. The central character, Flapping Eagle, and his companions travel from one place to another, seeking shelters for new free lives. Also, they seek the truth of life, knowledge and "new possible histories". Elfrida, a female character says, "There are a million possible Earths with a million possible histories, all of which actually exist simultaneously." (*Grimus* 53)

Rushdie's *Grimus* is made significant by his ability to build pluralistic worlds mediated by fantasy which permits entrance into alternative universe. In the novel, he uses the intervention of fiction to make the implausible possible. The alternative realities created in this novel, in particular is mediated by fabulation and fantasy to oppose the imposed rational reality and also as a technique that enable the excluded characters in the novel to escape the particular social restriction and conformities in their sad cities through the wings of fantastic imagination. Yet, the technique of fantasy in this novel serves to represent Rushdie's visions of "social change" and how history should be re-created to gratify the individual demands of new imaginative life. These pluralistic visions of realities and experiences indorsed in the novel form what we call "alternative versions" of history.

> "Alternative history" is a form of discourse which is constructed as a direct response to another form of discourse. It might also be viewed as a form of mythical narrative, which expresses a rejection to the realist political, colonial as well as patriarchal systems. It is also a method of analysis, which produces ideas and views which are used to defend certain values or attack particular dominant authorities. "Alternative history" can be described as a counter-narrative to the surrounding reality of repressive authority or colonial narrative: that is, to think of ideas and strategies that

> liberate people from the colonial supremacy. In the world of postcolonial fiction, the "alternative history" may signify a fictional narrative which functions as a form of counter, dissent and disruption against the repressive systems. This narrative has the meaning of confrontation and liberation, transformation and creation of new realities. In this case, the "alternative history" might be a creation of new fictions and myths against the fictions and myths of the dominant authority.

"Alternative history" is defined as "a genre of fiction consisting of stories that are set in worlds in which history has diverged from the actual history of the world. It can be variously seen as a sub-genre of literary fiction, science fiction, and historical fiction; different alternate history works may use tropes from any or all of these genres" (*Wikipedia*). In his *The Incoherence of the Philosopher*, Al-Ghazali defends the Islamic Ash'ari doctrine of a created universe that is temporally finite, against the Aristotelian doctrine of an eternal universe and proposed a modal theory of possible worlds (Kukkonen 479–502). "Alternate history is inherently presentist. It explores the past less for its own sake than to utilize it instrumentally to comment upon the present. Based as it is upon conjecture, alternative history necessarily reflects its author's hopes and fears." (Rosenfeld 93)

However, *Grimus* is considered by many critics as a science fiction, a term that encompasses novels and short stories that "represent an imagined reality that is radically different in its nature and functioning from the world of our ordinary experience" (Abrams 278). Hence, narrative is made to render plausible the fictional world by reference to known or imagined scientific principles whereby fantasy can be the appropriate device, especially in the issue of historical representation which is based on recreation. Fantasy then is used to enrich realism.

Science fiction is basically designed to provide an alternative version of reality and thus to create a possible way of looking to reality from different angles and dimensions. It is a mixed world of the real and the hyper-real and the events in this world move from temporality to timelessness, crossing the boarders of the actual and the mythical, the real and the hyper-real. On this basis, Rushdie's *Grimus* is considered as a science fiction because it makes use of these elements, and its themes have been conveyed within the frame of this genre. The novel makes use of technology and alchemy in order to highlight the themes of transformation, change and re-creation.

The blurring of the "real" and the "fantastic", and the past and present is a dominant feature of the novel. From the beginning of the novel, we read about the "elixir" which transforms the hero into an immortal and time-traveler being who breaks the boundaries between time and place. In his fantastic voyage, the Eagle explores and experiences many versions of life in the past and present. The multi- experiences of his journey enable him to predict and plan the shape of the realistic state of future. For this, we see him in the end of the novel giving his resolution to the conflicting views of the solid and stagnant state and the absolute liberal one.

Basically, science fiction is a form of literary work whose central concern is to research history, new imagined universes, and world of technology. The writer of science fiction relies on two major things: the advanced knowledge of technology and the exploration of new cosmos. In this case, Rushdie's *Grimus* searches for possible versions of histories and alternative realities, by focusing on the different experiences of his characters and by burdening them with the quest for a "history".

However, some critics argue that science fiction is not alternative history, but a fantastic story that deals with alternative reality in which the histories of the worlds being described do not connect with our own. Yet, Rushdie's *Grimus* is not actually a typical science fiction narrative that explores the future events and predicts new technologies. Rather, it is a narrative that explores within a science fiction narratology a possible version of history through dealing with different alternative realities. The main concern of Rushdie is neither the future nor the "the pastness of the past," but "its presence".

In the light of Rushdie's view, science fiction can then be described as a historical literature in which the alternative histories are achieved through the fiction narrative itself. In other words, alternative history is seen as part of science fiction. In every science fiction narrative, there is an explicit or implicit fictional history that connects the period depicted to our present moment, or to some moment of our past. Because no science fiction story describes the actual future that will ensue in the real world, one could even say that all science fiction narratives are alternative histories. Therefore, the relationship between science fiction and the writing of history seems obvious. Whatever else history may be, it is not an experimental science. The question is how we can make plausible conjectures. This is the way in which the alternate-history story was born. The common target of the two works of writing is to provide societies with imaginative frameworks to change the social and political environments. Ken MacLeod in this regard has argued that "History remains the trade secret of science fiction… History is an inexhaustible source of plots, and an indispensable map of the way in which societies work and how they can change." (8-14)

In fact, many fantasies and science fictions are set in a world that has a history somewhat similar to our own world, but with magic added. Some of these stories posit points of divergence, but some others feature magic, thus altering history all along. For example, Flapping Eagle's universe in the Calf Island is in part historically recognizable but also obeys different physical laws, reflecting the matter of India as history, and India as reality. The writer explicitly maintains that all possible decisions are made in all possible ways.

> I do not care for stories that are, so tight. Stories should be like life, slightly frayed at the edges, full of loose ends and lives juxtaposed by accident rather than some grand design. Most of

> life has no meaning so it must surely be a distortion of life to tell tales in which every single element is meaningful.
>
> (*Grimus* 141)

Grimus thus is a form of fantasy by which Rushdie deconstructs the concept of history as a given factual knowledge. Rushdie at the outset of the novel tells us that the central character, Flapping Eagle has lost his mother the moment he comes to this world. This kind of disruption that occurs in the life of the young Eagle registers a breakthrough in his life since it cuts him of his past. He has to experience a new reality in Axona. But, since Axona is the world of fixity and singularity in which there was only one version of life and one way of thinking, he was expelled for breaking the rule and having "strange attitudes". The god Axona imposes only one way of life: "The god Axona had only two laws: he liked the Axona to chant to him as often as possible, in the field, on the toilet, while making love, if concentration allowed; and he instructed the Axona to be a race apart and have no doings with the wicked world". (*Grimus* 16)

In fact, Rushdie's contention in this novel is that the individual can express his world views and live globally but thinking "glocally". Rushdie was not against the past or history, but he is against its totalitarianism. That is exactly what happens to Flapping Eagle. When he revolts against his past and begins searching for immortality (archetype) by drinking the magical liquid of elixir, he has bitten up by his sense of isolation and nihilism. His life in the Calf Island becomes monotonous and mechanical and has no meaning for human life. Rushdie here wants to suggest that immortals do not have history because their lives are governed by divine laws and therefore do not have variations. On the contrary, human life is nothing but an accumulative account of various forms of experiences and activities. It is then is subject to possible versions of realities and therefore cannot be narrated through a single view altogether. The novel at the outset deals with the re-creation of history. Mr Virgil

Jones, the philosopher and the guide of the Eagle gives his views about history. "An historian is affected by the present events and that eternally recreate the past." (*Grimus* 13)

Subsequently and soon, he recognizes his meaningless life of immortality and mechanicality in Calf Island, Mr. Eagle decides to reclaim his role as a social being and gets rid off this "given" life by battling with the monolithic Grimus, the official ruler of the land. He starts longing for his personal life and nationhood in Axona and therefore decides to make the Calf Island his alternative home that combines within itself the emotion of the "past memories" and his "present realities". As a result, the authority of the past has been modified by the reality of the present. This artistic representation that externalizes the ideas of monolithic version of history and the alternative or possible view of history is the underpinning element of the novel. Through the character of Flapping Eagle, Rushdie has shown us different versions of history from the conventional to the monolithic or from repressive to the political.

Flapping Eagle brings the conflicting forces of life together. After destroying the rational kingdom of the patriarch Grimus, who misuses the power of the magical Stone Rose in controlling the activities of the island's dwellers, he attempts to resolve the conflict between Reason and Emotion, and Rationality and Imagination. He says: "I began to re-create Calf Island, exactly as it was, with one difference: it was to contain no rose. I had decided that this was a better alternative than physically breaking the Rose." (*Grimus* 252)

Reality is "a timeless and spaceless community of spirits which perceive each other" (Ritvo 43). The problem with the Calf Island's ruler, Grimus is his obsession with the conceptualization of "dimensions" in order to fully control the movement of the immortal inhabitants. This is read as a patriarchal and monolithic discourse from the side of Grimus. Also, it tells us about the idea that there are no choices of experiences for the inhabitants who look the same thing and do the same activities. For this, Flapping Eagle leaves the K town:

> I am leaving K. It is a town made mad by a machine. Soldiers, policemen, actors, hunters, whores, drunks, wasters, philosophers, menials, morons, artistans, farmers, shoe-salesmen, artists, united by their common inability to cope with the world they have had imposed upon them.
>
> (*Grimus* 217- 218)

Flapping Eagle's power lies in his "fictive obsession" to explore the history of K town. He embarks on knowledge and enquiry to discover the truth. He is obsessed with a desire to "refute the Grimus myth" (*Grimus* 148). As long as there is a creative fiction, there will be a hope for re-creation of reality.Grimus himself on the Calf Island builds his power of controlling people from his invented myths and fictions in which the inhabitants believe. The relationship between fiction and reality is a central theme initiated in the paper. It is connected to the function and the primary interest of the postcolonial writer to build up his "fictional countries".

Nonetheless, *Grimus,* like much of Rushdie's work, undermines the concept of a "pure culture" by demonstrating the impossibility of any culture or philosophy existing in sterile isolation. This profoundly reflects the poststructuralist approach to culture which gains an overt expression in Mr. Virgil's comment on the limitations of aesthetic theories that attempt to suppress their own contingencies:

> Any intellect which confines itself to mere structuralism is bound to rest trapped in its own webs. Your words serve only to spin cocoons around your own irrelevance.
>
> (*Grimus* 91)

Rushdie relentlessly draws attention to the provisional status of his text's "truth" and, of course, the provisional status of any received account of reality, by using meta-text that foreground the unnaturalness and bias of the text's construction as an entity. Rushdie has argued that "one of the things that have happened in the twentieth century is a colossal fragmentation reality". (qtd. in Afzal-Khan 154) Hence, *Grimus* incorporates magic realism in order to transgress distinctions of genres, which mirrors the state of confusion and alienation that defines postcolonial societies and individuals.

Grimus is a critique of the concept of pure culture and monolithic history. Axona represents the authoritative vision of history which excludes any other interpretations, and everything recorded is fact and truth. We notice that Axona is governed by strict laws of morality and discrimination. "All that is Unaxona is Unclean" (*Grimus* 24). Beside this, god Axona has a law of punishment against those who might think to break the law of "purity" in the town. As a result, Flapping Eagle and his sister, Bird-Dog were exiled from Axona, simply because they broke the law and challenged the "oneness" and stagnation of the Axona system. Mr. Eagle is treated as a stranger simply because "first, my confused sex; second, the circumstances of my birth; and third, my pigmentation" (*Grimus* 18). Life and history in Axona are controlled by a pre-determined rule that prevent people even to dream or think of the world outside the kingdom. Axona town is represented as a closed world of rigidity and insularity. In other words, the traditional system in Axona does not accept the "difference".

Substantially, life is changeable, history is multifarious, truth is not absolute or final, reality has many versions, and culture is hybrid and has never been pure. These meanings and concepts are metaphorically and fancifully embodied in the character of Mr. Eagle—the symbol of alternity and social change. He has been described as thus:

> He was the leopard who changed his spots; he was the worm that turned. He was the shifting sand and the ebbing tide. He was

> moody as the sky, circular as the seasons, nameless as the glass ... He was the Eagle, prince of birds, and he was also the albatross. She clung round his neck and died, and the mariner became the albatross ... Several times he changed the name he gave to people.
>
> (*Grimus* 31-32)

He is looking for new ideals of identity, freedom, history and new culture, "I am looking for a suitable voice to speak in" (*Grimus* 32). To him, history is made of many voices and spoken by many languages. The protagonist, his sister and the other eternal birds are introduced as "anti-history" figures who act against the conventional history, which silences their voices and causes them to suffer their loss, "Frustration was building with Flapping, the frustration of centuries." (*Grimus* 35)

Contrary to the rational and fanatically religious Axona which embodies rigidity and insularity of historical truth and experience, K town is the magical world "full of secrets" (*Grimus* 20). It is a fictional life which is different from the reality experienced in Axona. It is a town, which is based on power of technology where things operate automatically and by gesture.

K town has a different type of life and reality in which the dwellers have different ways of living. It is a place of fantasy and fulfillment of desire. For instance, though Dolores O' Toole is a Catholic woman, she decides to follow her love desire. On the other hand, Mrs. Cramm is an eternal woman who submits her soul and body to the protagonist, Eagle. The sexual relationship between the two is part of the energetic life. This relationship is also an example of loose freedom on one hand, and cultural assimilation on the other.

K town is also a place of revelation and harmony. For the character, Ignatius Gribb, Calf Island "came as a happy revelation, here he found his self-respect and she returned her love" (*Grimus* 171). Ignatius Gribb describes this sort of power as "the supreme gift of the human race" (*Grimus* 161). Joel Kuortti comments that immortality in K town is based on obsession (43). Everyone is obsessed with his way of thinking. These examples tell that the secular life has many shapes of reality and that there is no one determined version of truth, and historical experience is not subject to the pre-determined rules and ordains of law. Moreover, the pluralistic views of these people signify a rejection of one imposed sort of life. The story of "K" inhabitants embodies the concept of "simultaneity of secular time" in Benedict Anderson's famous article, "Whose Imagined Community?" (24)

This contrastive image of Axona and K town represents two visions of historical representations. The first is a traditional view of history based on religious or divine truths. The second, however, identifies the fictive view of history that celebrates variety and difference. Yet, both visions evolve out of the extreme polarities. Historical truth is not a universal phenomenon or imaginary event. History is fact and fiction, a factual record and human experience, and a narration and interpretation. Subsequently, Mr. Eagle continues his "search of history" (*Grimus* 107). He denies the view of patriarchs and expresses a feeling of nostalgia for his past. This may tell us that the creation of new countries of free living can be achieved within the limits of temporality and spatiality. He says, "To be in "K" was to return to a consciousness of history, of good times, even of nationhood" (*Grimus* 130). Flapping Eagle becomes weary of immortal life at Calf Island, he decides to regain his nature as a human being and then re-create the land of Phoenix. Now he acts as a mortal being "I- Eagle". After experiencing "the vicarious joys and agonies of countless lives", he decides to use "the thought- forms" in giving "the Phoenix a new life, a new beginning." (*Grimus* 251)

The alternative vision that Rushdie provides through the experience of the Eagle is manifested in his projected reconciliation and resolution between Eagle the mortal and Eagle the immortal, and between Axona where historical truth is projected as a certainly given fact and Calf Island the place of illusionary truth. Subsequently, we come to notice that Grimus-

Eagle discovers that the people in the Calf Island are powerless and unable to draw the kind of life they want because their individuality is separated from the collectivity. He sees their fear of change: "the people of K reduced to a blind philosophy of pure survival, clutching obsessively at the shreds of their individuality, knowing within themselves that they were powerless to alter the circumstances in which they lived." (*Grimus* 251)

These lines show clearly the significance of the idea of re-imagining the past and how the Eagle emerges from his present home at "Calf Island" into the history of Phoenix to 'redeem' and 'reform' that history. We read in the passage that there is a longing for another history. The protagonist says, "To be in "K" was to return to a consciousness of history, of good times, even of nationhood" (*Grimus* 130). Joel Kuorti in her essay, "A View of History," argues that this longing connects the individual's identity to the national imagination (64). Flapping Eagle, Elfrida, Gribb, and Irina Cherkassov scuff off their immortal life in search for a new kind of earthly life, "It was because I thought life was sacred that I drank the elixir. One cannot take life." (*Grimus* 146)

The novel appears as a fictionalized picture of the writer's attitudes towards change and search for new realities. Flapping Eagle, experiences an unsatisfactory life in Axona. Similarly, he decides to break the sameness and mechanical material life on Calf Island by resurrecting the island without Stone Rose, the technological instrument at the hand of Grimus by which he controls life on the island. He rejects the views of god Axona as well as Grimus's because he seeks freedom from the force of authority.

Grimus presents a "multiple society" (Reddy 5) through a polyphony of voices. Each one of those characters represents a particular view of life and creates various versions of realities that cannot be interpreted by a single monolithic view. Joel Kuortti contends that the major problem of the Eagle is that he is burdened with history in terms of collective thoughts and that because of this he loses his home and belongings and things he owns. He is destined to be destroyed by racial, cultural, religious and political forces of history (65). Therefore, the Eagle searches for history not as a homogenous and "transparent truth" but as a process constructed from an endless number of events and stories. To develop this idea further, Rushdie seeks in his novel to undermine the authority of history by the use of fantasy, since fantasy represents a kind of truth where "real history is just another ideological fantasy." (64)

Rushdie's concern in this particular novel is the desire to offer an alternative version of history of the subcontinent and the postcolonial history in general by reworking the authorial view of historical experience and factual knowledge, and by simultaneously creating a fanciful image of historical realities similar to the postcolonial subcontinental history. The theoretical foundation of this is his rejection of what might be termed as "the totality of history" which results in "the loss of the individual". On this basis, Rushdie comes to establish his vision of history on the individual's position and role in society. The conventional history represents collective ideology which gives no regard to the individual's position in society, nor does it answer his hopes and expectations. Such an approach to history also depresses the individual, who, as a result, becomes without entity, family and history. In the light of this thought, the Eagle keeps searching for a history that privileges the "oneself" and the individual as a real element in history. The Eagle suffers the totalitarian and authorial history of Axona, and revolts against the mechanically assimilated history of Calf Island. In both "versions", this "fragmented subject" has not been given his weight as a "maker" of history or as a core of incidents against what is imagined as unified, complete and consistent with itself. By demythecizing the historical myth and mthycizing the ordinary events, Rushdie is instrumentally showing possible visions of history and realities.

By insisting on representing his protagonists as time-travelers and truth-seekers, Rushdie attempts to deconstruct the given facts and truth and subverting the concept of pure culture, absolute facts, and insular central pattern. Thus, his characters are either rebellious dissents or non-conformists. Consequently, if Axona represents the conventional view of history and Calf Island is the mythical version of history, the "I-Eagle" is the alternative history—a history formed out of recreating the "present" Calf Island and re-imagining the "past" Axona. This level of history implies that there is a room for interpreting its facts. Also, it implies that there is no final version of truth. Simply, Rushdie's method is based on exposing the problems of the individual and his sufferings under the "authentic history", which is very often collective and repressive. His approach of analysis deals, in brief, with the social and cultural realities in terms of ideas and visions and without any restrictions of dates, events and quantifiable time. Also, it highlights the role of the individual whose business is to search for alternative possibilities on the Earth. Through the Proustian device of "reclamation" Rushdie struggles "to bring the past back and recreate it." (Durix 12)

The alternative history in the novel takes three forms in Eagle's thoughts. First, the level of science with which he works to change the conditions and reality of the island governed by the tyrannical ruler, Grimus. The second is the level of politics in which he decides to go back to Phoenix to liberate it from repression. The third one is the level of fiction as a tool to create new realities. (Kuortti 34)

Fantasy, as alternative version of history in the hands of Rushdie, is closely allied with the fictional world of the novel and its controlling theme – i.e., search for the self and history. In this case, "fantasy is not the same febrile phantasmagoria but an energetic dramatization of a better future by people living in a concrete world" (Habegger 6). Therefore, fantasy in the novel does not oppose real conditions, but reflects them. Actually, it is rooted in the real conditions themselves—in the concrete social relations. Commenting on Rushdie's use of fantasy in the novel as a form of alternative reality, Syed Mujeebuddin notes that "in positing the real with the fantastic and story with history, Rushdie is presenting the reader with an 'anti-history' (131). Rushdie neither de-bunks the conventional histories of the glorious past nor acknowledges the fictionalization of historical reality.

Axona is an allegorical version of history of India in which "Rushdie's religious allegory is absorbed quickly into the political one because religion has always been a potent weapon in the hands of those who ruled India" (Banerjee 24). Religious truth, according to Rushdie, does not represent the universally historical truth since religion cannot escape the politics of collectivity. In his manipulation of the idea of timelessness and its relation to the concept of history, Rushdie suggests that there is a space of spatiality and temporality to create possible simultaneous versions of historical realities.

From the postmodernist view, *Grimus* translates the idea of authentic experience through Rushdie's approach to historical representation. Rushdie uses the idea of hyper-reality in representing reality as a natural and authentic experience. Life in Calf Island, therefore, is an excellent example of an authentic experience out of the limits of space and time in which the inhabitants fulfill freely and naturally their desire; they live their desire and not only dream of it. In so doing, Rushdie deals with the postcolonial issues in a realm of postmodernist world. Rushdie's postmodern world is seen as the alternative world where the symbol and image become reality itself. In this way, Rushdie has provided another vision of Indian history in particular and postcolonial world in general. To develop it further, Rushdie's approach to myth and history includes the postmodern concept of hyper-reality—reality as an image. Hence, as a fictional writer, his primary concern is to represent the historical veracities in a different way. It is significant to consider that Rushdie's opinion on the relation between novel and history is based on the idea that "knowing the world is a necessary first step towards changing it." (*Imaginary Homelands* 14)

From the postcolonial perspective, Rushdie tries to subvert the historical colonial accounts with its cons and pros by means of creating alternative histories and realities. The history of migration is also of Rushdie's main concerns in the treatment of history. The idea of alternative history takes into account the possible histories of immigrants as fragmented subjects who have experienced different forms of realities and divided between their national longing and the new cultural environment. This is just exactly the case of Flapping Eagle and his companions who have been expelled from their national land and experienced the life of migrancy, exile and assimilation in the Calf Island. Moreover, the instability of Eagle's character is also related to the idea of "unstable identity". His identity is made of different cultures. His identity is a process of cultural assimilation. "Several times he changed the name he gave to people. His face was such, his skin was such" (*Grimus* 32). Therefore, Rushdie's view of alternative history includes themes such as assimilation, alienation, loss, and longing. Despite of his postcolonial propensity, Rushdie's treatment of the compelling issues of migration, exile, political freedom, social change, and suppression of women and individual as historically fragmented experiences and stories underpin his engagement with the postmodern world. Fed up with her monotonous life of sameness on the Calf Island, Elferida bursts out profoundly:

> I don't like it [....] it's too pretty, too neat. I do not care for stories that are so, so tight. Stories should be like life, slightly frayed at the edges, full of loose ends and lives juxtaposed by accident rather than some grand design. Most of life has no meaning so it must surely be a distortion of life to tell tales in which every single element is meaningful.
>
> (*Grimus* 141)

Postmodernism denies "the fixity of the past, of reality, of the past apart from what the historian chooses to make of it, and thus of any objective truth about the past" (Himmelfarb 72). In other words, history is regarded as a text, "a discourse which consists of representations..." Louis Montrose explains the historicity of texts and the textuality of history in the following lines:

> By the historicity of texts I mean to suggest the cultural specificity, the social embedment, of all modes of writing [...]. By the textuality of history, I mean to suggest, firstly, that we can have no access to full and authentic past, a lived material existence, unmediated by the surviving textual traces of the society in question [...]; and secondly that those textual traces are themselves subjective to subsequent textual mediations when they are constructed as the 'documents' upon which historians ground their own texts, called 'histories'. (20)

The postmodern view of history thus "rejects the idea of "history" as a directly accessible, unitary past and substitutes for it the conception of "histories" as an ongoing series of human constructions" (Cox and Reynolds 4). Moreover, Himmelfarb develops the idea further to suggest that:

> To 'demythiciseze' or 'demystify' this history, postmodernism has to expose not only its ideology—the hegemonic, privileged, patriarchal interest served by this history—but also its methodology, the scholarly apparatus that gives it a specious credibility. (160-61)

At the end of the novel Mr. Eagle eventually declares: "I want to return to the human race" (*Grimus* 55). Thus, the alternative history in the novel takes the shape of "resolved conflicts" and balanced attitudes between given facts and fictional truths or between factual knowledge and mythical thought.

Works Cited

Abrams, M.H. *A Glossary of Literary Terms*. 7th ed.Australia, Canada, Mexico, Singapore, United Kingdom and United States: Thomson Heinle, 1999.

Afzal-Khan, Fawzia. *Cultural Imperialism and the Indo-English Novel: Genre and Ideology in R. K. Narayan, Anita Desai, Kamala Markandaya and Salman Rushdie.* University Park, PA: Pennsylvania State University Press, 1993.

"Alternate History." *Wikipedia: The Free Encyclopedia.* Wikimedia Foundation, Inc. 5 May 2011. Web. 21 May 2011. *<http://en.wikipedia.org/wiki/Plagiarism>*

Anderson, Benedict. "Whose Imagined Community?" *The Nation and the Fragments: Colonial and Postcolonial Histories.* Ed. Partha Chatterjee. Delhi: OUP, 1994. 3-37.

Banerjee, Ashutosh. "Narrative Technique in Midnight's Children." *The Novels of Salman Rushdie.* Ed. Taneja, G.R. and R.K. Dhawan. New Delhi: Indian Society for Commonwealth Studies, 1992. 23-32.

Cox, Jeffrey N. and Larry J. Reynolds. *New Historical Literary Study*. Ed. Princeton, New Jersey: Princeton: UP, 1993.

Durix, Jean-Pierre. "Salman Rushdie." *Conversations with Salman Rushdie.* Ed. Michael R. Reder. Jackson: University Press of Mississippi, 2000. 8-16.

Habegger, Alfred. "Fantasy in the Novel." *Gender, Fantasy, and Realism in American Literature.* New York: Columbia University Press, 1982.7-14.

Haffenden, John. "Salman Rushdie." *Novelists in Interview: Martin Amis, Malcolm Bradbury, Anita Booker, Angela Carter, William Golding, Russel Hoban, David Lodge, Lan Mc Ewan, Iris Murdon, V.S. Pritchett, SalmanRushdie, David Storey, Emma Tenant and Fay Weldon*. Ed. Michael Reder. London and New York: Methuen, 1985. 231-259.

Himmelfarb, Gertrude. "Telling It As You Like It: Postmodernist history and the Flight from Fact". *The Postmodern History Reader*. Ed. Keith Jenkings. London and New York: Routledge, 1997.158-203.

Kukkonen, Taneli. "Possible Worlds in the Tahâfut al-Falâsifa: Al-Ghazâlî on Creation and Contingency." *Journal of the History of Philosophy*. 38. 4. (2000): 479–502.

Kuortti, Joe. "*Grimus*: Fictions Where a Man Could Live." *Fictions to Live in: An Argument for Fiction in Salman Rushdie's Novels.* New York: Peter Lang, 1998. 43-66.

MacLeod, Ken. "History in Science Fiction: What (Hasn't Yet) Happened in History". *Histories of the Future: Studies in Fact Fantasy, and Science Fiction*. Ed. Alan Sandison and Robert Dingley. New York: Palgrave, 2000.

Montrose, Louis. "Professing the Renaissance: The Poetics and Politics of Culture". *The New Historicism.* Ed. H. Aram Veeser. London: Routledge, 1989. 15-36.

Mugibuddin, Syed. "Centres and Margins: Shame's 'Other' Nation." *Salman Rushdie: New Critical Insights*. Ed. Mittapalli_Rajeshwar and Joel Kuortti. Vol. 1. New Delhi: Atlantic Publishers and Distributors, 2003. 131-149.

Reddy, P. Bayapa. "*Grimus*: An Analysis." *The Novels of Salman Rushdie*. Ed. Taneja, G.R. and R.K. Dhawan. New Delhi: Indian Society for Commonwealth Studies, 1992. 5-9.

Ritvo, Rosemary Puglia. "A Vision B: The Plotinian Metaphysical Basis." *The Review of English Studies, New Series*, 26.101(Feb., 1975):34-46.

Rosenfeld, Gaveriel. "Why Do We Ask "What If?" Reflections on the Function of Alternate History." *History and Theory*. 41.4 (Dec., 2002): 90-103.

Rushdie, Salman. *Grimus*. 1975. Delhi: Vintage, 1996.

______ *Shame*.1983.Delhi: Vintage.1995.

______ *Imaginary Homelands: Essays and Criticism 1981-1991*. London: Granta Books, 1991.

9

The Spiritual Sense of Alienation in Diasporic Life: Reading Anita Desai, Bharati Mukherjee, Sunetra Gupta and Jhumpa Lahiri

—Amit Shankar Saha

Exile, in its literal sense, is a physical condition but the sense of exile is not necessarily a manifestation of a dislocated existence. Even if there is a geographical displacement, the exilic condition in many cases is only superficially physical and fundamentally psychological and spiritual. The external exile either compounds or, occasionally, suppresses these internal conditions. The Indian diaspora in the West has experienced a physical displacement but in a globalized world migrants are not treated as aliens, moreover the newer migrants have migrated of their own will, and hence there is little cause for them to feel the sense of being in exile. The world as a global village facilitates the feeling of being at home in the cosmopolitan urban quarters of the world. It is in these situations that the external circumstances of displacement become of less importance and the internal circumstances, that is the psychological and spiritual condition of the mind, gain prominence. Despite being in a diaspora there is little consolation of any hope of escape into any pre-exilic state. It is, as Rushdie says in reference to diasporic writers, a haunting of the mind:

> It may be that writers in my position, exiles or emigrants or expatriates, are haunted by some sense of loss, some urge to reclaim, to look back, even at the risk of being mutated into pillars of salt.

> But if we do look back, we must also do so in the knowledge – which gives rise to profound uncertainties – that our physical alienation from India almost inevitably means that we will not be capable of reclaiming precisely the thing that was lost; that we will, in short, create fictions, not actual cities or villages, but invisible ones, imaginary homelands, Indias of the mind.
>
> (Rushdie, *Imaginary* 10)

This mental condition can only be tackled by catering to the psychological and spiritual aspects of life – a self-fashioning of the mind and the spirit.

India is not merely a geographical space on the world map. It occupies a well-defined space both in history as well as in culture. Thus, the Indian migrants in the West look back not only at the spatial contour of the subcontinent but at its history, society, and culture too. This looking back is paradoxically aided by technological innovations that help keep intact one's link with the past – a past that reminds of one's roots. Films, music, magazines, the cyber communities, and all other media of communications continually keep refreshing the link. Hamid Naficy notes in the essay "Framing Exile: From Homeland to Homepage" that due to "the globalization of travel, media, and capital, exile appears to have become a postmodern condition" (Naficy 4). It is basically this postmodern condition that produces a gnawing feeling of being in exile for the Indian diasporic community despite having the advantages of easy telecommunication and speedy travel.

The trope of exile is a perennial presence in all religions. Its prototypical model can be found in the Jewish "exodus", the Muslim "hegira", and so on. Exile plays a pivotal role in both the two great Hindu epics *The Ramayana* and *The Mahabharata*. In fact, the Hindu pantheon of Gods and Goddesses is replete with the concept of mobility symbolized by the deities' "vahans" or the animals on which they ride – the lion for Durga, the ox for Shiva, the peacock for Kartik, the mouse for Ganesh, the owl for Lakshmi, the swan for Saraswati, and others. The psyche of the Indian immigrant fed on the mythologies of movement and exile is preconditioned to succumb to the sense of estrangement, alienation, non-belonging, and dislocation at the slightest pretext. Hence, physical displacement is only a catalyst that generally aggravates a pre-existing psychological and spiritual sense of loneliness. But this generalization is not sweeping because sometimes it so happens that physical displacement allays the cosmic sense of loneliness. It is because of this complex and apparently paradoxical nature of the exilic condition that it is equated with the postmodern condition.

Bharati Mukherjee's novel *Jasmine* traces the story of the eponymous heroine in her American odyssey. Jasmine, the Hindu widow, who leaves India for the US after her husband's death in a terrorist attack, is found to undergo a cross-cultural metamorphosis in her fractured life as an immigrant. The opening chapter of the novel starts with the words:

> Lifetimes ago, under a banyan tree in the village of Hasnapur, an astrologer cupped his ears – his satellite dish to the stars – and foretold my widowhood and exile. I was only seven then, fast and venturesome, scabrous-armed from leaves and thorns.
>
> (Mukherjee, *Jasmine* 3)

The astrologer goes on to allude to the story of Behula from Hindu mythology. Here Bharati Mukherjee is not just exoticizing the content of the novel through these allusions. She is defining the mental space of her seven-year-old protagonist. Jasmine's psyche is formed by the stories that her mother recited to her of "the holiest sages", the "third eye" they develop in the middle of their foreheads to peer "out into invisible worlds" (Mukherjee, *Jasmine* 5), and their likes. No doubt Jasmine's mind is spiritually inclined even though she challenges and revolts against customs and traditions.

Jasmine's decision to fulfil her husband's aspiration of going to America is guided by her spiritual beliefs as she acknowledges:

> I had not given even a day's survival in America a single thought. This was the place I had chosen to die, on the first day if possible. I would land, find Tampah, walking there if necessary, find the college grounds and check it against the brochure photo. Under the very tree where two Indian boys and two Chinese girls were pictured, smiling, I had dreamed of arranging the suit and twigs. The vision of lying serenely on a bed of fire under palm trees in my white sari had motivated all the weeks of sleepless half-starved passage [. . .]
>
> (Mukherjee, *Jasmine* 120-21)

The village girl from Hasnapur survives in America. She does not immolate herself because after landing on the Gulf Coast of Florida she is raped, and in turn she murders her rapist. This defiles her mission and death is denied her: "Lord Yama, who had wanted me, and whom I'd flirted with on the long trip over, had now deserted me" (Mukherjee, *Jasmine* 120). The transformation of Jasmine from the archetype of Sati to that of Goddess Kali as she towers over the man who violated her chastity, with blood oozing out from her sliced tongue, is a dramatic and violent imagery of self-assertion. The critic Nagendra Kumar notes that Jasmine's "decision to kill herself first, is a decision of a woman who lives for her deceased husband but the woman who kills Half-Face is prompted by her will to live to continue her life" (Kumar 110). Jasmine's journey from Punjab, through Florida, New York, and Iowa, to California depicts the various stages of her exilic condition. But these exilic locations are also representation of the spiritual states of her mind. Jasmine assumes different mythological avatars in her various exilic states: "I have been reborn several times" (Mukherjee, *Jasmine* 126). She shuttles between identities: "Jyoti [was] the Sati-Goddess, Jasmine lives for the future" (Mukherjee, *Jasmine* 176). Jasmine emancipates herself from being an illegal immigrant into a self-assured American woman but her spiritual call comes from India: "I am caught between the promise of America and old-world dutifulness" (Mukherjee, *Jasmine* 240).

The "old-world dutifulness" forms the spiritual make-up of Indian migrants to the West. In Jhumpa Lahiri's novel *The Namesake* the Bengali diasporic community in Boston religiously celebrate Durga puja and Saraswati puja. But for characters like Ashima such celebrations are less about religion and more about rejuvenation of the link with the old world – the home they have left behind. Ashima's life in exile is eased by the spiritual frenzy brought about by religious festivities. On the other hand, Gogol and Sonia, who are born and brought up totally in the West, find their parents' spiritual leanings intensifying their exilic condition. Their self-fashioning as Westerners receive a jolt each time they encounter certain aspect of their ancestry either corporal or spiritual. Sometimes the second-generation migrants revolt against their ambivalent position. The Gangulis celebrate "with progressively increasing fanfare, the birth of Christ, an event the children look forward to far more than the worship of Durga and Saraswati" (Lahiri, *Namesake* 64). But once Sonia, in one of her growing-up years, refused her Christmas gifts after taking a Hinduism class in college, "protesting that they weren't Christians" (Lahiri, *Namesake* 285).

In Lahiri's short story "This Blessed House", Twinkle fervently collects the Christian paraphernalia left behind by the previous occupier of the house that is newly procured by her husband Sanjeev. For Sanjeev, his wife's idea is outlandish. When Twinkle finds a "plaster Virgin Mary as tall as their waists, with a blue painted hood draped over her head in the manner of an Indian bride" (Lahiri, *Interpreter* 146) she decides to put it on the lawn to the shock of her husband:

> "Oh God, no. Twinkle, no."
> "But we must. It would be bad luck not to."
> "All neighbors will see. They'll think we're insane."
> "Why, for having a statue of the Virgin Mary on our lawn? Every other person in this neighborhood has a statue of Mary on the lawn. We'll fit right in."

> "We're not Christians."
> "So you keep reminding me."
>
> (Lahiri, *Interpreter* 146)

For Twinkle, her external exilic state suppresses her internal spiritual exile by giving her an alternative mode of belonging – to "fit right in." Twinkle's relic hunt in her newly possessed house provides her a mental connection with the past of the house to secure her sense of belonging. Salman Rushdie says that "the broken pots of antiquity, from which the past can sometimes, but always provisionally, be reconstructed, are exciting to discover, even if they are pieces of the most quotidian objects" (Rushdie, *Imaginary* 12). Though in Twinkle's case the objects discovered are not exactly common and have no relation to her past, they still bring peace to her mind, whereas, Sanjeev's psyche closes options for him, taking him to a spiritual isolation compounded by his external displacement. The psychological build up of each migrant is different and hence the varied responses to a similar situation.

It is often seen that the physical shift from one's place of origin to a new place of residence does little in itself to arouse the sense of being in exile. In Sunetra Gupta's novel *Memories of Rain* the protagonist Moni is the quintessential romantic who "had loved Heathcliff before she loved any man" (Gupta, *Memories* 177). She finds in Anthony a hero figure straight out of the novels of Jane Austen or Thomas Hardy. Anthony is to rescue her from India – "a bizarre and wonderful land" – to England – "this island, this demi-paradise" (Gupta, *Memories* 6). Incidentally, John of Gaunt, the Duke of Lancaster, in Act 2 Scene 1 of William Shakerpeare's play, *King Richard the Second*, composed in the 1590s and dealing with the subject matter of the early thirteenth century, speaks in very similar words ("This other Eden, demi-paradise"). This echo of lines spoken more than 750 years before Moni, and before Sunetra Gupta, show that for many middle class Indians, England is a cultural and spiritual state rather than a mere physical space. England is a space in Moni's subconscious mind. Moni has, as Amit Chaudhuri alludes, "the vague, intense longings of the feminized, adolescent imagination" (Chaudhuri 583). So, when Moni arrives with her English husband to an England that is vastly different from the England of her English literature class, she is in for a rude shock. Moni's psyche is fashioned by a life of sensation and when encountered with the bleak reality of a fast paced modern day England her sensibilities are brutalized. It is the irreconcilability of the life of action with the life of sensation that compounds Moni's exilic condition. Even the romantic consolation in sorrowful memories is denied her by the indifference shown to her by her husband, who is having an affair with another woman. Anthony is no Heathcliff and her dream of "wandering as a spirit with her beloved upon English moors" (Gupta, *Memories* 177) remains unfulfilled.

It is in the rains of 1978 Calcutta that Moni's brother brings home his English friend Anthony. Anthony is enamoured by Moni, the second-year college student of English. Later he recites from John Keats's "Ode on Melancholy" – "No, no! go not to Lethe, neither twist wolf's bane, tight rooted . . ." (Gupta, *Memories* 17) – and then to Moni's utter embarrassment he asks her to translate for him the Bengali song that she has been singing in the morning.

> Many years later, huddled in the deserted tin mine on the Cornish coast, she translated the same song for him, staring into the sheets of rain that ran by like frozen phantoms across the crumbling entrance, and he sat back against the moldy walls, paying only half heed to her eager, nervous translations, mesmerised instead by the duet of the storm and the sea, until, like the sudden spray it hit her that he was not listening, he was not listening at all [. . .]
>
> (Gupta, *Memories* 10)

Anthony is lost in his amorous musings of adulterous lovemaking with Anna and is blatantly indifferent towards Moni. It is the denial of even the "Beauty that must die", the "Joy [. . .] bidding adieu", and the "aching Pleasure" that bars Moni from entering Melancholy's "sovran shrine" (Keats 248). The psychological constraint of being deprived of the aesthetic response that one craves for in pain makes Moni's exile acute. So, when Moni decides to return to Calcutta a week before Durga puja, she reminisces how "every autumn she had watched the city burst into joy to welcome the Goddess Durga to her father's home" (Gupta, *Memories* 173) and realizes that "this year she will return with the Gods, a daughter come home" (Gupta, *Memories* 174). Moni reverts to her native spirituality as a consolation for her condition.

Anita Desai's novel *Bye-Bye Blackbird* has the Indian migrant Dev disillusioned by an England represented by the London of the 1960s because his mind has the image of an England as depicted in English literature studied in schools and colleges. Dev's psychology aggravates his exilic condition because his aesthetic sense cannot identify with reality. But when he visits the countryside he finds:

> this was the England her poets had celebrated so well that he, a foreigner, found every little wildflower, every mood and aspect of it eerily familiar. It was something he was visiting for the first time in his life, yet he had known it all along – in his reading, in his daydreams – and now he found his dreams had been an exact, a detailed, a brilliant and mirrorlike reflection of reality.
>
> (Desai, *Blackbird* 170)

Dev decides to stay in England after making this mental identification that eases his exilic condition. In St. Paul's and Westminster Abbey, Dev finds "little religious aura" (Desai, *Blackbird* 68) and "has an uneasy feeling that these are no temples of Christ, but temples dedicated to the British Empire" (Desai, *Blackbird* 68). It is in the countryside that he visits an "old, small and silent village church" (Desai, *Blackbird* 172) and on touching "the rounded pillars felt soft to his hand as do the stones in Hindu temples that have been touched by so many devout foreheads.

The stone tiles were curved beneath his feet as are those of temples on which Hindu worshippers kneel and walk incessantly" (Desai, *Blackbird* 171). Dev wishes that "he had a stick of incense to burn, a handful of jasmine or marigold to offer, Hindu fashion, to the grace of Christianity" (Desai, *Blackbird* 172). It is the aesthetic and spiritual familiarity that suppresses the psychological sense of exile.

In Sunetra Gupta's novel *A Sin of Colour*, physical relocation from India to England becomes too easy a form of exile to produce any sort of detachment. Debendranath wants to exile himself from his thoughts of forbidden love for his elder brother's wife Reba. Years later Debendranath's niece Niharika finds herself in a similar predicament when she commits the sin of loving a married man Daniel Faraday. Niharika also exiles herself though, unlike Debendranath, not away from the person of her love but rather with the person she loves. In both the cases their exiles are not mere physical dislocation but exile from society, exile from relationships, exile from a familiar world, exile from a former self, and an exile into anonymity. After twenty years when Debendranath comes back to Mandalay, the almost deserted house, Niharika summarizes his absence thus: "You were able to reinvent yourself entirely" (Gupta, *Sin* 134). This self-exile from one's identity, echoing the "agyatavasa" that the Pandavas suffered in *The Mahabharata*, transcends the concept of material displacement and takes exile to a metaphysical level. Exile becomes a panacea for the soul ailing from existential alienation. It is not only the contingency of the world but also, the contingency of one's very will that baffles. Debendranath and Niharika need to isolate themselves from the world of action because to act is to assert one's will. Hence, by faking death they somehow extricate themselves from the sin of their desires. The psychology behind their displacement becomes all the more important.

Jhumpa Lahiri's short story "A Temporary Matter" has Shoba and Shukumar in their diasporic life grieving for their stillborn child. They find solace by isolating themselves from friends and relations and starting to live life a little differently, fashioning themselves anew, and creating new identities for themselves. For them their exilic condition is superficially due to their diasporic status and is rather fundamentally psychological. At different levels this is precisely the case with most of the diasporic characters. Since by birth human beings are exiled from the womb; one's home, one's family, one's country, one's culture, and so on stand as metaphorical imagery of that natal refuge. This inherent mental condition either acts in conjunction with physical displacement or in opposition with it – either compounding the exilic state or suppressing it. That is why exile is taken as a human condition – some are exiles from happiness, some are exiles from peace, some are exiles from love, and some from their Maker.

Works Cited

Desai, Anita. *Bye-Bye Blackbird* (1971), Delhi: Orient Paperbacks, 2001.

Gupta, Sunetra. *Memories of Rain* (1992), London: Orion, 1992.

______ *A Sin of Colour* (1999), Delhi: Penguin, 1999.

Lahiri, Jhumpa. *Interpreter of Maladies* (1999), New Delhi: HarperCollins, 2000.

______ *The Namesake* (2003), London: Flamingo, 2003.

Mukherjee, Bharati. *Jasmine* (1989), London: Virago, 1998.

Chaudhuri, Amit (ed.). *The Picador Book of Modern Indian Literature*, London: Picador, 2001.

Keats, John. *The Works of John Keats*, Hertfordshire: The Wordsworth Poetry Library, 1994.

Kumar, Nagendra. *The Fiction of Bharati Mukherjee: A Cultural Perspective*, New Delhi: Atlantic Publishers, 2001.

Naficy, Hamid. "Framing Exile" from *Home, Exile, Homeland – Film, Media, and the Politics of Place*, Ed. Hamid Naficy, New York: Routledge, 1999.

Rushdie, Salman. *Imaginary Homelands: Essays and Criticism 1981–1991*, London: Granta Books, 1991.

10

Trimetric of Land, Culture and Identity in Indian English Fiction

— G.A. Ghanshyam

Indian English Fiction is a vast treasure-trove of fictional narratives that give an expression to the cultural ethos of the nation. The edifice of Indian English Fiction in fact stands on the trimetrical axes of land, culture and identity that defines and renders shape to it. Contemporary fiction, owing to the large scale influence of the Diaspora is replete with musings of 'home'. In other words, land holds an eminent place in Indian English Fiction as a symbol of 'home'; it is the roots that keep the individual grounded onto his native land and links him to his past through the inherited cultural ethos that he carries within his self. Land and culture are the essential elements that engender an individual identity thereby forming the important trimetric that characterizes Indian English Fiction. In other words this trimetric is the major concern of contemporary Indian novelists, who delineate them through their fictional narratives and characters.

Land is of prime importance in contemporary fiction. It is inter-related with the concept of roots or the home. Man being central to the narrative, it is natural that his association with land would be equally important. Land, roots, home or nation, whatever be the source of reference, an individual's identity is interminably bound to it. In fact land and culture are interchangeable terms, one being bound with the other, and an integral part of the other. Every land/home/nation has its own set of customs, tradition, ethics, beliefs and practices that contribute to the formation of the native identity. No matter where the person is placed, the individual always carries within the self, the influence of this native identity that is an amalgamation of his land and culture.

In the present scenario of a globalized world wherein an individual is displaced from his homeland and is an immigrant in another, the influence, presence and the expression of this trimetric becomes interlinked with the individual's need of assimilation into the new land; a new world of pluralistic and hybrid culture.

Land, culture and identity is fused together in the narrative of Amitav Ghosh's *The Hungry Tide* (2006), which is set in the Sunderbans. The novel begins with a comprehensive description of the landscape, alluding to the myth associated with the origin of the Ganges. Ghosh has very beautifully portrayed the river with the metaphor of a cloth; India's fabric, ". . . the ragged fringe of her sari, the achol that follows her, half-wetted by the sea." (*THT* 6).

The very character of the islands of Sunderban is defined and created by the landscape of the archipelago. The river forms various small channels that cut across the land, meeting to create confluences that are known as the "mohona" (*THT* 7). The place also referred to as the "bhatir desh – the tide country" (*THT* 8) is remarkable for its geographical bounds are determined by the tide. "This is a land half-submerged at high tide: it is only in falling that the water gives birth to the forest." (*THT* 8). This inconsistency of the land the inherent insecurity that is a result of the dissolution of borders influences the life and characters of the people living on the islands. Kanai, one of the protagonist found out that his western education and knowledge were inadequate in an environment where life was lived in close communion with nature; in fact dictated and directed by it.

If Sunderban is the landscape that dominates the narrative of Ghosh then the Kashmir valley looms large over the tale of Salman Rushdie's *Shalimar the Clown* (2005). The valleys, hills, the pine trees, the river Muskadoon, the village of Pachigam, the people and their Kashmiriyat hold a significant influence on the life of the characters even when the story shifts to the locales of the distant America. Even the names of the characters central to the tale are inspired by nature: Bhoomi (earth) preferred to be called as Boonyi, the local name for the "celestial Kashmiri chinar tree" (*STC* 46), while her mother was named Pamposh after the lotus but instead preferred the nickname "Giri, meaning a walnut kernel" (*STC* 51). The beauty of the Shalimar garden is depicted by the author enthralling the readers with its enigmatic splendour. India, the daughter of Boonyi and Max reconnects to her Kashmiri roots; "Kashmir lingered in her . . . She no longer saw this as an American story. It was a Kashmiri story. It was hers." (*STC* 372).

The pristine environment of Dehradoon is an integral part of Ruskin Bond's fiction. In his first novella, *The Room on the Roof* (1996), Bond details the local flavour of his beloved Dehra. The story begins with beautiful nature imagery, striking and vivid in its description.

> The light spring rain rode on the wind, into the trees, down the road; it brought an exhilarating freshness to the air, a smell of earth, a scent of flowers; it brought a smile to the eyes of the boy on the road. (*ROR* 545)

Land/Nature is the setting for all the novels: a basis, an inspiration, or an influence. In all three novels the presence of nature is unmistakably strong and integral. If land defines the narrative and character of Ghosh's fiction, then in Rushdie land is entangled with the political and emotional makeup of its characters, while it becomes an integral part of Rusty's life in Bond liberating him from his confined life.

Land and culture are intertwined. Researches have proved that land and environment affect and influence the cultural norms of its people. Rituals, customs, tradition, language and food habits depict this unique association of both. For instance, Eskimos have varied expressions for the word snow while the Marshalese has a variety of expressions for the coconut.

Ghosh details the native tradition and belief of the people living in the Sunderban in his narrative. The myth of Bon Bibi and her brother Shah Jongoli, Dokkhin Rai-the tiger demon and his demons, reveal the reverence for the land; the mystery and sheer power of nature. Till today the Sunderban is known for its ferocious tigers and the fragility of life held in balance at the mercy of nature: the man eaters, crocodiles, tides, cyclones and storms. Bon Bibi is the mother earth protecting her children from the tiger demon-Dokkhin Rai, while the dolphins are her messengers. The culture of the island is held in association with the land and land in Sunderban is not stable nor is life. Every step is taken in reverence to and with the blessing of the deified gods and deities of the forest for protection and prosperity.

Kashmiriyat is the culture represented in Rushdie. The village of Pachigam in Kashmir is an example of love and brotherhood. Divisions of race and religion are not a hindrance for its people and so Boonyi, a Brahmin girl is married off to a Muslim boy, Shalimar Noman with blessings and lot of goodwill. The traditional Kashmiri food, "the legendary wazwaan; the Banquet of Thirty-Six Courses Minimum." (61); the folk art from of "bhand pather or clown stories" (STC 61); co-exist with the myth sourced from a variety of various sources like Hindu mythology relate to the dance and influence of the shadow planets—Rahu and Ketu—over the human mind and passions, the presence of mystics like Nazrebaddoor and belief in totems and superstitions like the belief in snake luck by Firdaus Noman, displays the influence of the land on the culture.

The celebration of Holi in Bond's novella is resplendent with the coming of spring, a time for joy and merriness in every part of India. The natural vibrancy of nature's colours get mingled with the colours of Holi, moistening the lonely and desolate heart of Rusty.

> The walls of the houses were suddenly patched with splashes of colour, and just as suddenly the trees seemed to have burst into flower; for in the forest there were armies of rhododendrons, and by the river the poinsettias danced; the cherry and the plum were blossom; thin e snow in the mountains had melted, and the streams were rushing torrents; the new leaves on the trees were full of sweetness, and the young grass held both dew and sun, and made emerald of every dew-drop . . . Clouds of coloured dust rose in the air and spread, and jets of water—green and orange and purple, all rich emotional colours—burst out everywhere. (*ROR* 566-67)

Cultural ethos of a community or group of people are defined and directed by the land. The deification of nature and animals like tiger, projects the importance of nature that influences life in the islands of Sunderban wherein man lives life at the mercy of nature and the natural elements. The fusion of cultures and happy co-existence of the various ethnic and religious groups provides a benevolence of the land that generates a peaceful life and brotherhood in the pristine environs of the Kashmir valley, which is often referred to as the paradise on earth. In a similar vein there is the celebration of the coming of spring after a chilling winter; a breath of fresh air and new life that finds an apt expression in the jubilation of the people in the revelry of Holi.

Land and culture being complementary, they are the basis of an individual's self-identification. A person living in intimate interaction with nature inculcates the inherent simpler and natural life, devoid of all artificiality and superficiality, tuned in to the true spirit of life and nature. Modern, city life is however distanced from land and divorced from the genuine concerns and understanding of life.

In *The Hungry Tide*, Fokir is the character who is deeply imbued with the spirit of the land and nature of his environment. A fisherman by profession he lives in close communion with the land and earns his livelihood from it. The simplicity and rusticity of Fokir is evident from his innocence and a lack of greed. When Piya offers him money after being rescued from getting drowned, he is bewildered by the sight of so much money. Yet all he takes from her is the amount lost to the guard. Fokir stands in the novel in sharp contrast to the modern and educated Kanai, who with all his expertise and knowledge still falls short of his stature in a place that nullifies all superficial and worldly knowledge. On one of the excursion for the Irrawady dolphins Kanai is left behind on one of the islands and finds himself ill equipped to handle the dangers of the forest. The mysterious vision of the tiger strikes him with such fear that he faints and is rescued in time by Piya and Fokir. Even at the end of the novel it is again Fokir who saves Piya from the storm; shielding her and facing the wrath of its force on his own body. "She could feel the bones of his cheeks as if they had superimposed upon her own; it was as if the storm had given them what life could not; it had fused them together and made them one." (*THT* 391).

Fokir is a simple person without any affectations, completely harmonized with his environment and land while Kanai finds himself ill at ease in the islands. His westernized education and expertise are of no use. Even his knowledge of various languages is not essential for the illiterate Fokir to communicate with Piya. The sacrifice of Fokir transforms both, Piya and Kanai. They realize their true self and affirm to life and responsibility as is evident in Kanai's decision to return and Piya's to stay back and take the responsibility of Fokir's family.

A similar association with nature lends the freeness of spirit that Boonyi imbibes from her mother Pamposh. She represents the feminine principle of nature that cannot be bounded or restrained. When Shalimar refers to her as the earth, he is correct in his allusion but fails miserably in his assumption when he says, "She was the earth and the earth was the subject and he had grabbed it and sought to bend its destiny to his will" (*STC* 47).

Boonyi represents the free spirit of the land that transcends all societal bounds, yet comes back after her illusions shatter. The dull, debauched living of the city life leaves her bloated and in a degenerated state. But the valley restores her lost vigour and beauty back to her, and also her resilient spirit is revived that bravely waits for her end. Shalimar's identity is also defined by his relation to his art and the land where he practices.

The landscape of Kashmir abounds with tall trees like the pine, the chinar, etc. Shalimar literally walks on air as he balances himself on the tight rope. His flight does metamorphose into his voyage around the world; from India to America. His transformation into a killing machine reflects the problem of insurgency that has ruined the beauty and serenity of Kashmir and the loss of the Kashmiri way of life.

Land is also synonymous with home from where the individual is displaced and dispossessed in the modern globalized world. Shalimar symbolizes this displacement and so does Max and India. Maximilian Ophuls, a German Jew creates his identity under the shadow of the Holocaust and loss of home and family. Commenting on the process of self-identification he says, "The reinvention of the self, that classic American theme . . . began for me in the nightmare of old Europe's conquest by evil. That self can so readily be remade is a dangerous, narcotic discovery. Once you've started using that drug, it isn't easy to stop" (*STC* 162). This power of transformation or metamorphosis is best employed and imbibed by the migrant for whom the whole world is home; for him land is not a geographical area barricaded and confined. Yet the influence and pull of the land one originally belongs to is ingrained in the psyche through the emotions and experiences attached to the homeland.

Max experiences flashes from his past while visiting the Line of Control in Kashmir, which unsettles him. "Then his history reasserted itself and he climbed back into its familiar garments – in particular the history of his hometown . . . its people's lives"

(*STC* 180). India when she realizes her true identity conforms to the pulls of her roots that connect her to her mother and her past as Kashmira. She is all ice, cool and focused on her target when she faces her enemy and in the end "There was no India. There was only Kashmira, and Shalimar the clown." (*STC* 398).

The identity of Rusty is forced into confirmation by his disciplinarian guardian. English customs and traditions imposed on the young boy distances him from his land and culture; his immediate environment. The rain lashing on his face and the splash of colours of Holi, generates a new energy in him that helps him to break free from his guardian's house. His appointment as Kishen's English teacher and his growing attachment to Meena, Kishen's mother takes him forth on his journey towards maturity. His identity is mingled fully with his environ but does not realize it until he decides to leave. The decision to leave is also influenced by the absence of his friends, Somi, Ranbir, Suri, which makes him feel lonely and out of place. However the delinquent situation of Kishen makes Rusty reassess his decision and he decides to take responsibility of the child and return to the hills.

> They had to go back. To bathe at the water-tank and listen to the morning gossip, to sit in the fruit trees and eat in the chaat shop and perhaps make a garden on the roof; to eat and sleep; to work, to live , to die. (*ROR* 660)

Identity requires specificity of history and culture. In the modern times this specificity is temporal and shifting thereby lending a certain degree of complexity to the process of self-identification. No matter where a person is displaced, the influence and presence of his land and culture cannot be ignored or negated. It emerges either through the story, the theme, the characters or the situations inherent in Indian English Fiction. In fact it can be said that land, culture and identity are fused together to give a definite form and shape to the edifice of Indian English Fiction, which characterizes it as a unique expression of the life, culture and ethos of India and its people.

Works Cited

Bond, Ruskin. "The Room on the Roof" *Collected Fiction.* New Delhi: Penguin Books, 1999. 543-660.

Ghosh, Amitav. *The Hungry Tide.* New Delhi: Harper Collins Publishers, 2006.

Rushdie, Salman. *Shalimar the Clown.* London: Jonathan Cape, 2005.

11

Nayantara Sahgal's *Rich Like Us:* A Thematic Analysis

—Kiranjeet Kaur Bedi

The novels of Nayantara Sahgal deal with a wise gamut of themes ranging from personal dilemma and problems, joys and sorrows, fulfilment and frustrations of female protagonists to the political upheavals that India has experienced since Independence. Her proximity to political power has enabled her to project the kaleidoscopic view of the political changes in the country. She indeed is the ringside view of the happenings behind the political and bureaucratic curtains.

Rich Like Us portrays a nation which once embraced the hallowed Gandhian ideals and which in modern times has repudiated with a vengeance, as it were, Gandhi and all that he stood for in his life and politics. M.K. Naik observes that the real test of political novel is in its "preservation of the integrity of its fictional values of the ensuring that politics permeates the work either in the form of ideas and ideology or in respect of setting action as genuinely non-political literature."

Rich Like Us is set in the 1970s when the sacrifices and visions of the freedom fighters had been all but forgotten. It is complex novel with plurality of narrative voices and enigmatic ending and does not end itself to simple straight forward interpretations and characters. Judged from this norm *Rich Like Us* can be considered artistically successful novel.

The story of the novel is silhouetted against the backdrop of the Indian socio-political ethos, its economic disparities, rampant corruption, the hoary past with the cruel tradition of sati and the political upheavals of 1975. Sonali Ranade, an upright civil servant in the Ministry of Industry, is pitted against the contemporary bureaucratic regime.Sonali heroically fights the malice in the bureaucratic hierarchy which has seeped to the core and corroded the Indian society and its long cherished values. While most of the Indian novels in English portray the stereotyped versions of Indian womanhood. Sonali in *Rich Like Us* is made of quite a different stuff. A top-notch at the IAS competitive examinations, she has the intellectual strength to rebel against hackneyed thoughts, outdated customs anachronistic rituals. She knows and lets the world know that she is not out for an arranged marriage and the consequent life of intellectual inertia. Her destiny is elsewhere. After completing her studies in India she goes to Oxford for higher studies. Her rebellion against society is not merely a passive ideological resistance; it is a concrete manifestation of carving a new image in a new purpose to Indian womanhood. She has inherited her values and ideals from her conscientious who was an ICS officer in colonial India. With an admirable rare courage she refuses to grant permission to open the fizzy drink Hapyola factory to Dev, the spoilt son of Mona and Ram. She rebels overtly and fearlessly against the bureaucratic set-up. Patriotic, committed and honest that she is Sonali suffers a rude jolt when she gets her transfer order. Instead of receiving appreciation for having done her duty with a sense of patriotism, she is victimized by the bureaucratic system.

Ravi Kachru, an Oxford-educated officer, is an ardent supporter of the clannish dynastic succession (31). He replaces Sonali as joint secretary and thus her destiny comes to a dead end. After the death of her father she has none among his survivors who can measure and understand her deep sense of agony and isolation.

> The alienness of what had just happened, the midnights knock at mid day, for no reason. I could understand paralysed me, until I realized that nothing new or shattering had happened after all. No malign fate had singled me out for punishment.The logic of June 26th had simply caught up with me (32).

Sonali feels bitter and frustrated that the society she lives in rates those in power higher and more important than the honest and upright officers. She feels completely alienated and her sense of rejection reacts with a determination not to "grovels and beg favours and act like a worm instead of a person" (37). The strength of Sahgal's novel is in her honest upholding of human values. Sonali feels more human and less bureaucratic when she talks from Rose to her desk before she bids farewell to her office. Later in the story Sonali's sympathetic and an understanding friend Rose loses her life in the hands of her stepson Dev's hired goon. The tragedy reflects the bitter truth that women in India are mercilessly murdered by her own relatives when it suits them, whatever reasons. Sonali's great grandmother met with a similar fate in 1905. Rose's untimely death leaves Sonali bereft and lonely. Sonali and Rose share certain ideas and basic human approach to love its problem. Rose lends meaning to other people's life even after death. As an example, the beggar whom she used to feed and who finds meaning and purpose in life.

Nayantra Sahgal invests reality as a springboard to realize her vision of fulfilment in the life of her characters. Her novel proves that the theme shapes the form and the form of her novels is bright with the real life that becomes inseparable in her fiction. She explores the spirit of freedom through the consciousness of the heroine, and its significance in the lives of other less important characters like Kishorilal. *Rich Like Us* can be described as what John Barth calls the "literature of replenishment". Sahgal tells the story and looks at life, at least in the present novel, from two planes of view. One is the Omniscient author's and the other is Sonali the heroine's.

The novel is admired for its creative innovation and optimistic vision of life. Her story is told in the third person by the authorial narrative voice and in the first person in the voice of the heroine. By the artistic alternative of the focus between these two points of view are the two angles of the vision, the novelist projects a social-political reality at two levels: the level of the masses and the level of the individual. This symbolizes two classes into which the character in the novel seems to fall naturally. The technique of twofold vision enables Sahgal to portray vividly the two Indias—the India of the rich Western-educated, ruling elite, and Bharat, the India of a poor toiling mass of humanity which has been denied the fruits of India's independence. The two Indias do not complement each other; rather they are in sharp contrast to each other and with an unbridgeable gulf between them.

The novels make use of some editorials and letters written to the editors of the newspapers as a form of historical evidence. One of them is an editorial of the *Calcutta Gazette* of the 7 Dec. 1829 which expresses supreme pleasure and celebrates the Act of Abolition of the cruel sati passed by Lord William Bentinck. The English administrator is applauded for his reform which has ended "a system demoralizing in its effect on the living, a revolting system of suicide and murder."(134) Sonali discovers yet another instance of sati which dates back to 29 Dec. 1929 as recorded in the *Bombay Courier*. By quoting these documents the novelist juxtaposes the dead past with the living present, bringing both into sharp focus of contrast.

Sonali, instead of commenting on the observations of these news items, just shifts the focus of narration of her father's heroic efforts to avenge his mother's murder. It reflects her insight into the human spirit and its usage for justice and freedom in her present context. She juxtaposes the acts of injustice and cruelty of the past with those in the emergency regime of contemporary times. As an administrator she may be passive, but this technique of fusing the past with the grim present provides a ray of hope. She comments, "Not all of us passive before cruelty and depravity.

He [her father] had not been nor the boy in Connaught place."(152).

Thus, Sahgal in *Rich Like Us* uses the historical facts to enrich the form and content of her narrative. Sonali feels relieved at the end when Ram's old flame Marcella offers unstinted help and hope to Sonali's clouded future. She and Brian, her husband, encourage Sonali to take up a research project on seventeenth and eighteenth century India. Politics and the way in which historical forces and the individual interact and how major historical events shape individual lives have always been of interest to the creative imagination since the Greek and Roman epics and the *Mahabharata*. As Orwell wrote elsewhere, "There is no such thing as genuinely non-political literature."

Rich Like Us is set in the 1970s when the sacrifices and visions of the freedom fighters had been all but forgotten. It is complex novel with plurality of narrative voices and enigmatic ending, and does not lend itself to simple straight-forward interpretations. As Jasbir Jain observes, "*Rich Like Us* offers no easy solutions to mankind's problems on the contrary it challenges all known solutions . . . finally *Rich Like Us* is the about the complex nature of reality." The implicit suggestion of the novel is that personal feeling for others on a human and humane level can lead to redemption of a kind. There is certainly no conventional poetic justice in the novel. It is not a story where virtue is rewarded and vice punished but one of glorification, the courage and the good, attributing to them a kind of redemptive power even in death.

The politically committed character in the novel finds himself unable to sustain his Marxist ideals when faced with the real world. Ravi Kachru, at Oxford was a committed communist. Sonali, the Western-educated part narrator says: "Even when we did not agree with him he was the inspiration of all us radicals and we never did understand why instead of throwing in his lots with the commitments after Oxford changed his mind and joined the civil-service as I, in search of another kind of involvement had already decided to do. Within a few years Ravi is making his way up there hierarchy, and when the Emergency comes, he is one of Mrs. Gandhi's favorites. The 'higher-up'. (176)"

By the end of the novel, he falls from political grace but finally attains maturity to be honest on a personal level. After Ravi's plea to her of his continuing love, Sonali finds that: "This admission of waste, of years gone and opportunity lost, filled me with a sweet relief. Isolated from all that had happened outside our private creation it had the wonder for me of broken ends mending, Kachru becoming Ravi again, of friendship resuming, of love having been really love and not a mistake he had been trying to forget."(261)

Thus the strong political commitment of a young man is projected as merely a phase on the path to maturity.

Sonali himself has a set of ideas which are rudely shaken by the events of 1976. Her Marxist commitment had been different from that of Ravi's: "Our heart beats quite differently over our discovery of it (Marxism), his for humanity, mine for small actual conscience pricking images giving me a scratchy inner lining of anxiety" (110).

Already Sonali's commitment is closer to reality, and she refuses to be carried away by idealogy. Later she says: "Only the cloudness of commitment, like the perfect relationship, could be knocked sideways with a feather. It was doubts and uncertainties that kept things alive and kicking" (261).

"Her strong sense of service receives a blow when she is reverted from her responsible position in the civil service because she refuses permission for a preposterous proposal, requiring the import of more or less an entire factory" (29).

The unknown proposal to her has the blessings of her superiors: Despite her feeling that she is pretending that "the Emperor's new clothes were beautiful", it is implied that she would have acted in the same way even if she had known that the proposal had high political backing. Being impossible for her to continue working in such a corrupt environment, in any case: "The emergency has finished my career, but suddenly I did not want a career in the crumbling unprofessionalism that bowed and scraped to a bogus emergency" (36). Her father's stern decision not to compromise with dictatorship is regarded by Sonali as: "him at his strong and positive best" (175). Through grief-stricken at his death, she condemns "suttee' for its cruelty, I saw a world revealed by strangely enough it was not the evil in it saw . . . . . . Not all of us are passive before cruelty and depravity . . . . And I fell asleep to dream of heroisms whose company I was searcely fit to keep." (152)

The obvious message is: individual acts of bravery, to save one's loved ones or even oneself from death, degradation or disaster are always worth doing whether one succeeds in meeting or achieving one's ends.

Rose, the London-born second wife of a rich businessman, can be seen as epitomizing this ideal of redemption through personal courage. She risks marrying Ram despite knowing about his being married, and comes to India along with him. She saves Mona, Ram's first wife, from suicide and in spite of their initial antagonism, soon develops friendly terms with her. The crippled beggar completely neglected by the family is also helped by her. Her outspokenness and cockney bluntness—the principal characteristics—make her unplatable to her stepson, Dev. Though Ross, a brave women, is yet doomed by her honesty and her invidious position in Dev's household after her husband is incaparitated by illness. Her position as a virtual widow leads to her death arranged, as 'sati' usually is, by her husband's relatives and partly motivated by the same economic reasons. And Kishorilal, who is at first prepared to renounce his political allegiances to obtain his release from prison, finally refuses to be released and leave his young cell-mate behind. The brave, the incorrupt, the outspoken in the face of evil are admirable and inspiring, although they may not be rewarded either in this life or any other. It is certain that there is no religious orthodoxy propounded in *Rich Like Us.*

An over-dramatic and somewhat ridiculous Hindu rites are observed by Mona. Hinduism is not capable of explaining evil and hence rejected by Sonali's grandfather. In an interview Sahgal says that "Mortality is ingrained deeply in every one of us, thought may vary in details. The idea of individual morality seems to underpin her writing in *Rich Like Us.*"

Colonialism or Colonial Consciousness is another important aspect in the novel that requires to be defined. In 'Orientalism' Edward Said highlights the limitation imposed on a nation by colonial consciousness. One perceives oneself through the eyes of others and judges one by their standards by measuring oneself against their yardsticks. It is extracted that colonial consciousness consists of two stages: one of acceptance of the imperial model and the other turning away from it, both having dependent and imbalanced relationship.

The third and final stage is a moving away from these secondary positions to a position of critical identification of one's own culture, of being in position to sift and to criticize, a stance which is marked by an adult maturity. This transition to the postcolonial awareness is characterized by an ability to step outside the given and to reject the simplistic division of the 'good' and 'bad', and to forge an independent identity. This novel is remarkable for its non-emotional treatment of matters which had earlier forced the writer into a position of political partnership. This is attained by the gentle irony, humour and distance. The peculiar depiction is made of Dev's treatment of his wife Nishi and his stepmother Rose. Women like the colonial people are treated with indifference or with ruthlessness. Similar to the colonial word, their decisions are governed by the need to survive. Very often they are a long succession of compromises and sacrifices, a constant pushing of the 'I' into the background. As opposed to this, men ride roughshod over the women's emotional requirements and reject long-term solutions if short-term gains are in sight. Though it seems to be an over-generalization, yet mostly the men are found to be the exploiters. Divorce may be a way out for women, but bigamy is the rule for men; for instance, Ram having two wives in *Rich Like Us.*

It was always Sita who had to pray to be swallowed by the earth, and always a woman who had to climb her husband's pyre and be burned alive (67). This was a part of second relationship and as much colonial as the political relationship was with Britain, especially during the world wars when order had to be obeyed and not decisions independently arrived at.

In a colonial situation any act of defiance is viewed as treason, and the punishment for it or any act of questioning is death. Moral principles, concepts or right or wrong are waved aside in view of political expediency or goals. Such a situation is brought into being during emergency as described in *Rich Like Us.* Sonali is demoted and removed from her position in the ministry, and Ravi Kachru angles his way into the corridors of power. Rose is murdered and Dev gets away with the act of forgery. No longer is it a question of right and wrong but increasingly one of power vs. powerlessness. It is a repeat act and an eye-opener at that. *Rich Like Us* sets out to analyse the Indian heritage which is not all bliss and not all the same. The bits of evil which surface how are not all the result of a colonial aftermath; they are bits of the Indian heritage with its ratio, class-system and caste-division, and with India's inability to generate and persist in a native morality. The Gandhian episode begins to appear not as a continuation of a tradition, but a flash in the pan which is now over.

Rich Like Us is important for more Reasons than one: it comments on the political situation which has colonial overtones, it analyses the flow in the native tradition; and it justifies the moral struggle so important and significant for survival of the human being.

Works Cited

Naik, M.K. "The Indian English Political Novel" *Dimensions Indian English Literature*, (New Delhi: Sterling,1985).

Orwell, George, "The Prevention of Literature" in *The Orwell Reader*, (New York Jovaovich Harcourt Brace, 1965).

Jain, Jasbir, "The Emperor's New Clothes: The Emergency and Sahgals *Rich Like Us*" in *The New Indian Novel in English: A Study of the 1980s*, (New Delhi: Allied Publishers, 1990).

12

Postmodern Feminism in the Fiction of Indian Women Writers

—Vimmie Manoj

The Modernist thought is structured by a series of dualities including rational versus irrational, nature versus culture, subject versus object, reason versus emotion, absolute versus relative, and male versus female. The postmodern writings attack the dual dichotomy and the hierarchical modern thoughts. Postmodernism attempts to relocate the dual dichotomies, deconstruct it and reveal the assumed presuppositions. The discussions of postmodernism and feminism surfaced in the late 1980s and 1990s.

Judith Butler termed idiosyncratic approach to postmodern feminism. She argued that there is no real meaning to gender identity in the modernist and psychoanalytic theory, instead gender is constituted through the performance of gender roles. Her thesis was that gender identity legalizes the norms of heterosexuality. She conclusively asserted that the belief in gender identity thwarts to identify the political practice that produces coherent identity. Gender identity, therefore, instead of being the means of women's liberation, became the ground of women's oppression.

The postmodern feministic theorists oppose the gender based modernist thought that are rooted in the opposition between male and female resulting in the subordination of the feminine thus entailed. The French Feminists Luce Irigaray, Julia Kristeva, and Helene Cixous encountered postmodern themes and theorized the feminine within language and in particular of female sexuality. Concurring with the French Feminists and Butler, the postmodern Indian women writers have opposed the modernistic duality. Indian women writers of fiction like Shashi Deshpande, Anita Desai, Nayantara Sahgal, Bharati Mukherjee, Shobha De, Shauna Singh Baldwin, Jhumpa Lahiri, Kiran Desai, Namita Gokhale, Arundhati Roy and Shama Futehally reject the modern concept of male and female binaries that accept women as inferior to men. Their writing is an accord of the postmodern feminist theory. It reveals an attempt to deconstruct the thought and give a balance to the discord existing between the genders. It adheres to the idea that the opposition alters knowledge and presumes a false rivalry between the feminine and the masculine.

The Indian women writers have advocated this issue through their writings. They have rejected the modernist thought and shown little interest in the attempt to find universal truth, to fathom the social truth or to define the essential nature of woman. Through de-construction they have laid weight to shift these convictions, stressed on the ambiguous nature of social reality, and examined the method by which women's identity can be evasively reconstituted. Issues like marriage and individual identity are dealt with them making grounds for a new non-hostile environment for women in the postmodern world.

Indian patriarchal society uses marriage as a scourge to coerce and silence women. Using it as an institution it has placed women on a subordinate status and repressed their individual desires (although the basic concept of marriage designed in the Vedic era advocated equal partnership between man and wife). Indian women writers have rejected the Hindu laws propagated by Manu and his successors. The women characters they portray are no longer the long-suffering oppressed wives and mothers silenced by patriarchy. They slight the ideal traditional, oppressed woman that persisted in a culture infused with religious images of virtuous goddesses devoted to their husbands, projecting Sita, Savitri and Gandhari serving as powerful cultural ideals for women. The mythological dominant feminine prototype as of chaste, patient, self-denying wife that denied woman an existence apart from that of her husband are replaced by women characters who voice against the patriarchal hegemony and denote self-expression leading to liberation.

Shashi Deshpande, Anita Desai, Nayantara Sahgal, Bharati Mukherjee, Shobha De, Shauna Singh Baldwin, Jhumpa Lahiri, Kiran Desai, Namita Gokhale, Arundhati Roy and Shama Futehally through their writings suggest the remodelling of the existing norms since marriage as a legal institution focuses on the codes of sex stereotypes. They bring to light that marriage and sex stereotype have become so entangled that it is not possible to disaggregate them within the existing context.

In Bharati Mukherjee's novel *Wife* (1976) Dimple aspires to find freedom and love through marriage to an educated and a liberated husband but alienation from her husband disrupts the harmony and she feels "(...) bitter that marriage had betrayed her." Marriage cuts off her moorings and drives her to fits of psychic depression and eventual insanity. Bharati Mukerjee questions the roles assigned for husband and wife in the existing system of marriage.

In Nayantara Sahgal's novel *The Day in Shadow* (1971), Som feels threatened by the independent and individual existence of his wife Simrit. Later her refusal for physical intimacy with him offends his male ego and sanctions their separation. Nayantara Sahgal thus demands for a re-look into marriage as an institution, and demolish the difference in moral codes for man with that of woman.

Through Indu in *Roots and Shadows* (1980), Jaya in *That Long Silence* (1980) or Madhu in *Small Remedies* (2000) Shashi Deshpande exhibits the unequal stance granted to woman in marriage.

In Anita Desai's novel *Cry, the Peacock* (1963) Maya struggles against the cacophonous oppression due to the husband-wife alienation. Gautam, her husband, remains insensitive and his pragmatic approach adds to her trauma. Deprived of physically and emotional love she turns her into a schizophrenic who murders her husband and commits suicide. She accepts to kill and embrace death instead of being cowed down in the patriarchal system. However in her later novel *Where Shall We Go This Summer?* (1982) she exposes the repressed Sita who is aware of her "farce marriage." The insensate attitude of the husband Raman creates severe libidinous tribulations in the rational life of Sita. The novel ends with the writer suggesting the acceptance and adjustment adopted by both husband and wife in marital relationship.

Jhumpa Lahiri in her short story collection *The Interpreter of Maladies* (1999) voices the unrhymed distortion that exists in marriage through Shoba in the story *A Temporary Matter* or Twinkle in *This Blessed House.* Shoba decides to break the marriage whilst Twinkle refuses to undergo any change, and thus compels her husband Sanjeev to submit to her eccentricities. These women writers thus endeavour to restructure the institution and end its deleterious impact upon society.

Postmodern Indian women writers expose that the root cause of inequality is sexuality that is constantly controlled to highlight women's subordinate position. Though the Indian society implements rigid norms on men and women individually, ironically men supersede since physical pleasure and social life is not amorphous regarding their requirements and desires.

Catharine MacKinnon proposes a dominance viewpoint to establish if a rule or policy discriminates on the basis of sex, and it contributes to women's subordination to men since it treats similarly situated women and men differently.

A. Carter rightly quotes that "morality as regards women has nothing to do with ethics: it means sexual morality and nothing but sexual morality...it is far easier for a woman to lead blameless life than it is for a man; all she has to do is avoid sexual intercourse like the plaque. What hypocrisy!" Shobha De's writings oppose the male domination. Her women character Asha Rani, the celluloid actress in *Starry Nights*(1992) does not hesitate to explore her physical desires. Although initially the protagonist is a victim of the male domination, later she uses her body to gain her aspirations. Similarly Nayantara Sahgal's novel *Storm in Chandigarh* (1969) is a story of Saroj who struggles against the domineering dual standards and supercilious outlook of the patriarchal society.

Shashi Deshpande's *The Dark Holds No Terror*(1980) narrates the self exploration of Saru who turns down her husband, Manu's sexual overtures. She turns to Booze, Padmakar and then to Madhav to fulfil the vacuum. Saru justifies her advances "(...) wasn't it always a solution for woman who found no happiness with one man to try and find it with another?" But all men fail her mainly because both man and woman as partners do not stand on the same echelon in the societal plane, and the failure results in Saru feeling guilty, for a woman's craving to gain physical desire is not acknowledged. The novel ends with Saru waiting for Manu's arrival.

Ammu in Arundhati Roy's *God of Small Things* (1997) explores forbidden love. Shauna Singh Baldwin in her novel *What the Body Remembers* (1999) narrates the story about Satya, the barren wife, and Roop, the second wife, who becomes the child-bearer for Satya. The novel annotates on the right of a woman to own her body, surrogate motherhood and "the two strains of feminism, strident and persuasive". Shauna argues that a woman needs to be considered as a person. In the Indian society women like Indu or Saru are dependent on their male counterparts in emotional and social perspectives irrespective of their being financially constrained or unconstrained.

Paro in Namita Gohkale's *Paro: Dreams of Passion* (1984) with an appetite for life and sex is a seductress. Paro, the symbol of pure love and devotion of a maiden Indian, as depicted in *Devdas,* the Bengali Classic by Sharat Chandra, is replaced by the contemporary Paro as an alluring and voracious young girl. Paro here is more like the seductive prostitute Chandramukhi in *Devdas.* In Jhumpa Lahiri's *Interpreter of Maladies* (1999) Mrs. Das's son Bobby has been born out of adultery. She yearns for togetherness that is devoid in her marital life. Kiran Desai in *The Inheritance of Loss* (2006) does not hesitate to describe Sai's physical indulgence with her tutor, Gyan. The physical crush without any emotional borders proposes Sai's freedom to own her body. Anita in Shama Futehally's *Frontiers* (2006) has an extremely passionate date.

The women writers expose the stark reality regarding difficulty in individual struggle for survival, security and emotional equilibrium for Indian women like Saru, Indu, Simrit, Asha Rani, Saroj, Satya, Mrs. Das, Sai, Roop or Paro. The fulfilment of physical desires in women is till date considered a taboo, and women who write demanding it are labelled as of a perverted mindset.

Shobha De and Kamala Das have been criticized for their bold style of writing, and Namita Gokhale's frank sexual humour in her novel too has generated furore amongst the puritans and rendered as 'unwomanly'. Such allegations however fail to curtail their voices; instead postmodern women writers have accepted the challenge with added aggression.

Conforming to Donna Haraway's argument that women in the postmodern age need a new identity that can substitute the constructed fundamental identity of socialist feminism, Indian women writers have established how the postmodern critique of identity can be used to devise feminist views suitable to the postmodern era, and redefine women's identity. It is evident that for the past four decades the image of women in fiction has undergone a change. Women writers have moved away from traditional portrayals of undeviating, self-sacrificing women toward conflicted female characters searching for identity, no longer characterized and classified as victims. The female characters in the postmodern era are bold, confident and courageous, who acknowledge themselves and defy marriage and motherhood. The women writers have turned away from the quest for universal truth, a meta-narrative aspect, and turned instead to the specific definition of woman's identity established by discourses within the Indian society.

Gayatri Spivak has argued against the approach towards postmodernism as exclusively a white male theory, and highlighted on its extension to the issues involving gender, race and colonialism. She has stated the usefulness of deconstructive methods to define postmodern feminism. The Indian women writers do not discard the ideologies of Michel Foucault, Jacques Derrida, and Jean-Francois Lyotard that emphasize on the role of language and discussion in the construction of sexuality and the structure of gender relations. Depiction of sexual freedom and relationships outside marriage or even incestuous relationships are described in their writings.

The Indian women writers do differ from the Western postmodern feminist writers in the sense that they have not shunned the union of the man and woman, instead they have pointed towards an equalized society, a society where men and women acquire their assigned status and not that of being a dominating or a dominant being. Lesbian or philanderer issues (except for a few occurrences) are rarely dealt by them. The future writing does not necessarily determine the resistance to these issues. The sordid side cannot be veiled in the postmodern era, and women writers have valid reasons to present it amiably. The Indian women writers cater to the varied aspects related to the image of the liberated woman that is deconstructed from the traditional one. The writings of these women writers are justifiably postmodern feministic.

Works Cited

Butler Judith, "Contingent Foundations: Feminism and the Question of 'Postmodernism,'" *Praxis International* 11.2 (July 1991): 150-165.

Carter, *A. Wayward Girls and Wicked Women: An Anthology of Stories,* London: Virgo, 1986, Introduction x.

Desai, Anita *Were Shall We Go This Summer,* New Delhi: Vikas, 1975, 145.

Deshpande, Shashi, *The Dark Holds No Terror,* New Delhi: Vikas, 1980, 120. <<Bold Type Essay by Shauna Singh Baldwin.htm>>

Haraway Donna "A Cyborg Manifesto: Science, Technology, and Socialist-Feminism in the Late Twentieth Century", in *Socialist Review 1984* <<en. Wikipedia.org/wik/Gayatri_Spivak>>

MacKinnon, Catharine *Sexual Harassment of Working Women,* 1979.

Mukherjee Bharati, *Wife*, Delhi: Sterling Paperbacks, 1976, 101.

13

Sociological Status of Women in Gita Mehta's *A River Sutra*

—D. G. Thakor

The novel written in the last two decades of the twentieth century had inextricable links with the socio-political milieu as it struck deep roots in the Indian sociaty. By imaginatively treating the contemporary themes, the postmodern English novelist's sought to explore and interpret India significantly in its various aspects. Gita Mehta's *A River Sutra* reflects contemporary society by describing six stories, through which people's money-minded attitude, indifference to the poor or low profile people, jealousy, anti-socialness, in-safety of women, optimism, kind nature, women empowerment, metaphysis, etc. are clearly evidents. The present paper focuses on the social status of contemporary women and its their importance in creating a healthy society depicted in Gita Mehta's novel *A River Sutra.*

Inspired by the exigencies of socio-political history of the country, the Indian novelists took upon themselves the responsibility of giving artistic articulation to the problems of the contemporary society to make the reader aware of the current situations as well as to force their mind indirectly to think over the burning issues like the tyranny of poverty, illiteracy, suffering, superstitions, caste and sex, political issues, Indian culture, challenges etc. The postmodernist novelists with the adoption of structuralism try to convey a certain message diluting the main theme of the novel into their imagination through selecting the protagonist from the different sectors of the society like farmers, labourers, factory workers, and virtuous women fighting against a zamindar, landlords, factory owners or hard-hearted men—maybe their husbands. We may say that the postmodernist novelists have succeeded in their efforts to portray creatively in a realistic manner the whole of India.

Gita Mehta's *A River Sutra* can be described as "Metaphysical Novel", narrated with multiple narrative directions and a protagonist who does not have direct involvement in the all subplots. The passive hero attempts to narrate his story, but at the same time he is told many stories by others. A bureaucrat at the age of retirement tells this story but in this story-telling there are small stories of the Monk, Executive, Courtesan, Teacher, and Minstrel, and within the stories, there are stories of Shiva, Narmada etc. Even though there are several stories the narrator without having any pause switches over from one incident to another easily. The narrator becomes the speaker and listener at a time. This narrative technique of the writer holds the readers' passion to move forward or to read the novel at a single sitting.

Almost all the main characters, including the protagonist, try to escape from everyday reality, inhumanness and materialistic approach of the whole society. At first sight they seem to be far away from women as they realize during their personal relation with women that women become hurdles on carting on their lives to the immortality or to be free from mental disturbance. This novel reveals social status of contemporary society in different ways. The Monk, without thinking of his wife, gets ready to give up his wife with wealth, children and all the comforts, only taking for granted the worthlessness of life without thinking about his wife's feelings. The orphan boy's story reveals the tragedy of such children's life. He is offered to sing songs at the cost of a very nominal amount of five thousand rupees to the Great Sahib. Later on he is forced to sing and he sings such notes that they spoil his voice. Suddenly the Great Sahib slits the throat of the boy, kills him as the boy seems unworldly to him. Generally women are considered merciful and kind but here the boy is forcefully offered to the inhuman character by the wife of Master Mohan.

The Executive's story shows the modern attitude of lustful eyes to use and throw women as they wish. The story of the Courtesan reveals the current situation of male-dominated society, unsocial men's kidnapping of girls and their emotional blackmailing. The story of the Musician's daughter describes the reality about how any female of the society is exploited as a daughter in the hands of her own father and as a beloved in the hands of her lover. The male characters think that to get higher enlightenment in the life women become hurdles so she should be avoided. This attitude of some religious people is still exists in our society. They don't want to look at a woman's or to have their shadow on their lives. This attitude shows negligence of the female section of the society which will be harmful towards the reformation of a healthy society. Women never become obstacles in anyone's life journey. On the contrary, so many examples women are there in our history, who have supported mankind for their better inner and outer progress. Shakespeare had rightly said, "Behind every successful man there is a woman", as a woman is always an idol of sacrifice and renunciation. The main thing is that human beings must conquer their instincts, senses which misguide them towards a rude or unhealthy behaviour.

The status and predicament of women in Indian society have been yet another motivating force for the Indian novelist with a social purpose. Despite the fact that woman can contribute to social regeneration as much as to the cause of family welfare she has become a victim of social prejudices and male chauvinism. However, Gandhi's call to the Indian women to participate actively in the freedom movement made them conscious of their duty and rights which have changed their lives to some extent. They have started to fight against ignorance, superstition and backwardness, harmful to them. Indian English novelists have begun to treat women's status as the central theme for their purposeful social novels. Their efforts are to be relevant to their culture by presenting characters and situations rooted in Indian ethos.

The postmodern Indian English novelists like Anita Desai, Shashi Deshpande, Salman Rushdie, Shashi Tharoor etc. have tried to depict the political, economic or social oppression of individuals in their novels. Their novels do not deal with a personal and private predicament. But, what we have to keep in mind is that these novels are more concerned with presenting the entire picture of society, the contemporary problems and topical events in life. They are born because of the writers, consciousness about the phenomenon occuring around them. We have to note that "contemporary novels are the mirror of an age, but a very special kind of mirror, a mirror that reflects not merely the external features of the age, but also its inner face." (Walter Allen, *Reading a Novel*, 18.19)

The novel *A River Sutra* depicts women's situation in the contemporary society through very few subplots. In the novel there is no search of identity with a woman's point of view as far as women characters are concerned but their life incidents show how they have been treated since a very long period, and continuous to be so in the twenty first century. Very few women's status has changed since the society has not given total freedom to them to do what they like at the cost of only their duty towards the family or the society.

The first story is of a young man, the monk, who renounces the world at the cost of 62 million rupees and freely chooses to change his status from the richest of the rich to the poorest of the poor. As a prosperous diamond merchant's eldest son, Ashok has known the satiety of wealth-pleasure-power. He is shocked at the conditions under which the diamonds are mined, distressed by the poverty of the minors, which had left his father, the practising "non-violent Jain, undisturbed. The son realizes the absurdity of this hypocrisy and challenges his father. He is very much disturbed by his father's dehumanized acts. The Monk suddenly decides to give up wealth, wife, children, friends and all the comforts of a luxurious living. He accepts the life of a hermit, maybe welcoming the decision but at the same time he has to think about his wife also. In our human society, most of the husbands are entitled to take any decision without consent from their wives. Sometimes, they simply inform them about their decision but do not ask for their suggestions.

The second story, told by the Teacher Tarig Mia, is a story of a music teacher who has adopted a blind orphan boy to teach him music. After sometimes it is found that the boy's singing has become very popular. The Great Sahib of the village invites the boy to sing at his place. Master Mohan doesn't like the offer, so he rejects. Master Mohan's wife wants to make some money out of the offer. So she accepts the offer herself without discussing the proposal with her husband thus showing her empowerment. She sells the boy and receives five thousand rupees. Her attitude is the depiction of Gita Mehta's positive reflection of women empowerment. But the wife's negligence towards the death of the boy is a very simple example of today's money-minded women's attitude which is quite contradictory in comparison to the river Narmada, the merciful Goddess who gives peace to these who surrender themselves at her feet. Such kind of women are also present in our contemporary society. They feel themselves so powerful while taking any decision like men. Perhaps this is the impact of Western culture on them. This "The Teacher's story" is told to the narrator by a man who is accused of murder. Actually the music teacher, Master Mohan, has a gentle nature. Even though he is unhappy about his life as he is kind to others and being a poor fellow married to a rich woman, he has no right to do what he likes. He gets engaged to a rich woman by his father because he has lost his property. When this rich woman sells the orphan blind boy Imrat, whom he met during a Quawwali

Concert, to the Great Sahib, the latter cuts out Imrat's tongue as he is jealous of his voice thinking "such a voice is not human". Mohan becomes very upset and commits suicide but the rich woman has no concern with the act. For such a woman this sort of poor people are another commodity, purchasable at a certain prize. As women's attitudes are the base of a healthy society, the society never expects such an act from women.

When such evil is prevailing in the society for unsocial men, women will always remain objects for them; they can be sold and purchased anytime easily. In the novel we find a statement uttered by a drunkard, "What's the woman's price, pimp? Offer me a bargain. She won't find another customer tonight" (64). Even today girls are sold and purchased not only by men but also by women, to engage them in satisfying the carnal pleasures of men.

The Executive's story shows another reality of lustful eyes. It is the story of an urbane and sophisticated Westernized executive who gets infatuated with a tribal girl, Rima, a coolie's wife, in his remote tea estate after making love to her in darkness for several nights. When he returns to the city and gets lost in the glitter of society ladies, he still is haunted by the love song of the tribal woman. The deep love for the girl makes the executive Nitin Bose visit the tea estate again. When he encounters Rima again he is subjected to some kind of tribal magic. He starts to think that he himself is a woman. Then he goes to River Narmada to get cured. This story reflects three things. One, that first he exploits the married girl physically and then after that he finds himself trapped in her love. Second, even though he knows that he loves that married woman, he leaves her to her own situation and goes to a place where again he feels himself attracted towards the modern city women. Lastly, when the married woman realizes that the man has left her forever there is something like revenge working in her mind. Perhaps that's why during her first encounter with Nitin she possesses him with her tribal magic. Thus this poor lady seems powerful, empowered. At the same time this short incident also describes the social milieu that poor women are easily available for rich men whenever they want.

The story of the Courtesan, narrated by her mother and herself, is a tale of belief and faith based on intuition. The mother, courtesan by generations, fails to protect her daughter from the increasing indignity around her, which is directly related to the growing pollution of a heartless society ruled by money-power-muscles nexus. Rahul Singh, the notorious bandit, kidnaps the young courtesan and keeps her in captivity in a cave. She refuses to surrender herself physically at the feet of the unsocial element. The person is so intelligent. He exploits her emotionally by telling her that she had been his wife in many births before this one. Thereafter, she starts to think about her previous births. One night, when he touches her, she realizes, "Guided by his touch, I learned, I had known his body in a hundred lifetimes before he took me again a virgin on the thin quilt which was all that shielded our bodies from the ground"(184). Rahul Singh has also been a victim of this society. The two victims by force come to love each other, and their only shelter is the forest. When he is caught by the police, the girl ends her life. Her mysterious disappearance near the cliffs never disturbs the mother. For her it is normal thing. This story reveals that to some extent, today's women have been appearing in the front row of the society becoming less emotional. Professional approach of the society has diverted their mind because of which, sometimes they feel alone, totally free from anything or independent. Nothing can captivate them deep-heartedly. They are not like Savitri, that they run after the god of death to save Satyavan, Savitri's husband. They think if something is left, leave it and go ahead or try to capture something else which is more beneficial. There may be some women like Savitri, who try to regain the lost things. But their number might be less.

The Musician's story is about a girl who has become "dead inside", to express desire in music. She has come to the river as a possible source of inspiration when she tells her father that she learnt music along with another young man on the condition that the young man would marry her. She strongly longs to marry the unknown. But when that fellow gets married to someone else, she is left much disturbed. Besides consoling her by supporting her feelings, her father insists on her going to River Narmanda to be cured of her deepest attachment for the fellow and marry music. He wants to make her Ragini to every raga for which she has to surrender herself fully to the music by becoming the bride of it which she does not like. In this male-dominated society, sometime it happens that the father fails to fulfil his promise given to his daughter. In this story, we can see that the father has turned off his face from his responsibility to fulfil his daughter's very common desire of marring someone whom she loves and wants to make him her life-partner. The music would not be able to satisfy her physical necessity. Thus, one daughter's common requirement, the desire to marry someone, is killed by her own father. Even today in many houses a female child is not given that much importance that is given to a male child in the same house by the same parents. She has to do what her father expects from her as a daughter, what a husband demands from a wife or in her old age what her son orders her to do.

In the novel, the main woman protagonist is River Narmada. She is depicted with motherly love, who always welcomes her children to relieve them from mental and physical sorrows or disorders. It is the central character of the novel like a women character in Lakshmi's *Kaveriai Pola*, a Telugu novel. She is described as "The most dangerous of her kind: A beautiful virgin innocently tempting even ascetics to pursue her in flaming their lust by appearing at one moment as a lightly dancing girl, at another as a romantic dreamer" (8-9). It is this character around whom all the subplots are woven. Any virtuous women can be proved to be a pain-reliever to anyone, maybe in the form of a daughter, a sister, a wife or a Mother. For example, mother Teresa, Mataji, Kasturba, Sarojini Naidu, Rani Lakshmibai, Maa

Sharda, etc. Any sufferer can have shelter in their heart. In the novel, it is depicted that almost all the sufferers find relief by surrendering themselves at Mother Nature's lap, River Narmada. Thus, she is depicted as an empowered woman who can contribute a lot in creating a healthy society. (88)

The novel *A River Sutra* is one of pilgrimage or of people who have a strong quest for some power or peace in nature. They are attracted towards Mother Nature to lead their life peacefully. It shows the importance of mother, a woman who can guide the one who comes to their shelter with tender love, if she is respected whole- heartedly. Otherwise she can be like a demon, which can ruin the unsocial elements. In the novel, many social evils are described directly. But its deep reading leads us towards the social condition of the women of the contemporary society, before 27 years when the novel was published in 1993 and its relevance to the present society. Very few dialogues and characters are used to unravel the present status of women in the society. But the depicted dialogues are so powerful that you can have the image of it in the novel. The novelist has tried to shape it in an artistic form. The creative artists have depicted postmodern period social situation in terms of life rendered artistically through frictional devices and techniques. Really, this novel has conveyed its message powerfully as it is "a vivid interpretation of life." And "a vehicle of truth," the most chosen theme for creative art by a postmodern English novelist.

It is the Goddess River to which various sorts of suffering people can get themselves related in meaningful ways. In this novel, six stories are described to depict the potentiality of River Narmada. When the Monk realizes the hypocrisy of his father while giving answer to his question regarding the pitiful condition of the diamond minors: "How can you worry about a dead insect more than you care about a human being?"(25), he feels: "Wealth had exercised my father's emotions freeing him to examine people as if they were abstractions. His benevolence had a cold mathematics." And he decides to live a hermit's life by renunciation of his father's property alongside the holy river. Thus the Monk surrenders himself to the river mother. When the music Teacher sees that the murder of the innocent orphan blind child, Imrat, by the Great Sahib goes unpunished because of his money-power, Master Mohan soon on his way back to Calcutta commits suicide in the river water he free from grief. To get back his manliness, Nitin Boze performs the rites at the shrine, which is "on a big Banyan tree" (141) on the river bank and he comes back cured. When Rahul Singh is caught by the police, the girl whom he had abducted and later on accepts as his wife, ends her life in the Narmada. The minstrel story is about one Naga Monk. When he comes to the Narmada, he takes a child from a brothel and saves her from a miserable life of violence and corruption in a society. She is taught that the Narmada is her home and mother. She is renamed as Uma and brought to the river bank to plunge in the cold water. Thereafter, she is supposed to become the daughter of Narmada. It is significant that as she later chants her hymns to the river, she seems "ageless to the narrator."

Works Cited

Bhatnagar, M. K. (ed.). *Comparative English Literature,* Atlantic Publishers, New Delhi, 1999.

Kundu, Rama. *Surfacing And A River Sutra: A Comparative Study of Two Pilgrimages.*

Meheta, Gita. *A River Sutra,* London, Viking, 1993.

Rammoorthi, P. *Triumph of Desire Over Renunciation: Gita Mehta's A River Sutra.*

Reddy, K. V. and Reddy P. B. (eds.). *The Indian Novel With A Social Purpose,* Atlantic Publishers, New Delhi, 1999

14

The World of the Marginalised in Mahasweta Devi's Play *Mother of 1084*

—G. Gulam Tariq

Mahasweta Devi was born in the year 1926 and belongs to Bengal. She began to show a keen interest in literature since the young age itself. This can be witnessed in her contribution of several stories to the various literary magazines. Her first novel *Nati* was published in 1957. Gradually she raised herself to the level of a writer activist as she spent many crusades for the rights of the tribals. From 1980 onwards, she has been actively associated with many grassroots level social movements around the plight of bonded labour, persisting feudalism in rural polity, state negligence especially to the marginalized section of the society which includes communities like untouchables and tribals.

In recognition of her social activism through the media of literature, she has been honoured with Padma Vibhushan, Magsaysay and Padma Shri awards for her activist work amongst dispossessed tribal communities. Besides this, she is the recipient of the covetous, India's highest literary award, Gnanpith Award (1996) and Yashwant Rao Chavan National Award for 2010 "for her contribution to national integration, democratic values and the socio-economic development of India." Recognizing the work of the writer and social activist, the Human Resource Development Ministry has appointed her as National Research Professor for a second term of five years from February 2011. This honour fetches her Rs. 75,000 a month. This has added another feather to the crown of her glory as a dynamic writer. Being a social activist, this octogenarian recently actively took part in issues like Singur-Nandigram political controversy, undocumented plight of the tribals in Gujarat. Her plays:

> represent a profound concern for human predicament and sincere hope for the *better future of mankind.*

Before acquainting ourselves with the plight of the marginalized, to know the exact meaning of the term 'marginal' or 'marginalized' is of vital importance. According to the *Oxford Dictionary* the concept 'marginalize' means 'to make somebody feel as if they are not important and cannot influence decisions or events; or to put somebody in a powerless position'. So, the word 'Marginalized' refers to the group of people who are deprived of their minimum rights and are exploited.

In postcolonial dialects the term 'marginalized' occupies a prominent place. The term 'subaltern' or 'marginalized' incorporates the entire people who are subordinates in terms of class, caste, gender and office. It is the subject position that defines marginality. The lack and deprivation, loneliness and alienation, subjugation and subordination, the resignation and silence, the resilience and neglect, mark the lives of the 'marginalized', even when they resist and rise up. They feel bounded and defeated by their subject positions. They have no representatives or spokespersons in the society they live in and so helplessly suffer and get marginal place or no place at all in the history and culture of which they are the essential parts as human beings.

The Naxalite movement of the late 1960's and early 1970's was also an important influence on her work. Devi, in a 1983 interview, points to this movement as the first major event that she felt

> an urge and an obligation to document.

This leftist militant movement, which started in the Naxalbari region of West Bengal, began as a rural revolt of landless workers and tribal people against landlords and moneylenders. In urban centres, this movement attracted participation from student groups. Devi's *Hajar Churashir Ma* ('Mother of 1084') is the story of an upper middle class woman whose life is shattered, when her son is killed for his nexus with the Naxalites.

The play *Mother of 1084* is the original translation of Mahasweta Devi's Bengali play *Hajar Churashir Ma.* It has the best illustrations for the marginalized category. The neglected and suppressed plight of the woman is represented by Sujata Chatterjee, mother of the protagonist of the play, Brati Chatterjee, whose ideology, i.e., commitment to the revolutionary and Communist Naxalite movement has labelled him as a rebel, and killed ruthlessly by the police in an 'encounter'. In the play *Mother of 1084* Sujata Chatterjee, a traditional apolitical upper middle class lady, an employee, awakens one early morning to the shattering news that her youngest and favourite son, Brati, is lying dead in the police morgue bearing the corpse no.1084. Her efforts to understand her son's revolutionary activism leads her to reflect on her own alienation from the complacent, hypocritical, bourgeois society against which he had rebelled.

The play moves around Sujata, belonging to a 'bhadralok', bourgeoisie Calcutta family. Born into a conservative, affluent family, she is advised to pursue her B.A. so that it helps her marriage prospects, but is ultimately married off to Dibyanath Chatterjee, a chartered accountant, despite his unsound financial situation. In 34 years of their married life, she gives birth to four children, two sons (Jyoti and Brati) and two daughters (Nipa and Tuli). When the novel opens, two of her children are already married, Jyoti to Bina and Nipa to Amrit. In the eyes of the world, all of them are leading perfectly happy and settled lives, but as Sujata goes on to discover later, this happiness is only superficial.

Significantly, Sujata makes several other discoveries, only after the sudden and mysterious death of Brati, her younger son, with whom she had always shared a very special relationship. For instance, she discovers that all her 34 years of her married life, she has been living a lie, as her husband, being an incorrigible philanderer, always cheated her with his mother's and children's tacit approval. He fixes up a petty bank job for her, when Brati is barely three years old, not out of any consideration for her economic independence, but essentially to help the family tide over a temporary financial crisis. And, as soon as the tide is over, he wants her to give up the job, which Sujata simply refuses.

Later, she also discovers that her children, too, are leading lives very similar to her own. If there is someone who has dared to be different, it's Brati. Sullenly rebellious, right from his childhood, Brati has made no secret of his disregard, even contempt, for his familial code and value system. Turning his back upon this decadent and defunct code, he decides to join the Naxalite movement sweeping through the State of West Bengal in the late 1960's and early 1970's.

Unaware of his secret mission, Sujata is not able to dissuade her son from joining this movement. During his period of struggle, he comes into contact with a young girl, Nandini, who is also a member of the underground movement and with whom he shares his vision of a new world order. On being betrayed by one of his comrades, Brati and three of his close associates, Somu, Parth and Laltu, are brutally murdered by the hired assassins of the police.

Later, the police call up his father, asking him to come and identify the dead body of his son, who has in the meantime been divested of his identity as a person, and given another 'dehumanized identity' as corpse number 1084. Not only does the father refuse to go, but he also forbids other family members from doing so. Outraged at the manner in which his associates, his immediate family and the state have abandoned the dead Brati, his mother, Sujata decides to go, throwing all pretensions to false social respectability and the fear of public censure, to the winds.

Dibyanath Chatterjee, father of Brati Chatterjee, is represented, as an honest representative of the male-dominated society. As soon as he comes to know about the news of his son, instead of rushing to the police station he tries to hush up the matter. Sujata is aghast to see the indifferent behaviour of her husband. He is least bothered to talk about this matter to his wife Sujata. The following sentences reveal very clearly how much she is neglected by him:

> "Sujata : (uncomprehending, in a panic). What will you hush up? What are you talking about?
>
> Dibyanath : Jyoti, there is no time to waste. He goes out.
>
> Sujata : Jyoti! (Jyoti busy in dialing a number. He does not reply) Jyoti! (Reproving). Jyoti! What's happened?

From the above lines one can easily conclude that Sujata has been neglected though she is the second important member of the family. Dibyanath Chatterjee bothers to consult his son Jyoti rather than his wife Sujata. Sujata feels shocked when Dibyanath Chatterjee refuses to go to the police station with the fear of stigma in the society for his son's involvement in anti-government affairs. In the words of Sujata:

> "But that soon? Even before the body's been identified? A father gets the news on the telephone and does not even think of rushing to have a look? All he can think of is that he'd be comprised if his car went to Kantakapukur?"

The four chapters in the play mark a new stage in the evolution of Sujata's consciousness, as it enables her to re-order her fragmented and chaotic life in search of a cohesive identity. Every time she visits her own past or that of Brati, Somu's mother or Nandini, her long-suppressed personal loss is slowly released into the ever-widening, spirals of betrayal, guilt and suffering. From a weak-willed, hopelessly dependent and a non-assertive moral coward, she is transformed into a morally assertive, politically enlightened and a socially defiant individual.

In the first chapter, significantly titled 'Dawn,' Sujata primarily returns to her interior, private world of personal suffering, torture, betrayal and loneliness. Negotiating the inner time in relation to her immediate familial situation, she becomes aware of how she and Brati are not just fellow sufferers but also soul mates.

In the second chapter, 'Afternoon,' Sujata's visit to the bank to get jewellery from the locker is only a pretext for her to visit the house of Somu's mother. A close associate of Brati, Somu has been killed in the same encounter. More significantly, Brati has spent his night in Somu's house before his mysterious disappearance and death.

While Sujata goes to Somu's mother with the specific aim of retrieving the memories of Brati's last few hours, it turns out to be her entry and initiation into another world altogether. It is the world of primitive squalor, filth, poverty, degradation and subhuman existence that only hovers tentatively on the margins of 'bhadraloks' consciousness. She enters into the little known world of slum dwellers. The sight of Somu's ageing mother, her disgruntled daughter and that of their ramshackle tenement with a straw roof is enough to complete the rituals of initiation.

In the third chapter, titled 'Evening,' when she visits Nandini, who apart from being Brati's comrade-in-arms, is also his beloved. It is Nandini who reconstructs for Sujata all the events leading up to Brati's betrayal and murder. In the process, she also initiates Sujata into the little known world of the underground movement, explaining to her the logic for an organized rebellion, giving her first-hand account of state repression and its multiple failures. It's through Nandini that Sujata is finally able to understand the reasons for Brati's political convictions and his rejection of the bourgeoisie code. All this leaves her so completely bewildered that she openly admits to Nandini, "I didn't really know Brati."

In the last chapter of the novel titled 'Night,' we meet a transformed Sujata, one who is more self-assured, morally confident and politically sensitive. She decides to leave the house in which Brati never felt at home, where he wasn't valued while he was alive, nor his memory respected after his death. Having found a soul mate in Brati, she turns her back on Dibyanath and his decadent value system.

Bound by a sense of moral responsibility, she does go through all the rituals and ceremonies connected with Tuli's engagement, but during the party, she maintains a stiff, studied silence. Her insistence on wearing a plain, white sari for the party is also a significant gesture. Her feelings are not respected but misinterpreted by the members of the family. The given conversation between Sujata (Tuli, the second daughter of Sujata) and Tuli represents this thought:

> Tuli : Didn't Brati laugh at other people's beliefs?
>
> Sujata : Brati's belief was so different from your belief in the Swami, or Bina's in her prayer room, that it sounds utterly absurd when you drag his name into the same context.
>
> Tuli : The same thing again! You will react every time we mention Brati.
>
> Sujata : Yes.
>
> Tuli : Are we not worthy enough to pronounce his name?
>
> Sujata : The way you pronounce it! To hurt me!

On one occasion Dibyanath Chatterjee accuses Sujata for misleading their son which has led him to become a rebel. The egoistic nature of the father is understood in his words:

> 'Bad company, bad friends, the mother's influence'

It is a well-known fact in the society that father and mother play an important role in bringing up the children. But it is ridiculous to notice that when the children get spoiled, complete blame is thrown on the mother. Being physically weak and fragile (for a few years, she had been living with a rotten appendix inside her system), and traumatized by her younger son's death and subsequent repression of grief, she simply gives up on life. When she screams and collapses into a heap, her husband is quick to react that her "appendix" has burst. Whatever the symbolic overtones of his statement, she certainly succumbs to the slow process of inner-outer rot and decay. Finally, as she herself says, "Now that Brati is dead, I, too, wouldn't like to go on living." She discovers her inner self but on the whole loses her will to live and survive.

Time constantly swings back and forth, and so does the pendulum of two interconnected, intertwined lives, that of Sujata and her son, Brati. Interestingly, it is death that unites them both, irrevocably asserting the authenticity of their lives too.

Mahasweta Devi's predominant concerns are the tribal backwaters, the "exploitations of the Adivasis by the landed rich or the urban-administrative machinery callously perpetuating a legacy of complicity with the colonizers, bonded labour and prostitution, the destitution and misery of city dwellers who are condemned to live at the fringes and eke-out a meager livelihood, the plight of woman who are breadwinners and victims of male sexual violence, dependent widows, ill-treated wives, and unwanted daughters whose bodies can fetch a price – are adequately represented".

From the above situations, one can infer the insignificant role of Sujata in the play *Mother of 1084*, as a woman who has been relegated to the position of a neglected, suppressed, ill-treated, mechanical and marginalized in all forms in the male-dominated society who consider woman as an object of sex, only to reproduce, bring money when needed and does not possess even a voice to express her own concerns.

Works Cited

Bandyopadhyay, Samik. *Five Plays.* Seagull Books Pvt Ltd, Calcutta,1986.

Devi, Mahasweta. *'Anthology of Five Plays',(1997),"Mother of 1084"* Seagull Books Pvt Ltd, Calcutta.

Sen, Nivedita and Nikhil Yadav. *Mahasweta Devi: An Anthology of Recent Criticism.* Pencraft International Publishers. 2008.

Sharma, Ram. *A History of Indian English Drama,* Baraut,Baghpet, U.P.

15

Nergis Dalal's *Skin Deep*: Sister-Knot in Conflict?

— G. Sundari

> ...That women writers are likely to place their sense of values is likely to differ and that they will deal with what may appear trivial to male readers because it appears to have less consequence than the usual male consequences do, with what is less solid and tangible than the concerns of most men that is, less with action, experience and achievement, and more with thought and emotion and sensation.
>
> —Anita Desai

The role of women writers is a topic of concern in the present scenario for, being a woman and a creative writer, she has some distinctive perception of life to comprehend the world. Though Indian Writing in English was shaped and sustained by male writers, it was women writers who struggled to create a new and unexplored space for women. They have really made miraculous feats with words blended with the kind of robustness of language and fertility of ideas, which churn inside the kernel. Most of the women writers today are all time icons because the old pattern is no longer applicable. Women have broken through the mould and their mindsets have changed, and they seem to be liberating on several levels. Women today are no longer the victims of patriarchal society that subdued them to silence. The image of the New Woman and her struggle for an identity of her own also emerges as a dominant theme in the Indian English novel. The introspective novel consists of the " objects that are hidden and reveal themselves to the avid look that establishes meanings by composing experiences in polithetic act, that is knowing a being or a thing, loving something, yearning for something, all things considered in the plural." (http://www.highbeam.com/doc/1G1-169876970.html)

At the outset, Indian women writers relished the idea of making an extensive exploration of Indian myth and legend but Nergis Dalal delved deep into the layers of the human mind and gave ample evidence of her prosodic skill in portraying the sister relationship. Having been written in English, a work of this scope of psychoanalytical depiction of the intricacies of mind between sisters is no mean a feat that evolved the imperatives of the form of the novel in artistic utterance.

Psychoanalytical problems evolved out in the twentieth century fiction, bringing in its wake, the introspective novel. Thus, a considerable part of literature was based upon the psyche and its inner conflicts, paralleled with the struggle for social existence. Since the origins of psychoanalysis, the field has displayed a powerful set of connections to literature that embarked upon breaking new ground in women's psychology that led to an intrinsic exploration of the intricacies of life's conflicts, and love in the bonds between sisters. Moreover, the image of women in fiction has undergone a change during the last four decades. Women writers have moved away from traditional portrayals of enduring, self-sacrificing women toward conflicted female characters searching for identity, no longer characterized and defined simply in terms of their victim status. The theme of East-West encounter, contemporary social practices and political issues, Indian immigrants and many a varied theme were treated deftly by the Indian women writers.

In the novel *Skin Deep,* the concept of "sisterhood" was taken as a causative theme by Nergis Dalal for, "where everything in the novels can be imbricated with biographical revelations and thus psychologised or approached formalistically so as to focus on the technical expertise with which she deploys what are taken to be characteristic themes in her work." (Ruthven 49-50)

The writer herein takes the idea of an unconscious, a submerged iceberg, and transformed it into a dynamic force with awesome power and often cruel and crippling consequences. How the unconscious is not under the control of civilization, or any other relationship remaining as a voice within that rebels against the demands morality of the main protagonists of the novel, is an explorable question.

The most engrossing feature of a woman writer's creative art was its vitality which exposed her individual talent to the optimum and her capability of extending her writing to scale on to the peak of artistic control and an agile consciousness of the abiding values of Indian life.

In 1974, Juliet Mitchell, in *Psychoanalysis and Feminism,* signaled the redemption of psychoanalysis as, at the very least, a tool for the exploration of the unconscious and as an explanation of the construction of subjectivity and subject's sense of sex and gender. (Stimpson : 188)

Nergis Dalal, in exploring the relationships between the non-identical twins, Yasmin and Naaz, who were often freighted with a rocky mix of emotions and most of the time they disregard and envy each other, leading to anguish and confusion on the playground, in the home, and in the school, is sought to exploit psychoanalysis by the novelist, for her creative purpose focusing on the twin's experiences negotiating their layered feelings toward each other sister, shapes their psychology as forcefully as their relationships do, with their parents. Naaz in her heart of hearts thinks:

> No one loved me, I cried, because I was not pretty like Yasmin, and Sophie deliberately dressed me in clothes that made me look ridiculous. I hated those horrible dresses she forced me to wear. (24)

Her grandmother helps her to get educated and become skilled in areas such as efficient management of finances, running a smooth household and developing her personal poise in a dignified manner. She always used to motivate Naaz by saying:

> You have to make the most of everything you can do and Yasmin can't – you are clever and can work hard to do better, not only better than Yasmin but better than everyone in your class. Don't try to compete with Yasmin. Be different, make people look up to you because of your exceptional abilities and focused work ethic. (25)

Structurally, psychoanalysis in general elicits and tells stories. Psychoanalysis explores the complexities of the human soul, which emanated as a major preoccupation of literature. Psychological and ideological conflicts are part of human life which reveal as much about her own personality as well as Yasmin's, "her sister, her twin, her enemy". Naaz is the teller of the tale and the novel is structured around her narratives, mediated by the language employed by the writer.

The novel starts with the awaiting of Yasmin's visit to Dehradun where Naaz had a beautiful house, "something that Yasmin, for all her beauty, has never had". She starts her narration as her emotions of confrontation race back and forth between envy and appreciation and probably "Beauty and Brains" could be best used to describe Yasmin and Naaz, individually. Naaz, emerges out as a secured woman and Yasmin as a failure in life. Until then Naaz lived a peaceful and serene life but after her sister's arrival she happens to read "sinister meanings into everything around her", looked depleted of her with and moreover, she is subjected to a kind of psychological harassment and it is well communicated as such in expressing the emotions and feelings in varied forms. Their expressions look very ordinary but on second thoughts, they carry profound meaning, result of a deep psychological analysis.

> Yasmin said, 'The house looks enormous...Why do you need such a big place?' (18)

> With Yasmin here I felt the old sense of insecurity, never quite knowing what the day would bring. (20)

Skin Deep is one of Dalal's finest novels reflecting upon the concept of sisterhood bond in the family. She emphasizes on the psychoanalytic technique and dwells on the role of the nuances of the psyche's ponderings mostly of the two twin sisters. Their past and their childhood scenes are brought before the reader's eyes in flashes and images and the formative years of the two sisters lack any sentimental significance which is termed as an inevitable ingredient of the labyrinth of human relationships between the sister siblings in the family.

The novelist portrays the visible and vibrant dissimilarities of the sisters in a heart rending manner, that most often the reader sympathizes with Naaz. According to practical psychology, a child's behaviour is scrutinized to understand the adult behaviour because any kind of a present problem, has its roots in the past. Yasmin staunchly felt that life would provide everything for her because she entertained utmost confidence in herself that the world of female magic and her beauty would fetch anything that she wanted in life but everything evaporated into thin air after clashing against the harsh realities of life. Love and affection that is received through the bonds of human relationship brings out the best in the humans because an element of growth is visibly present. Yasmin does not adapt to situations and the state of evolution was utterly absent in her way of doing things and establishing a relationship with Ramesh that is termed frivolous by Naaz.

Freudian theories point out that adult problems can be traced to unresolved conflicts from certain phases of childhood and adolescence. With Yasmin's arrival, it seems as though the past continues indefinitely in the present life. And so, Naaz very often gets reminded of her childhood, where she suffered the manipulated, exploited and jealous-filled experiences with her sister Yasmin.

> The true heart of darkness has no real physical location, and even after all these years I can find myself there. (13)

As in Freud's psychoanalysis the patient gets isolated from external stimuli that his mind may play over his past and link it to the present, and so Yasmin without any self-analysis seduces her sister's husband. At times, Naaz's mind reflectes the feelings that she has about her sister as if, "the sip may evoke other coffee-drinkings that in turn flood out memory as if it were a flickering cinema that pulls together images and words"(Leon 28). Somehow life becomes conflicted for her because of the intense emotions that she experiences in their childhood in the household.

> In the mind past and present merge: we suddenly call up a memory of childhood that is chronologically of the distant past; but in it memory becomes instantly vivid and is relived for the moment that it is recalled. (Leon 41)

As viewed by Padilla-Walker, in the August 2010 issue of the *Journal of Family Psychology,* "An absence of affection seems to be a bigger problem than high levels of conflict".

The tragedy in relationship is that Naaz's past fears are brought into the present that produce much of the unexpected outcomes. She cannot preconceive the other's point of action or any notion. Even when she tries to free herself from the past traumatic circumstances, we certainly notice that her childhood experiences have their impact on her which again would turn out to be the most painful adult experiences. As a child she was always looked at with a feeling that she was not as beautiful as her sister. Her primal experiences and her understanding have produced in her the decision that she is not that beautiful to attract, her thoughts go unpleasant which are preoccupied with her sister Yasmin. At times in relationships sharing one's true feelings is also not safe. The more Naaz tries to bury a negative thought with positive thinking, the louder the negative thought becomes. At times, the tenacity of what Naaz resists turns out to be the most powerful reality of change. The more she tries to suppress the sadness with an impoverished state of feeling and seemed of false happiness, the less credible and veritable she feels.

Naaz constantly blames a painful childhood. We always see that her twin has an agenda opposite and rarely at one's best interest. One should be endowed with an enormous appetite towards life and concern towards sibling relationships, in order to support our perceptions towards life. Twins are born with the full potential that they can make things happen but at times never achieve tangible results. Constant discussions and debates go on inside the twins' heads regarding certain situations disturbing the calm and peace. The louder the chatter, the fiercer the battling in their head becomes and more difficult for us to comprehend their actions in life. "Anytime, there exists opinionated, serious and critical dialoguing in their mind which does enable us to tap into our personally manifested destiny waiting to be unexplored." (Jasbir 296)

There is more of "emotional chronology", as Keatly points out. "Childhood is important. In out formative years we are fed with bits and pieces of emotional and factual information. We do not store images in a chronological order but according to their sentimental significance".

The sister relationship in life can turn out to be a curse than a blessing, like an unfulfilled dream, Naaz childhood haunts her in such a way that she cannot articulate and be logical with her reasons because she suffers most and begins to buy into her own rationalizations. Somewhere, deep down inside her, she confidently knows that Yasmin is not true. When intensions go unexplored, they leave a tremendous hole in the soul. Any substitute remedies may not be available for, all those are the indirect sources of satisfaction but the quest for fervance in relationship only bestows a fulfilment in life.

At certain times Naaz's thoughts are uncomfortable and unpleasant, as if inviting a sister to her house becomes a self-inflicted torture. In such circumstances negative thoughts grow too large in Naaz's psyche that they become very influential, leading her to visceral experiences in life. Naaz allows intolerable thoughts, feelings of the kind that coexist within her, but when they exceed the limit, she losts her peace of mind. Her main error is putting too much trust in her husband Ramesh when he is before the out-of-control and dominant sibling as Yasmin and so, she cannot gain back her earlier command of her life. Her relationship with Yasmin and Ramesh demands too much of an effort and causes her much of life's struggle and pain.

Yasmin's throbbing sense of insecurity makes her seduce Ramesh, so that she can be satisfied with the feeling of having taken vengeance on Naaz for the past. We wonder what world we are in when we understand her strange way of thinking about how the sisters were brought up in a family, in which the past virtually engulfs the present. Certain layers are so dense that they remain obscure to any, and Dalal has rendered these obscure layers with remarkable dexterity. Her approach in rendering of the novel was treated with sensitivity and charm that rose above the plain of commonplace sentiments and traditional expression that urged upon flashy incidents in life, an astounding peculiarity of one whose vengeance was beyond question resulting in seducing one's own sister's husband.

At times, we wonder whether Nergis Dalal is primarily a novelist or a psychologist.

Ayn Rand, the famous fiction writer, explores certain philosophical thoughts to make things clear in one of her books entitled *For the New Intellectual: The Philosophy of Ayn Rand* . When she was constantly questioned by her admirers, of her philosophical explorations even in her novels, she states in her preface of the book:

> I am often asked whether I am primarily a novelist or a philosopher. The answer is: both. In a certain sense, every novelist is a philosopher, because one cannot present a picture of human

> existence without a philosophical framework; the novelist's only choice is whether that framework is present in his story explicitly or implicitly, whether he is aware of it or not, whether he holds his philosophical convictions consciously or subconsciously. This involves another choice: whether his work is his individual projection of existing philosophical ideas or whether he originates a philosophical framework of his own. I did the second. That is not the specific task of a novelist; I had to do it, because my basic view of man and of existence was in conflict with most of the existing philosophical theories. In order to define, explain and present my concept of man, I had to become a philosopher in the specific meaning of the term.
>
> (Ayn Rand vii-viii)

In a similar way we can understand that Nergis Dalal, consciously or subconsciously, endures the trait of understanding the deepest feelings and attitude of her characters' psyche. The kind of psychological excavations that she goes for is complete with undoubted dexterity, that she explores the mindscapes and many-layered complexities of human relationships.

We understand that the author is with total creative independence, but also driven by her intuition and emotional urges of some strains of her own life because she believed that originality of vision would gain newness of ideas which could make her fiction to be approached, to learning and assimilation. Nergis Dalal is one such writer, whose work is marked by an impressive feel for the language, and an authentic presentation of conflicted female characters searching for identity. They are no longer characterized and defined simply in terms of their victim status but are depicted twofold, i.e; by the diversity of women and the diversity within each woman, rather than limiting the lives of women to one ideal.

Mrs. Dalal drew her sustenance from the Parsi identity in India and its tradition as inspiration that made her to be very conscious of Indian culture. Her originality and novel approach in weaving out the sister relationship makes her identified in the ambiguous definition between the foreground and background space of the mind's mystical aura which created the sister-knot. Moreover, Sigmund Freud's psychoanalytic theory, the human mind is said to be operating on two levels of consciousness, the 'Id' and the 'Ego'. The Ego represents the conscious level of behaviour while the Id is where the repressed and frustrated emotions are stored. And so, the novelist focused on the inner recesses of her characters for a better manifestation of the sensibilities of the characters in the novel.

"Freud further developed the iceberg metaphor. Just as the vast bulk of an iceberg is submerged below water, most thoughts, wishes, motives, and so on remain out of consciousness. The small fraction of such psychological experiences that do come to consciousness show themselves as the 'tip of the iceberg' above water. Most onlookers are only aware of the 'tip of the iceberg', but to understand the movements of the iceberg it is important to be aware of its submerged bulk. In essence the submerged part of the iceberg, the unconscious, has an enormous impact on behavior, but remains out of sight." (Moghaddam 44)

The fair idea of what is going on in Naaz's mind when Yasmin questions about Ramesh's sudden demise and speaks about his leaving of some fortune for her, does not reveal her relationship with him. Naaz, is very much conscious of her sister's affair with her husband but does not intend to express anything to her, she questions herself thus: "I wonder, did I intentionally create the confrontation which brought on Ramesh's fatal heart attack? Was I unconsciously or even consciously, hoping it would happen? It is a question I prefer not to answer." (301)

Works Cited

Ayn, Rand. *For the New Intellectual – The Philosophy of Ayn Rand,* Random House,Inc., New York 1968.

Dalal, Nergis. *Skin Deep,* Penguin Books India, 2005.

Edel, Leon. *The Psychological Novel,* Kalyani Publishers, Reprinted 2002. Ludhiana.

Jain, Jasbir. *Women's Writing : Text and Context*, Rawat Publications, Jaipur, 1996.

Moghaddam, Fathali M. *Great Ideas in Psychology: A Cultural and Historical Introduction*, One World Publications, England, 2007.

Ruthven K.K. *Feminist Literary Studies: An Introduction*, Cambridge University Press, Cambridge, 1991.

Stimpson, Catherine R. *Where the meanings are : feminism and cultural spaces*, Routledge, New York, 1989.

16

Poile Sengupta's *Thus Spake Shoorpanakha, So Said Shakuni* as a Postmodern Text

— L.V. Padmarani Rao

> Literary criticism as such perhaps be called the art of re-reading.
>
> —Barbara Johnson

By mid-fifties the modernist tendency in literature has run its course, as it were. Modernism in the hands of Eliot, Joyce, Faulkner and their imitators had practically turned the pursuit of literature into a 'criticism industry' for the enlightened academics. With Modernist texts like *The Wasteland* or *Ulysses,* with its invitation to enormous textual exegesis and New Criticism, for all its rejection of biographical and historical criticism, literature and criticism were increasingly becoming something especially meant for academic consumption and it intended to entertain less. Hence is the post-war artist's frustration with regard to modernist art. The passing away of modernism was mourned / celebrated by W.B. Yeats in 1919 in the following lines.

> Things fall apart; the center cannot hold;
> Mere anarchy is loosed upon the world...
> The best lack all convictions, while the worst
> Are full of passionate intensity.

Leslie Fiedler (1982) would be a good representative who first coined the term 'Postmodernism'. And his essay *Cross the border*

– *Close that Gap: Post modernism* is still a good introduction to the subject. Edward Arnold (1992) argues that modernism and postmodernism give great prominence to fragmentation as a feature of tweneeth century art. The modernist laments fragmentation while the postmodernist celebrates it. The current use of the term 'Postmodernism' was used in the 1930's by Jean Francois Lyotard in his essay the *Postmodern Condition: A Report on Knowledge.* Lyotard's essay *What is Postmodernism?* (1982) breaks the meta-narratives that purport to explain and reassure are really illusions, fostered in order to smother difference, opposition and plurality. Derridian Deconstruction, Lacanian Psychoanalytical Criticism and the Feminist Literary Criticism of the 1960s and later are the postmodern support of Lyotardian petite-narratives.

Decline of faith in the keystone ideals and ideas of the Enlightenment like liberty, truth, subjectivity, humanity, progress etc are the postmodern outlook which completely believes in fragmentation and plurality. Gyno-criticism and Gyno literature along with the minority and subaltern voices became an important postmodern phenomenon. Not only do the postmodern texts vary in form and content but postmodern outlook gives a new meaning and interpretation to the old and established renowned epics and texts.

Poile Sengupta was born in 1948 as Ambika Gopalakrishnan. She is one of the foremost Indian writers in English especially well known as a playwright and writer for children. In addition, she has been an accomplished actor on stage and in film (The Outhouse). She is the founder of Theatre Club, a Bangalore-based amateur theatre group. *Thus Spake Shoorpanakha, So Said Shakuni* (2001) is one of the six plays included in her book *Women Centre Stag: The Dramatist and the Play (2010)* in which she brings in the two villains from the two great Indian epics, the *Ramayana* and the *Mahabharata* together at one platform in the modern world. Shakuni from the Mahabharata, hated even today as the man who fanned the conflict and later led to war between the Kauravas and the Pandavas and Shoorpanakha from the Ramayana, a villain who is more seen with ridicule and contempt because of which Sita was abducted by Ravana, Shoorpanakha's brother and thereby led to the war between Rama and Ravana, meet in the modern age in an airport at the waiting lounge. The entire play is set in the airport, within the context of delayed flight and the threat of terrorism. During their talk with each other, another angle of their personality is brought out while also justifying their actions and blaming the misunderstanding and misrepresentation of their respective characters in the epics and by the people later. In fact, both are victims and vengeance seekers and throughout the play the theme of vengeance runs in both of them.

From the dramatic technique point of view, the play is highly innovative, for, the stage has the centrestage with two chairs, which is the acting area and the down stage with the left and the right two clearly defined areas. The down stage is in the full view of the audience, each of which holds the props and costumes needed for the action. What is more interesting is that it also has a make-up kit and a mirror so that make-up is done to the artists either by the make-up artistes or by the actors themselves on the stage itself. The director is also free to place chairs behind the acting area on the centrestage to simulate the airport waiting lounge and whatever happens behind, the actors are not to be disturbed. The very stagecraft of the play is novel and postmodern in its approach, with the touch of the Brechtian model of Epic Theatre.

There are two characters in the play, the WOMAN and the MAN. They are not named and are dressed in contemporary travelling clothes. This is how the characters are universalized and belong to the past, present and of all times. The WOMAN has a bulging handbag and a glossy magazine, while the MAN has a heavy briefcase picked up from among the props down stage. The

WOMAN sits very comfortably in the chair seriously examining the cover of the fashion magazine. From her appearance, her eagerness to hide her spectacles and the way she tries to read the magazine from upside down, it is clear that she does not know to read and write. The MAN tries to sit by her side and looks as if serious and dislikes everything around him. The very erotic and feministic talk of the WOMAN makes him even more irritated. The language of the play is contemporary and postmodern and the idea of the occurrence of a bomb in the vicinity is floated in the beginning of the play by the WOMAN.

> WOMAN: You know these people who've got late for the flight and they call and tell the airport that there is a bomb on the plane. And of course everybody knows it's a hoax but you can't take a chance, can you? You have to search the aircraft and everybody waiting. (248)

Both these characters strongly feel that they have been wrongly interpreted by history and they are made villainous by unfolding partial truths related to them. Both feel that they are innocent and they played an important role in the respective epics but are not given due importance in the epics; on the contrary they are portrayed as vicious, villainous and neglected. Both the characters are with anger and vengeance to undo the injustice by history and prove their innocence. The MAN and the WOMAN feel that even in the contemporary era they are similarly exploited and neglected, and hence find a parallel to the epic characters of Shakuni and Shoorpanakha. In fact, the MAN carries a bomb in order to take revenge. They come down to the down stage and pickup from the props so as to make them look like the epic figures. This type of stagecraft, transformation of characters on the stage where the characters move continuously from present to the past and vice-versa reminds the audience of Salman Rushdie's magic realism. Like Rabindranath Tagore (as in *Chitra*) and Girish Karnad (as in *Yayati*) mythology is perfectly blended with the contemporary situation. The play rather is a retelling of the epics in a contemporary situation with the help of two characters who are the icons of the two minor but villainous characters from the respective epics, who move continuously between the past and present. This very idea is postmodern in its origin.

The WOMAN first divulges her identity as Shoorpanakha with the words "It's my story. (Pause.) I was her" (255). She narrates the incident that was responsible for the epic to commence. While Rama, Sita and Lakshmana are in the forest, it is Shoorpanakha who expresses her love and sexual desire for Rama first and then to Lakshmana, but both the brothers refuse her.

> WOMAN: You know what they did to me...the two brothers...theylaughed. Laughed at me. They teased me. Mocked me. The older one said, ask my brother...he might want you...the younger one said... I can't marry without my brother's consent...ask him... . They tossed me this way and that, as if...as if I did not deserve any more respect. As if I were a broken plaything. (261)

The ridicule of the two brothers and the chopping off her nose, ears and breasts enrages Shoorpanakha who says that "I wanted love...just a little love...for a little while" (262). Her brother Ravana is filled with anger and goes to take revenge for her sake, but soon "fell in love with Sita and took her away to his palace" (269) and as a result the epic turns around the triangle of Rama, Sita and Ravana and finally ends with the death of Ravana. In this entire epic, Shoorpanakha remains as a villain and she feels that the epic/history did not give her justice and so she wants to take revenge.

> WOMAN:What was Shoorpanakha's crime? That she approached a man with sexual desire?
>
> Shoorpanakha merely wanted love. (277)
>
> They assaulted a defenceless woman. (278)

Since then Shoorpanakha wants revenge on history and on people; she also wants a justified place to be given to her. The MAN joins the WOMAN and says, "I wanted revenge too. Hot...bloody... fanged revenge." (262). The MAN identifies himself with Shakuni, the villainous character from the *Mahabharata* and announces, "I am an illusionist. Like you." (263) Long before Drutharashtra marries Shakuni's sister Gandhari, the Kuru soldiers defeat the Gandhara princes of whom Shakuni is the youngest. The Kurus imprisons the Gandhara princes and feed them all with a handful of grains. The brothers feed their youngest brother, Shakuni, with all the grains and they die one after another in front of him. Shakuni is filled with revenge for the Kurus, but when he is released, he is very surprised to see the blind Kuru prince, Drutharashtra getting married to his own sister, Gandhari, who willingly blinds herself for the sake of husband, by wearing "a dark, thick, bloody bandage over her eyes" (265). As Shakuni is destined to take revenge on the Kuru clan, he accompanies his sister to Hastinapur and pretendes to be a friend of the Kurus.

> MAN: When you want revenge, you should be completely focussed...every part of you must plan the revenge. (269)
>
> I pretended I was the friend of the Kurus...that I was on their side. (269)
>
> But when plotting revenge, nothing else is important...not my nephews...not me...Finally...not even my sister...I wanted to turn everything to dust. Dust and ashes. (269)

To play the game of chance, i.e., the game of dice with the Pandavas is also according to the plan of Shakuni. He plays on behalf of the Kurus and he doctors the dice as the dice is made of his brothers' bones. Naturally the Kurus win and the Pandavas are easily defeated. Shakuni starts the war and gets the Pandava brothers to kill all the Kurus.

> MAN : It was all part of my plan anyway. The five brothers and the wife were exiled for thirteen years and they

left city as the crowds wailed... But I did not let my bloody nephews forget their hate. I coaxed their hatred...fed it...I inflamed it and finally there was war. (271)

WOMAN : I started a war too. But it was not fought for my sake. (271)

MAN : I felt that Shakuni hadn't been given his due..... ...I realised that he was a victim. (276)

WOMAN : Like Shoorpanakha.

The revenge motto brings both the characters together. While the WOMAN feels that Shoorpanakha merely wants love and she is not only disappointed but neglected by history, the MAN feels that the second epic is only because of the Aryan greed, their striking race superiority and their arrogance like a bloodthirsty sword where Shakuni plays an important role but not given due place in history.

The MAN and the WOMAN in modern times also are the sufferers still. The WOMAN still doesn't get true love for which she has been searching for centuries. The MAN's land, in the modern times, has been torn apart and his brother has been taken away by branding him to be an informer and killed him later. His 13-year-old sister has also been kidnapped, raped and killed. Hence the MAN decides to take revenge by exploding the bomb at the airport.

WOMAN : Love. Hate. Bomb. All four-letter words. (279)

Sengupta has finely blended the modern terrorism with the old revenge. By making the marginal characters of the epic to be the important and emphasizing, she brings out the central place for the subalterns. The dramatist has finely fused the past and the present; the illusion of the modern characters with the epic characters; the marginal and the minor characters of Shoorpanakha from the *Ramayana* and Shakuni from the *Mahabharata* to dominate the entire drama where both are filled with the feeling of injustice not only in the respective epics but in the recent times; and their revenge to be exercised in the world with bomb blasting is the postmodern way of looking at the epics. The skilful handling of the plot, merging of the two epics, the domination of the plot by the minor characters of the epics, the blending of reality of the modern times with the illusion of the past, the continuous movement of the characters between present and past and the modern use of the language by the characters add to the stunning effect of the play. The play abandons the nostalgia of the epics for the 'one and all' and realizes the intervention at the micro and local level in the Lyotardian sense. Both the characters are consumable, in which the medium becomes the message, and truth is just another illusion in a Baudrillardian dictum. If the postmodern age is full of simulations and the 'loss of the real', the text represents a typical postmodern condition.

Works Cited

Benjamin, Andrew, ed. 1989. *The Lyotard Reader*. London: Blackwell.

Conner, Steven, 1989, *Postmodern Culture: An Introduction to the Theories of the Contemporary*, London: Blackwell.

Lyotard, Jean Francois, 1984. *The Postmodern Condition: A Report on Knowledge*, Manchester: Manchester University Press.

Sengupta, Poile, 2010. *Women Centre Stage: The Dramatist and the Play*. New Delhi: Routledge (All references are from this text).

Waugh, Patricia, ed. 1992. *Postmodernism: A Reader*, London: Edward Arnold.

________ 2006. *Literary Theory and Criticism*, New York: OUP.

17

Soul-Body Concept in the Selected Novels of R.K. Narayan

— R. Jothilakshmi & G. Meenakshi Sundara

R.K. Narayan has a very strong background firmly fixed on the Vedic injunction. He never fails to extol the Vedic perspectives in his novels. How he impregnates the essential concepts of Vedic philosophy into the sequence of events in his novels are indeed worth admiring. In the most expected places he inserts the profound philosophy which provides the reader with a sudden insight into the concept of 'WHO AM I?'

The question 'Who am I?' is the basic principle on which the entire *Vedas* is built. One who is a 'jnani' or scholar, in whose mind this question arises, is considered eligible to pursue the study of Vedic literature which includes the four *Vedas (Rig, Yajur, Sama, Atharva)*, 108 *Upanishads*, 18 *Puranas*, the *Itihasas* and *Brahmasutra*. In *Brahmasutra* the philosophical treatise on the *Upanishad*, the first verse says.

atato brahma jijnasa

which means an inquiry into the knowledge about the self, which again is "who am I? The answer to this profound question is the prime subject of the entire *Vedas* as already mentioned. One who has cherished this question in his mind is rightly motivated to pursue the ultimate reality of life-becoming aware of the self.

This profound question is being repeated on many occasions in the novels of Narayan. Srinivas is one of the main characters in the novel Mr. Sampath. Narayan portrays Srinivas as quite philosophical. After his graduation he spends years reading the *Upanishads* and not in the least bothered about earning a livelihood. The mystic purity of the *Upanishads*, which in terms of human existence means restrained and regulated life becomes Srinivas' dominant passion in life.

When Srinivas approaches the old landlord for a house, the old landlord asks him, "Who are you?"

"It is a profound question"[replies Srinivas]. "What mortal can answer it?"(Sampath 9). While he thunders against municipal or social shortcoming a voice goes on asking, "Life and the world and all this is passing—why bother about anything? The perfect and the imperfect are all the same. Why really bother?"(30)

This statement is the natural conclusion for his questioning mind and he has to find an answer for question.

His interest in the *Upanishads* leads him to ask, "Is it right to be family centred?" He says that "every activity in this world is centered on false ego [I am this body-(i.e) My] and real ego [I am a soul—(i.e) I]." While he is reading the *Upanishad* he is totally absorbed in it. All his domestic worries and all these questions of prestige seem ridiculously petty. "My children, my family, my responsibility must guard my prestige and do my duties to my family-who am I?"(13)

Srinivas considers this to be far more serious a problem he has to face. These are meant to encourage gradual development of self-realization.

The Vedic wisdom advises how to live and get rid of the material entanglement. The chance for spiritual realization is offered in the form of the *Upanishads*, which are the part of different *Vedas*. Thus reading few lines from *Upanishads*, Srinivas involves himself in deep inquiries above his own self which is the beginning of self realization. "Till I know 'who I am' how can I know what I should do?"(13).

Narayan is at his best when he deals with it for he deals with it for he has got a very strong foundation of Vedic literature. The same idea is very much echoed in Narayan's *A Tiger for Malgudi*, which is considered to be a very profound work by almost all the critics. This novel is about a tiger possessed of the soul of an enlightened human being who tells the readers the story of his life.

For example, the master who is the chief protagonist is questioned by someone among the crowd:

"Who are you?"

The master replies, "You are asking a profound question. I've no idea who am I! All my life I have been trying to find the answer. Are you sure you know who you are?" (*Tiger* 118)

Being steeped in the Vedic philosophical attitude to life, in the acceptance of self realization, Narayan reflects his own response to the deeper needs of life. Thus he is in search of real identity "Who am I?.

The inquiry of *Vedanta Sutra* "Who am I?" I am a spirit soul.

This can be understood very easily from Srila Prabhupada's teachings found in the *Topmost Yoga System:* "I am' not this body, because at the time of death the body remains-although everyone cries, 'Oh the poor man is gone!' the man is lying there. Why do you say he is gone? He is lying there! At that time we can come to our senses, the body is not the man. The real man is gone-that is the soul" (9).

When one understands that he is not his body and is a spirit soul, he comes to his real ego. In the Vedic literature [*Brhad-aranyaka Upanishad* 1.4.10] it is said, "aham brahmasmi". (I am a spirit soul). The quality of a spirit soul is explained in the *Bhagavad Gita* as follows:

avinasi tu tad viddhi
yena sarvam idam tatam
vinasam avyayas yasya
na kascit kartum arhati.

(That which provides the entire body you should know to be indestructible. No one is able to destroy that imperishable soul.) (96)

This verse more clearly explains the real nature of the soul, which is spread all over the body. Anyone can understand what is spread all over the body. It is consciousness. This consciousness is the symptom of the soul.

In the *Bhagavad Gita*, Lord Krishna says that the soul is the maintainer of the body.

antavanta ime deha
nityas yoktah saririnah
anasino 'prameyasya ...

(The material body of the indestructible, immeasurable and eternal living entity is sure to come to an end.) (98-99).

The material body is perishable by nature. It may perish immediately or it may do so after a hundred years. It is a question of time only. There is no chance of maintaining it indefinitely. But the spirit soul is so minute that it cannot even be seen by anybody. In the *Vedanta Sutras* the living entity is qualified as light because he is part and parcel of the Supreme light. As sunlight maintains the entire universe, so the light of the soul maintains this material body. As soon as the spirit soul is out of this material body the body begins to decompose: therefore it is the spirit soul which maintains this body.

The same idea is repeated in *The English Teacher*. The novel is undoubtedly the most personal and autobiographical of Narayan's novels. It is a direct result of the agony of Krishna's losing his wife, whom he loved very clearly. The novel is indeed based on the need to understand and realize life and death which are two different states of existence where two entirely different systems of values exist. There is certainly a deliberate contrast in the novel between the visible bodily world of human being and the invisible world of spirit and dead.

He establishes the universal truth that the fulfilment of man's desires and aspirations is limited very much by forces outside the control of the human will. There are certain facts of which death is the most obvious which no aspiration and no force of man can conquer. There is a sort of stubbornness in the stuff of experience which frustrates and resists the human desire. This idea of fatalism as well as helplessness gets more affirmed when the doctor says, "What can we do? We have done our best" (*Teacher* 94).

Narayan here drives home the point that the human body is perishable, whereas the soul is eternal. He establishes this fact while talking about how Krishna succeeds in communicating with the spirit of his wife. Here the readers of Narayan get the answer to the question which his characters like Srinivas and the Master ask the question 'Who am I?'. Narayan had a definite idea about human problems like birth, death, old age and disease which cannot be conquered by any living entity.

While talking about the loneliness and separation, which is caused by the sudden death of his wife, Narayan, the master craftsman, puts the same idea that the soul – the maintainer of the body which is not perishable by nature. He says there in no escape from lonelincss and separations:

> Wife, child, brothers, parents, friends ... we come together only to go apart again. It is one continuous movement. They move away from us as we move away from them. The law of life can't be avoided. The law comes into operation the moment we detach ourselves from our mother's womb. All struggle and misery in life is due to our attempt to arrest this law or to get away from it or in allowing ourselves to be hurt by it. The fact must be recognized. A profound unmitigated loneliness is the only truth of life. All else is false (177).

One can come across the same idea repeated in *A Tiger for Malgudi* which may be considered to be the masterpiece of Narayan.

"No relationship human or other association of any kind could last forever. Separation is the law of life right from the Mother's womb." (*Tiger* 174)

The *Bhagavad Gita* confirms this idea:

> na Jayate mriyate va kadacin
> nayam bhutva va bhuyah
> ajo nitya sasvato yam purano
> na hanyate hanyamane sarire

(For the soul there is neither birth nor death at anytime. He has not come into being, does not come into being, and will not come into being. He is unborn, eternal, ever – existing and primeval. He is not slain when the body is slain.) (101-102)

For example, in *The English Teacher* Susila, who is no more, tries to send a message to her husband through a medium. This proves that her physical body is destroyed but not the soul.

> This is a message for Krishna from his wife Susila who recently passed over .... She has been seeking all these months some means of expressing herself to her husband, but the opportunity has occurred only today, when she found the present gentleman a very suitable medium of expression. Through him she is happy in another region, and wants him also to eradicate the grief in his mind. We are nearer to each other than you understand. And I am always watching him and the child ...
>
> (*Teacher* 106)

It is quite distinctly stated in all Vedic literatures and especially in *Bhagavad Gita* that death is not an end:

> jatasya hi druvo mrtyur
> dhruvam janma mrtasya ca
> tasmad aparihaye rthe
> na tvam socitum arhasi

(One who has taken his birth is sure to die, and after death one is sure to take birth again. Therefore, in the unavoidable discharge of your duty, you should not lament). (110-111)

This piece of thought is very clearly substantiated in the *The English Teacher* as well as in *A Tiger for Malgudi.* We find Krishna lamenting over the sudden demise of his wife. At that time he is not aware of the fact that death is not an end of life. He comes to know about this reality when his wife communicates with him and enlightens him about the fact that the soul is eternal.

Krishna tries to gather more information about the life after death. He confirms from Susila's spirit that the soul never perishes. Though Susila is physically no more Krishna experiences her presence by his side on the bed and converses with her. When she leaves him in the early morning he utters the following words, "We stood at the window, gazing on a slender, red streak over the eastern rim of the earth. A cool breeze lapped our faces. The boundaries of our personalities suddenly dissolved. It was a moment of rare, immutable joy – a moment for which one feels grateful to life and death" (*Teacher* 184)

While acknowledging the fact that any artist is bound to improve in his art as he gains experience, the researcher is inclined to conclude that the realization about the law of life Narayan gained out of loneliness caused by the separation of his wife played a greater role in bringing about a great change in his philosophy of life and his ability in creative writing. Indeed this realization has not only touched the recesses of his mind and soul, but also ignited a sort of enlightenment in Narayan which can be confirmed from the fact that the novels which follow *The English Teacher* show a maturity of mind, art and tightness in structure. The analysis of the novels like *Mr. Sampath, The Man Eater of Malgudi* and *A Tiger for Malgudi* may hold testimony to this view. This realization would have helped Narayan to create characters like Sampath and Srinivas in his novel *Mr. Sampath* which follows immediately after the *The English Teacher.* One finds Sampth being very materialistic right from the beginning of the novel. But Srinivias views everything in the larger context of time which is cyclical.

In *Mr. Sampath*, the quest for self-realization is the main theme. When one analyses the characters like Sampath and Srinivias in *Mr. Sampath* one may be tempted to believe that Narayan would have had the same line of thought in his mind. Sampath is completely materialistic and he always runs after sense gratification. He does not find time to pose and think for a moment anything about self-realization. Perhaps that may be the reason why Shiva. K. Gilra says, "Sampath and Margaya uproot themselves from their traditional ethos to run after illusions of material success". (40)

One may find from the beginning how Srinivas is slipping away even from his family life and going towards the quest for self-realization.This can be understood easily from the conversation between himself and his elder brother.

> His brother asked, "What exactly is it that you wish to do in life?" Srinivas flushed for a moment, but regained his composure and answered: "Don't you see? There are ten principle Upanishads. I would like to complete the series. This is the third."
>
> (*Sampath*12)

Through Narayan depicts Srinivas as a totally different character from the other characters in the novel, he faces the same kind of mutual crisis just like any other man who is caught between worldly duties and the quest for self-realization.

> He asked himself, "Family duties come before any other duty. Is it an absolute law? What if I don't accept the position? I am sure, if I stick to my deeper conviction; other things like this will adjust themselves." (33)

Though Srinivas is the scriptwriter for the film 'Burning of Kama' about the success of which everyone is very speculative, one may find him being very much balanced by understanding the meaninglessness behind the mad rush for worldly things. Perhaps that may be the reason why he is not at all disturbed when the attempt for the film making got completely wrecked all on a sudden.

After a long silence of seven years of the publication of *The Painter of Signs* in 1976 one can hardly disagree with the verdict that Narayan is at the peak of his creative originality in *A Tiger for Malgudi.* Like all fables, *A Tiger for Malgudi* tells a good story. As the story proceeds one is made aware of much more clarity in design and intersection in the narrative momentum. In an unusual prefactory introduction, Narayan reveals how he came to write this novel. He had read newspaper report of a tiger faithfully hermit during the Kumbhamela festival and speculated on its possibilities for a novel. He writes, "It also occurred to me that with a few exceptions here and there, humans have monopolized the attention of fiction writers."(*Tiger* 7)

He then emphasizes the moral basis of this novel. "Man in his smugness never imagines for a moment that other creatures.....I made a tiger the central characters in a novel" (7-8).Like Narayan's other central characters, the tiger too, experiences fear at first but eventually triumphs over it. The tables are turned and the population melts out of sight as the tiger roams the street of Malgudi. Raju witnesses the cowardice of mankind. Their sense of insecurity and the irrational dread of losing their assets lie behind this behaviour. The tiger takes refuge in the headmaster's room of a local school and the door is bolted on the outside with the unfortunate headmaster trapped in the attic. The tiger's redeemer arrives, none other than the master who admonishes the crowd for using words such as 'beast' and 'brute' for the tiger.

> They are ugly words coined by man in his arrogance. (118)

When their attempt to shoot the tiger fails, again due to the psychic aggressive powers of the master, he succeeds in subduing the tiger and walks away with the animal at the heels.

The religious aspect takes over from the moral and the social on the next stage of the tiger's life is one of the gradual transformations, equivalent to the Hindu ashrama of sanyasa. It is here that Narayan perfects the theme of renunciation and creates a real sanyasi in the Master, instead of the earlier fake Sadhu Raju, the guide. The master is neither animal trainer, nor is he an ordinary man. Once a respectable and prosperous man of the world, a man of property, and one who had taken an active part in the politics he gives up everything. Like Siddhartha he renounces the world because of an "inner compulsion," in order to merge his could with the universal soul and attain the spiritual insight of a mystic. (38)

The tiger, ferocious in nature is calmed by the power of the Master's suggestion alone. He stands head and shoulders above humanity in general and is a symbol of the perfection that man can reach through the pursuit of ancient wisdom.

> Life or death is in no one's hands: you cant die by willing or escape death by determination. A great power has determined the number of breaths for each individual, who can neither stop them not prolong ... that's why God says in the Gita "I am life death: I am the killer and the killed... (142)

The first lesson the tiger learns is that it is not a tiger. It must learn to transcend the self – a lesson that does not come easily to man. As old age advance, Raja learns to appreciate the companionship of the forest animals. Self-realization can only come through acceptance rather the rejection.

In spite of the fact that the world around Narayan changed at a fast phase, his novels maintained the slow phase, which he had developed since the 1930. He was deeply rooted in tradition and religion. In his novels the conflict between tradition and modernity is very common, but in the long run, he holds to the deep-rooted tradition.

Though he maintains an objective detachment from his themes and characters, a close scrutiny reveals his Indianess: and even detachment is an essentially Indian quality. This is reflected in the character of Srinivas in Mr. Sampath. It appears that Narayan believes that society is not man-made by choice; it is a part of the universal order. Therefore if one wants to appreciate his work, one must understand his view of man's life relation to the cyclical universal order and his attachment to the wheel of existence, which is purely Indian. According to the Hindu philosophy in which Narayan's faith is unshakeable as evident in his novels, this mundane world is not the real world and so is ultimately insignificant. Being essentially Hindu in his attitude, custom and practice, he views every phenomenon as illusion (*maya*). Through characterization he filters the unique Hindu philosophy. The lives of his major characters revolve a particular obsession which may be ambition as in Srinivas of *Mr. Sampath.*, *A Tiger for Malgudi, The Man-Eater of Malgudi*, the main characters prove to be truly Indian in spirit as they strive for their true identity. Srinivas in *Mr. Sampath* is a classic example. As he experiences Ravi being exorcised, he experiences the necessity on a person's part to achieve true identity. This realization frees him from the shackles of involvement in the mundane world.

As R.K. Narayan acquired the universal truth from the Vedas that the soul is eternal, he developed the character of Krishna in *The English Teacher* and made him realize at the end that death is not an end. The realization is that only the body of his wife Susila perished and he could communicate with the spirit soul which is eternal.

The same idea is reinforced in *A Tiger for Malgudi.* According to Narayan the tiger and the Sannyasi were brothers in the previous life, which amounts to prove that the soul is eternal and only the body is changed.

Conclusion

Narayan proves to be very victorious in characterization by portraying characters like Srinivas, Master, Tiger and Natraj who are the product of the true Vedic spirit. The novels *The English Teacher, A Tiger for Malgudi, The Man-Eater of Malgudi* and *Mr. Sampath* become all the more popular among the Indian readers for this philosophy of life which is a part of the mass consciousness of the Indian people.

Works Cited

Narayan, R.K. *The Man Eater of Malgudi,* (Mysore, Indian Thought Publication, 1988).

______, My Days: A Memoir, Mysore, Indian Thought Publication, 1979.

______, R.K,*The English Teacher,* (Mysore, Indian Thought Publication, 1986.

______, R.K, *A Tiger for Malgudi,* London,Penguine Books, 1983.

Srimad Bhagavatam. Los Angeles: The Bhaktivedanta Book Trust, 1972.

The *Topmost Yoga System.* Mumbai: The Bhaktivedanta Book Trust, 1972.

www.sacred-texts.com

www.bhagavatgita.us/bhagavatgita famous comments.htm

www.indiadivine.com

18

East-West Encounter in R.K. Narayan's *The Bachelor of Arts*

— Kapil Dev Sharma & Pradeep Kumar Talan

The theme of Europe vs. India that critics usually term as East-West theme in Narayan, is embodied in Chandran's character. Narayan is trying to portray the dilemma by introducing this cultural conflict right in the beginning. He brings 'India' as it was the 1930's and 1940's into sharp focus. A sense of social inequality and that of economic and racial exploitation are the main issues, which Gandhian thought emphasized. To know India and to be an Indian was in the air all around during the 1930's and 1940's. Chandran's idea of self-respect for a nation, as his speech at the historical association meeting implies, necessarily makes him seek personal independence as a man. The quest for personality on Chandran's part will, in Malgudi milieu, involve him in comic imbroglio, and this comic imbroglio functions in the novel, as intended, as an educational process for the protagonist.

By this research paper my focus is to explore the East-West conflict and portray the dilemma and social inequality, economic and racial exploitation due to the East-West encounter in R.K.Narayan's *The Bachelor of Arts.*

R.K. Narayan's *The Bachelor of Arts* was first published in 1937. In this novel the theme of Europe Vs. India which critics usually term as East-West theme in Narayan novels is embodied in Chandran's character. He asks very basic questions which every sensitive Indian faced during the 1930's and 40's. Through Chandran's character Narayan is trying to portray the dilemma, as A.N. Kual says, "A consideration section of Indian society striving to live its daily life in a definite historical situation".

Chandran reflects deep-seated cultural prejudices when he says, "Remember that he is scoundrel at heart".

The theme of the futility of English education in India continues in *The Bachelor of Arts,* The novel significantly participating in the debate on the topic "Historians should be slaughtered first." Students' need to put India's past and correct perspective is provoked by false presentation of Indian history by British rules. The debate in which Chandran is participating, naturally introduces the theme through the protagonist's conflict with persons and institutions that represent alien culture. Mr. Brown, the English Principal of Albert Mission College, provokes Chandran into a sense of racial antagonism. Chandran keeps gagging at Brown's pink face and this is what strikes him:

> He is not here out of love for us, but merely to keep up appearances. All European are like this. They will take their thousand or more a month, but won't do the slightest service to Indian with a sincere heart. They must be paid this heavy amount for spending their time in the English club. Why should not these fellows admit Indians to their Club? Sheer colour arrogance.

Chandran is freed from all the "distracting illusions and hysterics" and he accepts life in all its sanity and common sense.

Narayan's critic of examination system gives an extra dimension to the protagonist's response to the colonial situation. Chandran talks of examinations as the 'final trial' that produces a peculiar hysteria. But instead of preparing for the examination, he gets involved with the historical association as its secretary. It is significant that the beginning of the session has led to the formation of a proper historical association. Its aim is to assess Indian history in its proper perspective. Ragvachar, the history professor, emphasizes its importance by saying that "If he were asked what the country needed most urgently, he would not say self government or Economic Independence, but a clarified, purified Indian History."

Gandhian thought with its reinterpretation of India's part culture was responsible for creating a sense of history. It provoked an individual to understand himself in the context of history of his country. Narayan's protagonists refuse to live in the image of an Indian created by English rulers. Actually this explains Narayan's characterization as a mode of moral analyses. His presentation of Indian characters as it was being changed under Gandhi's leadership is, as Yasmine Gooneratne rightly says, an attempt creating a "New literary mythology" and "setting the record straight".

Chandran the bachelor is presented as rather romantic and heroic and therefore a comic character in Narayan's vision. Apparently an important student member of Albert Mission College, he is an eloquent public speaker with a nucleus of friends where he dominates— Veeraswami, revolutionary, and Mohan, the poet. Veeraswami contribute a paper entitled, "The Aids to British Expansion in India". The narrator informs us that "It pilloried Great Britain before the Association, and ended by hoping that the British would be ousted from India by force". This creates pre-censorship on all papers by Principal Brown. As a protest Veeraswami offers to read another paper entitled, "The subtleties of imperialism." The narrator's comments on this character give us a clue to Narayan's point of view which does not seem to approve of violence.

> Veeraswami bristled with prejudices and violence, Imperialism was his favourite demon. He believed in smuggling arm into the country, and on a given day, shooting all the Englishman.

Part-II of *The Bachelor* relates Chandran's life after graduation till he arrives and settles down as a newspaper agent in Malgudi.

But his smooth life has once been disturbed by Chandran's romantic love for the girl in 'green sari' whom he had seen at the Sarayu beach. This brief episode of his love sickness provides Narayan an opportunity to define his hero's romantic excess before he is returned to Malgudi with sanity and equilibrium.

Narayan's treatment of man-woman relationship is very close to the Indian social reality of times. Unlike the pre-1930 romance writers like Cornelia Soabji, S.M. Mitra, Sirdar Jogendra Singh and Bal Krishna who depicted love scenes in imagination of the English novelists, Narayan's treatment of man-women relationship is realistic. His portrayal of married love as against the romance before marriage is traditional but authentic. Narayan is conscious of the difference between the two words as he underlines in an article:

> In the English novel, for instance, the theme or romance is based on a totally different conception of man-women relationship from ours. We believe that marriage is made in heaven and bride and groom meet, not by accident or design. But by the decree of fate ...... the eternal triangle, such a standby for a western writer, is worthless as a theme for a India, our social circumstances not providing adequate facilities for the eternal triangle.

And if we remember the Malgudi ethos of 1930's, it would be easy to understand that there could have been no freewheeling by Narayan in the passing of love. Keith Gorebian aptly remarks:

> The Indian principle of order has to be followed if Narayan is to represent his society with authenticity, and this principle conceals the eternal triangle of romance (found so commonly in Western literature) in favour of arranged Marriage.

If the caste created no problem, un-matching horoscopes horoscope are there to lead to Malgudi marriage to someone else. Chandran's bout of romantic involvement, of course, compels him to leave Malgudi for Madras, and after a brief halt at Madras, he adopts the role of sanyasi.

Preoccupied with the Guru theme and with exploring its comic potential from different angles, Narayan is usually attracted to the character of trickster sadhu. This trickster sadhu in Narayan may take on that garb in mere self-delusion in the beginning but as the plot unravels, Narayan's hero usually ends in genuine self-realization and return to the Malgudi world of common sense. The narrator tells us that Chandran was "different from the usual Sanyasi, other may renounce with a spiritual motive or purpose, but chandran renunciation was not of that kind. It was an alternative to suicide. He was a sanyasi because it pleased him to mortify his flesh. His renunciation was a revenge on society, circumstances, and perhaps, too, on destiny".

After eight months of aimless wandering Chandran reaches Koopal village. The villagers take him at his face value and pamper his with gifts and devotion. He cannot remain self deceived anymore. He finds it ridiculous to dress in ochre garbs for nothing better than a girl's love.

It is, therefore, through the character of Chandran that Narayan presents the influences of Western culture on Indian society and conflict between the East-West culture in the 1930's and 40's. The protagonist is restored to Malgudi normally. Freed from illusion and hysteria, he appears to be changed from within –with no more plans to go England for higher studies.

Works Cited

Garebian, Keith 'Narayan's Compromise in Comedy' in *Literary Half Yearly*, vol. XVII, No.1, Jan.1976.

Gooneratne, "Yasmin Traditional Elements in the fiction of Kamla Markandaya, R.K. Nrayan and Ruth Prawar Jhabwala", *WLWE*, vol.15., No.1, April 1976.

Narayan', 'R.K. English in India', *Common Wealth Literature, Unity and Diversity in Common culture,* ed. John Press, London: Heinemann Educational Books, Ltd, 1965.

Narayan, R.K. *The Bachelor of Arts* (Mysore; Indian Thought Publication, 1937).

19

Theme of Love in Manjul Bajaj's *Come, Before Evening Falls*

— K.K. Sunalini

Come, Before Evening Falls is a novel which weaves the story set in the year 1909 in Rohtak Division of the erstwhile Punjab province. Though the story has past historical reference, it has the stark and brutal choices that confront young people as they try and find a way between the impulse of love and the dictates of duty to their families, remain largely unchanged.

Raakha, the protagonist, is a problem child. He perceives the awkwardness and shame in his mother's marriage. His mother is the second wife to his father. Raakha considers his father ruthless as he exploits his mother for his own pleasure. As a young girl, his mother was sent to assist her sister's delivery who in turn got pregnant twice and later discarded to her fate. Her older sister hats her and blames her for seducing her husband and also for his transgressions. Raakha, along with his mother and younger brother, has slowly been edged out. They live like servants in their own house. If it wasn't for his mamaji, Raakha would not have got education.

Jugni is Chaudary Hukum Singh's niece. They are Jats. It is a society governed by strict marriage rules and the diktats of the Khap panchayat. The village is Kaala Saand named after a dead bull. Jugni is the first person to see the new teacher Raakha. She feels a thrill run through her body when she sees him. She wonders at the unknown reason that causes her heart to shrink at the thought of Raakha.

Jugni and Raakha have their first acquaintance at the family well. Since then he visits her house regularly to meet her uncles Chaudary Hukum Singh and Tau. Once, he stops her by holding her wrist saying that they make better friends rather than enemies. It becomes difficult for her to come out of the first crush. Since then she eagerly waits for their next encounter. She was no fool for she knows exactly what happens between men and women. What she wants to know is what happens underneath that happening. She not only mulls between the chemistry between men and women but also how life can cut a person in a zigzag way, the loyalties on one side and the personal interests on the other. Her loyalties lie with her Dadi, Tau and Chaachi who have nurtured her with utmost care. The novel gives explicit statements regarding womanhood and marriage. Chaachi says, "Womanhood was a bottomless well" (Bajaj, 2010, 29). In another context also she says, "Nothing remained your own after you get married. Not your body, not your sleep – not even your tears" (ibid.).

Bajaj endows Jugni with two persons: The insider and the outsider. In her mind she pretty well knows that she is clear-headed and sensible. She is alerted by the impulses incapacitated at the sight of Raakha. She wonders what if the insider in her entirely takes over and makes her do stupid things, and brings dishonour and shame. She imagines her body hanging from the peepal tree in the chaupal at the centre of the village, Tau crying into the turban, and her brothers tip-toeing through the village hanging their heads – in permanent shame. She dares not take any chance.

Raakha develops a love for Jugni. Every morning when he wakes up, her face flashes up across his sleepy brain. Her eyes, the tilt of her chin, the arch of her foot, the gold of her skin, the toss of her plaits and the curve of her waist. All these cause a happy smile to flash across his face. Jugni, on the other hand, is a self-controlled girl. Though the word 'love' keeps inserting itself into her head, she keeps sending it away. She tells herself that nothing can happen unless one permits it to happen. The words 'disgrace, dishonour, and death' whisper themselves in her head. She does not prefer to choose the words. She is also aware that love begets bastard children. And girls who fall in love either become corpses hanging from the trees or doomed to fates worse than death.

Considering the consequences of love, Jugni pleads with Dadi to get her married as soon as possible. However, Raakha cannot keep his mind off Jugni. He tries to impress her wherever he meets her.

Jugni is just an ordinary village girl – unlettered, outspoken with piquant looks, not beautiful by any standard, still the moment he lies on his bed, he feels that she is no girl but a woman, his woman especially created to wrap herself around him, her body fusing with his. At 24, Raakha is a man, a grown man who has known many women but none like Jugni. He has always felt drawn to the company of women. The warm softness of their bodies is a reprieve from the harsh coldness of the outside world. The light of longing in their eyes succeeds in momentarily vanquishing the shadow of rejection that follows him everywhere. The thrill of a new conquest always helps him lose sight of himself of the battle that can never be won. Making love to a woman no space for pain, it is pleasure but with Jugni he imagines that it will be different. He thinks that he will not lose himself but will find himself in her. He remembers his first and latest experiences, his step-brother Malakhan's wife who had seduced him when he was eight, to the very last - a migrant cattle-herder from the Thar desert. He carries the separate odour of each in his nostrils. The differing touch of each upon his palms. Not one has he forgotten. Even the prostitutes, he thinks back of fondly. Married women, prostitutes, widows, are his priority in the order of safety. To him, married women are the safest because they never cry or try to blackmail. By chance if they become pregnant, no one searches for the father of the child.

Jugni finds herself helpless because it becomes difficult for her to come out of Raakha's love. She is annoyed with herself for asking Dadi to get her married off quickly. Once, Raakha dreams of Jugni running away from him. He pleads with her saying that he is not a predator. He imagines a tiger pouncing upon her and ripping open her blouse. He wakes up from the violent dream. The last image is unforgettable to him. Jugni's bare breasts, in the centre of her naked girl–woman's breasts written unmistakably in the schoolmaster's neat handwriting are two letters – Raa kha. The image is vivid in his head – her naked breasts clearer, more real to him, than those of any woman he has ever slept with.

In reality Jugni is sure that she will not go when Raakha calls her. However, he doesn't call her. She is torn between herself and the insider. Her heart wants to feel the warmth of his eyes. She fails to understand the reason behind her disappointment. It may be because he doesn't call her as her nerves are all on edge from the waiting, and partly because the Nayin always leaves some new tit-bit of a tale corroborating her theory of Raakha's interest in Kamala, the potter's middle daughter. But mostly, she weeps from the sheer confusion of not knowing how to stop the shouting, slanging voices that have begun to live inside her head; not knowing which is her real self; not knowing which voice to be nurtured and which throttled into silence.

Jugni meets Raakha in the field and asks the reason for his not calling her. In this meeting both of them try to know each other's psyches regarding their commitment to love. Jugni's meetings with Raakha in the clearing field fall into a pattern but still she cannot speak of it as love to Raakha. The thought of speaking about love is to end it because it makes her increasingly anxious at what is happening to them, setting a constant war within her. Nothing in her short life has prepared her to face the tumult of what is happening. Meeting him is utterly reckless, dangerous beyond contemplation, putting her life at risk. Yet each time she reaches the clearing field and finds him waiting for her seems like a home-coming to her soul. She knows no place in the whole world that feels safer than his arms.

The thought of Jugni getting married to somebody else brings him a thought to "Runaway. She will not say no. Far away, to a place beyond gotra rules, the diktats of the Khap" (Bajaj, 2010, 143). He also gives another thought, "But in what currency would he measure the grief of the girl he loved more than anything else on earth when he separated her from everyone and everything she had ever known and loved since birth?"(ibid.). Jugni and Raakha enjoy a lot of liberty, sharing his romantic tales over which Jugni getting possessive gives a picture of their congenial relationship. He often pulls her leg about her name. He says, she is born fitted with a light inside, like the firefly she is named after, shining her torch inquisitively into the dark corners of other people's souls. Ferreter of secrets, he calls her. He cares a lot for her feelings. Though he gets a chance to make love to her in the clearing field he never forces her. He thinks, "If he were to push her down into the warm mud and begin to make love to her, as he wished to at that moment, he knew it would end badly for them both. Her body would stiffen" (Bajaj, 2010, 149). There is a lot of compatibility and also a lot of uncertainty in their relationship. She always instinctively knows the right thing to do: when to question and probe and when to retreat and console. What would he do when she is gone? This village, this job – nothing would be the same without her. How could it be, that she who has meant so much to him, is not meant for him at all?

Raakha has a lot of uncertainty regarding Jugni's love because she prefers the love of her Tau, Chaachi and Dadi, and never does anything to hurt them even if it kills her – still Jugni risks her life in bringing a kurta for him to wear to Hissar but he shakes and abuses her for being very selfish in coming to see him only when she pleases. She considers him angry, irrational and cruel. She thinks, "Perhaps, he was incapable of love. Distrust and anger were his nature. She was lucky to have got out of lt like this. A broken heart can be hidden. In time it would heal. At last she had not sullied her face and blackened her family's name. Atleast her Tau's reputation was safe" (Bajaj, 2010, 185).

For a days on, he has rung the temple bell and waits in their clearing field but she does not come. He waits for her, "Come, Jugni, come. Come before evening falls" (Bajaj, 2010, 194). But she never turns up. Talking about family honour Tau tells Jugni," "A family's honour was everything. A family was like a tree, its honour was not to be violated like this. Honour was the main trunk, if you struck at it, everything else – the branches, the leaves, the flowers, the fruit – they just fell, collapsing in a dead heap around it." (Bajaj, 2010, 199)

Raakha goes crazy without Jugni's love. He asks, "Jugni. Just tell me whether or not you will come with me .... Jugni, you are my woman. How do you expect me to live with the thought that I let you marry another man without making any effort to stop? I will die for you. Jugni, before I let that happen" (Bajaj, 2010, 206)". She thinks that there is no greatness in dying for love. She wants to say that those who die untimely, violent deaths do not bring ashes. They become guilty scars on the flesh of the living. They become wounds that never heal no matter how much time passes. Raakha repeatedly pleads with her to run away with him. She feels that it is not just to build one's own happiness on other people's grief. She doesn't wish to be branded as a truant daughter, a runaway bride, a blot on her family's history, a corpse hanging from some tree.

Twenty-five days before Jugni's wedding, Tau dies. At the final prayer, Chaachi's eldest brother takes Raakha's *chaddar* and wraps it around his sister (chaachi). A deathly disbelieving hush descends on the gathering. Jugni runs outside, full of impulse to throw up violently. He and Chaachi, the thought of them together, is hideous. This is the man who has held her in his arms and called her his rose-petal girl. And now he is married to a twice-widowed woman.

Jugni thinks, "She was to be a second wife to him! A chattel with no status, a woman the whole world would look down upon as a kept woman, a marriage breaker? A southan, a rival to her own Chaachi?" (Bajaj, 2010, 225). Raakha justifies himself by saying that this is the only way for them to be together. Towards the end of the novel Raakha and Chaachi are murdered dy Dadi for the sake of family's honour. While dying, Chaachi comes out with the truth that she poisoned Tau. It is Raakha who plans to kill Tau by supplying poisoned tobacco through Chaachi. Jugni finds "The man she had loved had killed her uncle and seduced his wife because he saw it as the only way he could make Jugni his own" (Bajaj, 2010, 235).

Manjul Bajaj makes a difference in the portrayal of the theme of love. She deals with the theme in a pragmatic way. The closing lines of the novel discriminate the men and women's attitude towards love, "A woman's way is different. Violence is man's way, a woman's resilience. She asserts that women know how to live on. To choose life over death, love over anger, peace over war, making over destroying, each time and every time, no matter what the circumstances are." The novel ends with an optimistic note of Jugni's perception of womanhood. She once thought that womanhood was a bottomless well. But now, with a new perception she thinks it is wrong. Instead, it is a way to explore the darkest recesses of one's own experiences and find the sweet, life–sustaining water within.

Work Cited

Bajaj, Manjul. *Come, Before Evening Falls* Gurgaon: Hachette India, 2009.

20

Shiv K. Kumar's *A River With Three Banks*: Revisiting Partition

— P.R. Shewale

A River with Three Banks, the most ambitious novel by Kumar, deals with the theme of the partition of the Indian subcontinent. Kumar has described the tragic consequences of the partition vividly in this novel. The merciless killing and bloodsheding in the wake of communal violence, the abduction of young girls, the loss of faith, the migration of a large number of people from both sides of the border are some of the tragic consequences of the partition. The river-India appears troubled by the inner currents of brutality. The title of the novel is highly symbolic. Hinduism, Islam and Christianity may be taken as three banks that condition the flow of the river-India's life-stream. Thus Shiv K. Kumar's *A River with Three Banks* is a symbolic record of the consequences of the partition of the Indian subcontinent. About the partition of India D.R. More in his book *India and Pakistan Fell Apart* rightly observes:

> The partition of India in 1947 was the most fateful incident in the history of the Indian subcontinent. It made a very great impact on the Indian people, turning the Hindus, Sikhs and Muslims who for a considerably long period unitedly fought against the British, into one another's enemies. In this civil war, thousands of men from both sides were massacred, a great number of women raped and abducted, children mutilated and property destroyed. A bilateral communalism – Hindu and Muslim or Sikh and Muslim– caused the carnage of thousands of innocent people. (More 1)

A River with Three Banks is also a story of marriage and divorce, love and hate and forgiveness and revenge on the backdrop of the partition.

Gautam Mehta, a journalist in Delhi, manipulates his divorce from his adulterous wife, Sarita through his conversion to Christianity. One day his close friend Berry tells him to spend a night with a call girl. Gautam falls in love with this call girl Haseena, a Muslim girl, who has been kidnapped from Allahabad by a gang of abductors headed by Pannalal, a pimp. Gautam helps her to escape from Delhi to Allahabad. Gautam is persuaded by Pannalal, catches him on the banks of the Ganges. In a duel, Pannalal gets killed. Gautam later on converts himself to Islam in order to marry Haseena. At the end of the novel, while Haseena's family migrates to Pakistan, she stays back but not as Haseena Mehta but as Haseena Gautam. They decide to start a new race– sans religion and sans caste.

The novel opens on a relatively calm note: "It was the quietest day of the week – comparatively speaking, of course" (*River* 1). But soon the plot of the novel starts unfolding rapidly. The novel begins with Gautam's proceedings to get divorce from his wife. Gautam Mehta, a Hindu journalist working for *The Challenge*, goes to Father Jones, a bishop, to convert himself to Christianity. He manipulates the bishop about his conversion by saying that this is a matter of spirit and heart, he also adds that he was influenced by cardinal Newman, and Catholic writers like Francois Mauriac, Evelyn Waugh, Graham Green, etc. Actually he decides to embrace Christianity not because of his love for the religion but for securing a divorce from his wife Sarita. "The certificate of baptism was all that he wanted to grab. That was his Passport to freedom" (8). What implies Gautam to get divorce from his wife is her illicit relationship with Mohinder, a fellow journalist of Gautam. The partition, in the novel, is at two levels – division of the family and division of the country. Gautam's parents have migrated to Delhi from Lahore due to the partition of the country. They suffer not only from the partition of the country but also from the partition of the family:

> His parents arrived in Delhi after many harrowing experiences on the way from Lahore. Though they were fatigued and their nerves were frazzled, Gautam could not keep them with him for more than a few days. They had been looking forward to seeing their grandson but soon they felt unhoused – their second partition .... (31)

Kumar has attempted to weave the domestic division as well as the political division of the country into the texture of the novel. The domestic drama of divorce takes place during the partition riot. When Gautam goes to the church to meet the bishop he witnesses a murder of a Muslim called Abdul, by Hindu fanatics. He discovers a letter in the dead man's pocket which reveals that Abdul was in search of his abducted daughter Haseena.

After having got the divorce, Gautam and his friend Berry go to Neelkamal Hotel which "offers its patrons everything – wine, woman and song – to use an apt cliché" (16), to celebrate the occasion. Though Gautam is a gentleman he is forced to visit a prostitute by his friend, Berry. In the hotel both of them happen to meet a pimp called Pannalal. Coincidentally, Gautam meets Abdul's daughter Haseena who was abducted by Pannalal during the partition riot. Here begins the story of Haseena as a partition victim. Pannalal had abducted her away from Allahabad when she was an undergraduate student and forced her into the business of prostitution. The abduction of women was a common thing during the partition. The story of Chandani in Chaman Nahal's *Azadi* and Haseena in *A River with Three Banks* represents this aspect of the partition.

When Gautam learns that Haseena is actually the daughter of Abdul who was killed before the church, he decides to release her from the clutches of Pannalal instead of using her for his sexual pleasure. Out of the crisis evolves a romantic love story of Gautam and Haseena in the novel. He falls passionately in love with her. Here, Shiv K. Kumar has followed the love affair of a Hindu boy and a Muslim girl, repeatedly found in many partition novels. While commenting on the love motif in the partition novels D.R. More in his book *The Novels on the Indian Partition* says:

> Almost all the novelists have used the motif of love as a means of bridging the emotionally divided minds by way of a love episode. For instance, a love episode of a Hindu or Sikh boy and a Muslim girl is necessarily woven into the plot. (More 242)

Both Gautam and Haseena decide to run away from Delhi. Finally they are helped by Berry to escape from the shackles of Pannalal. Thus Gautam's elopement with Haseena and Pannalal chasing the lovers provide a romantic tinge to the love story. If the Gautam-Sarita relationship represents divorce and hate, the Gautam–Haseena relationship represents union and love.

Gautam, thus, falls in love with Haseena, and puts the proposal of intending to marry her before Haseena's mother. When he is asked to convert himself to Islam, without hesitation he embraces it and assumes the name Saleem. Gautam, thus, crosses religious barriers to serve his convenience. Though born as a Hindu, he converts himself to Christianity for the sake of divorce and again to Islam for the sake of marriage. Pannalal too comes to Allahabad in search of Haseena and he happens to meet Gautam. He threatens to kill him if he does not disclose Haseena's whereabouts. In this encounter Gautam kills Pannalal, which unfortunately takes on the communal colour that "a member of the majority community was brutally killed last evening by a member of the minority community." (*River* 163)

After Haseena's marriage with Gautam, her family decides to go to Pakistan. Through Berry's British connections Gautam safely escorts the family of Haseena across the border risking his own life. The couple decides to start a new race of humanity. Protesting against her wish to be addressed as "Haseena Mehta"

Gautam says: "No my love, ...Not Haseena Mehta...Just Haseena Gautam – our first names only ... Yes we'll start a new race – sans caste, sans religion, sans nationality" (214). At the end of the novel there is a description of clouds sail across the border with a flock of birds winging away into the sky. It symbolizes the message of a universal religion which Kumar wants to convey through the novel:

> The sky was now covered with mountains, clouds – white, inky blue and grey. They assumed all sorts of fantastic shapes – of giant dinosaurs, their long necks craning forward, of the skeletal remains of some primordial, mammals, of an army of soldiers on the route. Ceaselessly, they sailed across the bridge from India to Pakistan casting fugitive reflections In the tawny waters of the river. (214)

Thus, like other novels on the theme of partition, Kumar's *A River with Three Banks* too ends on a strong note of optimism. Kumar advocates that we should cross the religious and communal barriers for a better future through this novel.

Basically *A River with Three Banks* narrates two stories: the story of Gautam – his conversion to Christianity for the sake of divorce and again conversion to Islam for the sake of marrying a Muslim girl, and the story of Haseena – her ups and downs as a victim of the partition. Both the stories are interwoven on the background of the partition. Gautam and Haseena are the two central characters portrayed well in the novel by Shiv K. Kumar. The impact of the partition is pronounced on Gautam and Haseena. Gautam's father has migrated to Delhi from Lahore facing the harrowing experience of the partition of the country. Haseena is abducted, her father is killed and her family migrates to Pakistan due to the partition. Haseena represents the hundreds of unfortunate women abducted during the partition. Neither Muslims, Hindus, nor Sikhs but women of all these communities are the most suffered victims of the partition. Women were abducted, raped paraded naked in public streets, forced to prostitution, and put to death. According to Urvasi Bhutalia,

"The history of partition was a history of deep violation – physical and mental – for women." (Bhutalia 131)

The theme of woman's exploitation and forced institution has been depicted very effectively in the short stories by Saddat Hasan Manto. But Haseena's character in *A River with Three Banks* is quite different from that of the women characters portrayed by Manto in his stories. Haseena is not corrupted by the institution of prostitution. Even though she is abducted and kept in a brothel, she remains unprostituted. Her first encounter with Gautam turns into love.

Pannalal, a pimp, is a selfish man. He is a villain and gets killed at the hands of Gautam. Thus the novel observes poetic justice. Another important point to be noted here is that Pannalal and Suleiman, a man connected with the business of prostitution, work together in their business. At this level there is no scope for communal rivalry.Therefore, the Superintendent of Police comments: "Here is a real intercommunal home, with Pannalal and Sulieman Gani as its heads" (*River* 131). It is ironic that we find communal hatred only among the politicians and not among the people like Pannalal and Suleiman.

There are other references to the partition in the novel. The episodes like the public rape of a woman and stabbing of her brother, and Haseena's father dying before the church are witnessed by Gautam in the novel. The brutal killing, the rape, the forced prostitution, the abduction of women, the naked parades of beautiful women are common episodes in the partition novels. In this context, Saros Cowasjee observes: "Though partition offered a variety of subject matter, the majority of the writers chose to deal with violence of one kind or another – abduction and rape being particular favourite." (Cowasjee, 1995, xiii)

The partition was a complex phenomenon. It had many aspects – historical, political, economical, psychological, religious etc. Thus Kumar's novel *A River with Three Banks* is concerned with those people who have a definite past, their present is disturbed by the partition of the Indian subcontinent but the future is possible for them. They can hope for a better life in future. Thus Kumar's novel ends an the optimistic note.

Works Cited

Bhutalia, Urvashi. *The Other Side of Silence.* New Delhi: Penguin Books, 1998.

Cowasjee, Saros and K.S. Duggal, eds. *Orphans of the Storm.* New Delhi. UBSPD, 1995.

Kumar, Shiv K. *A River with Three Banks.* New Delhi: UBSPD, 1998.

More, D.R. *India and Pakistan Fell Apart.* Jaipur: Shruti Publications, 2004.

______. *The Novels on the Indian Partition.* Jaipur: Shruti Publications, 2008.

21

From Routes to Roots: Diaspora in the Novels of Salman Rushdie

— Janmejay Kumar Tiwari

Displacement has no replacement and this is the reality of diaspora. Since the inducement of humanity, people have been straddling throughout the world without having any theoretical knowledge of boundaries. Man has always been suffering from the disease of alienation without realizing the actual outcome of migration. However, in the twentieth century, the concept of coming and going was theorized and immigrants and migrants were compelled to be aware of the plight. India, once being the colony of the British Empire, has been suffering from her internal malady and misery. The plight and predicament of the native have also been miserable. Moreover, in search of food and other necessities, they had to be dependent on their rulers and the later caught the nerve and exploited the former to the lees. The Indians had to migrate as indentured labourers for the sugarcane farming either in Caribbean countries or in South America.

The writers of the previous century have done extensive research in and into the diasporic field from external to internal, from geographical to psychological and from virtual to real. They have left no field unravished for literary enjoyment. Even in the era of global township, the home has become more significant than it used to be. Authors like Naipaul have been edifying houses for Mr Biswas, and Rushdie has no home but imaginary homelands. Writers like them have left their homelands not once but several times and still breathing the same oxygen. Imagination makes virtual homes but the fact is that virtualism is not realism.

Salman Rushdie is the author who inaugurated the field of postcolonial diasporism with his debut novel *Grimus,* which was an experiment to show the plight of estrangement and alienation. The story deals with immortality, generated worlds, surreal things, other scopes both interior and exterior, and castaways. The story follows Flapping Eagle, a young Indian who receives the gift of immortality after drinking a magic fluid. Flapping Eagle, an Axona Indian, is ostracized from the society because of his fairer complexion. His mother perishes just after few moments of his arrival in this mortal world. His sister Bird Dog shelters him and offers him with the preparation of interminable life and after that, she evaporates mystifyingly from the terrestrial of the Axona. Flapping exiles from his people, and mooches the world for centuries in search of his sister and his identity and in this mission, after wandering for 777 years, seven months and seven days; he falls through the fleapit in the Mediterranean Sea. Because of his eternity, he lands in an equivalent dimension at the preternatural Calf Island. People of this island are consecrated with immortality yet fed up with the monotony of life. However, they are disinclined in giving up their immortality and happen in a stagnant community under an understated and creepy authority. In the search of his identity Flapping is weary of the mundane reality of immortality hence wants to get rid of the Grimus effect. The novel apparently demonstrates that migrants have no future, neither on Mortal Island nor on immortal one. They can wander wherever they wish but without having their heart with them.

Midnight's Children, Rushdie's *tour de force*, paved the path for postcolonial literature in India. He began to decolonize English from the English and his programme is still in furtherance by him as well as from others. Like him, the protagonist Saleem Sinai wanders among three countries, i.e., India, Pakistan and Bangladesh but is unable to find a proper place to live in. *Midnight's Children* is a narrative of displacement and rootlessness that is caused by relocation. Many of its characters are migrants drifting from shore to shore in search of some "imaginary homelands" and obviously, the author identifies himself with his migrant personae. As Pramod K. Nayar opines:

> Much of diasporic writing explores the theme of an original home. This original home as now lost– due– to their exile–is constantly worked into the imagination and myth of the displaced individual/ community. (Nayar 191)

And:

> Diasporic writing captures the two invariables of their experience: exile and homeland. All diasporic literature is an attempt to negotiate between these two polarities. The writings of exiled/ immigrant writers undertakes two moves one temporal and one spatial. It is as Meena Alexander puts it, "writing in search of a homeland. (Nayar 188)

Exploding the myth of home Salman Rushdie speaks of "imaginary homelands, Indias of the mind" (*IH* 10). In the process of searching the homeland, he as well as his characters lost their roots, routes and identity. All Midnight's Children, Saleem, Shiva, Padma, Parvati face a calamity of identity, disintegration of disposition, geographical as well as cultural dislocation. As Rushdie clarifies:

> When the Indian who writes from outside India tries to reflect that world, he is obliged to deal in broken mirrors, some of whose fragments have been irretrievably lost. (*IH* 11)

Cultural displacement has forced the immigrant writers to accept the provisional nature of all truth and certainties. It is almost impossible for migrants to be unable to call to mind his native place and nativity emotionally. Consequently, this displacement constitutes a double identity that is at once singular, plural and partial. In *Imaginary Homelands* Rushdie echoes:

> Our identity is at once plural and partial. Sometimes we feel that we straddle two cultures, at other time we fall between two stools. But however, ambiguous and shifting this ground may be it is not an infertile territory for a writer to occupy. (15)

In *Midnight's Children,* he pictures this trauma of fluid identity. In his first migrated country Saleem becomes a dog; a member of the Cutia Unit. Consequently, his body has gone fully numb, the only sense active being his sense of smell, "anaesthetized against feeling as well as memories" (*Midnight's Children* 353). His fellow soldiers start calling him "'Buddha' because there hung around him an air of great antiquity" (349), though he is 24 years old at that juncture. Here Saleem Sinai is presented as the microcosm of all the diasporic generation; how they are treated in the newly inhabited territories; how the venom is thrown upon them and the current example of this venom throwing is Australia. Saleem, being the mouthpiece of his creator, expresses the feelings that Rushdie feels while living in an adopted land.

Shame, the most political adventure of Rushdie, exhibits the trauma of migration that he has been facing throughout his life. *Shame* is a novel about migration. At several places, Salman Rushdie emerges as the narrator and narrates the deplorable conditions of migrants; as he confesses in one of his interviews with Ashutosh Varshney:

> It's a novel about the changes that happen to individuals and communities under the pressure of migration… I wanted to talk about the immigrant community in London particularly the South Asian immigrant community, and at that time what I wanted to say about it is, " Here's this enormous community of people who are, it seems, invisible–their concerns their lives you know, their fears, and so on, somehow invisible to the white population". (Herwitz and Varshney 19)

Like all migrants, Salman Rushdie has not been able to shake off the idea of roots and identity. Roots, as he says in *Shame,* are "designed to keep us in our place" (86). These roots help the migrant to be in touch of his nativity and the effect of these pedigrees could not be eradicated easily. One is bound to have an origin without that one's derivation is meaningless.

The theme of root, route and rootlessness has become an explicit and intricate part of Rushdie's plot. His novel delineates the psychological crisis resulting from the forfeiture of identity and roots, and this happens to almost each and every diasporic and postcolonial author. In his authorial intervention in *Shame*, Rushdie depicts the actual position of migrants what they get and what they lose:

> When individual come unstuck from their native land, they are called migrants, when nations do the same thing (Bangladesh), the act is called secession. What is the best thing about migrant peoples and seceded nation? I think it is their hopefulness... . And what is the worst thing? It is the emptiness of one's luggage. I'm speaking of invisible suitcases, not the physical, perhaps cardboard, variety containg a few meaning-drained mementoes: we have come unstuck from more than land. We have floated upwards from history, from memory, from time. (86-87)

And Rushdie describes his own position in these words:

> I am an emigrant from one country (India) and a new comer in two (England, where I live and Pakistan to which my family moved against my will). (85)

The core issue of this expat cognizance is the question of identity. As an immigrant moves from place to place, region to region, his identity becomes hybrid and fluid because of these geographical movements. The migrants may live in new places but that is only as imaginary homeland— they never feel comfortable in their newly occupied home/country. They live, as Bhabha states, "in between two geographical cultural locations, which is often perilous and marginalizing," and these "in between places provide the terrain of elaborating strategies of selfhood singular or communal–that initiates new signs of identity" (Bhabha 17).

Rushdie in this context of migration brings the theory of fantasy, according to him, all migrants like him are fantasist. For him fantasy is not only a part of reality but it helps him to rise above reality and it pronounces a seeming freedom of creativeness as the distinguishing feature of art. It not only hassles the fictive elements in the plot but also is revelatory of the mind behind the work. Imaginary nation states are fabricated on existing ones. Imaginary and real countries, both have to deal with the question of history, and to some extent, they thrive in fluctuating it. A migrant writer's position has an attention-grabbing benefit as it affords him with conflict to cultural authoritarianism and its claim to speak the absolute truth, and thus to pull to bits a treatise of western historiography.

The Moor's Last Sigh is the first major novel that Salman Rushdie produced after "The Rushdie Affair". The novel narrates the story of last Muslim ruler of Spain, Boabdil who lost his empire to the Catholic conquerors Ferdinand and Isabella of Spain. *The Moor's Last Sigh* refers to a geographical point in Andalusia from where Boabdil looked at Granada for the last time before the conquering armies of Ferdinand and Isabella finally captured this legendary city. Commenting upon the diasporic nature of the novel Minoli Salgado remarks:

> The novel appears to replicate the author's predicament by foregrounding a sense of banishment and impending death, opening and closing the eponymous Moor's narrative with his premature death in exile. Exile and death thus frame the rich narrative collage that constitutes this saga of Catholic-Jews Da-Gama-Zagoiby family, containing the events in a foreclosed temporal register that offers the cultural and historical density of text. (Salgado 153)

The Ground Beneath Her Feet is the novel where Rushdie expresses his diasporic views ostensibly. The novelist is entailed in sketching a textual diasporism in the novel. All the three major characters, i.e., Ormus Cama, Vina Apsra and Umeed Merchant a.k.a. Rai experience the predicament of migration, as Rai describes:

> Ormus, Vina and I: three of us came West and passed through the transforming membrane in the sky. Ormus, the youthful proselytizer of the here and now, the sensualist, great lover, the material man the poet of the actual, saw visions of the otherworld and was transformed into an oracle, a ten-year monk and an Art Decorated recluse. As for me, I must say at last that I passed through a membrane too. I became a foreigner. For all my advantages and privileges of birth, for all my professional aptitude, I was turned by the fact of leaving my place of origin into an honorary member of the ranks of the earth's dispossessed. (418)

Rai starts feeling that he has started becoming peaceful when he looks at his new house that he shares with three other photographers, namely, Mack Schnabel, Aim'e-Cesaire Basquiat and Johnny Chow:

> So this is what they feel like, I thought: roots Not the ones we're born with, can't help having, but the ones we put down in our own chosen soil, the you could say radical selections we make for ourselves. (414)

Like all migrants, these characters feel infatuation with their second country where they migrate Salman Rushdie himself Rai starts loving America:

> ...America below fourteenth Street, loosey-goosey and free as air, gave me more of a sense of belonging that I'd ever felt back home. Also, with the dream America everyone carries round in his head, America the Beautiful, Langston Hughes's country that never existed but needed to exist with that like everyone else, I was thoroughly in love. (419)

In spite of the blind love towards America, a man of exile is unable to forget his past. He feels nostalgic, as nostalgia is the measure sub-theme of theory of diaspora. In the migrated country one feels himself thrice removed from reality: (1) he is geographically removed and in this way he loses his cultural environment in which he was brought up, (2) he is removed from his language and is forced to adopt a different language, (3) he is dislocated from his own mental territory. The love quoted in the above paragraph is textual, ephemeral and virtual not real. In reality, the situation is quite unlike:

> ...the day doesn't pass when I don't think of India, when I don't remember childhood scenes: Dara Singh wrestling in an open air stadium, Tony Brent singing, Sherpa Tenzing waving from the back of an open car outside Kamla Nehru Park. The movie *Mughal-e-Azam* bursting into color for the big dance-number. The legendary dancer Anarkali strutting her stuff. The nonstop sensory assault of that country without a middle register, that continuum entirely composed of extremes. Sure I remember it. It's the past my past. (416)

The point is that a diasporic man may become hilarious for a period only; happiness is not an everlasting one in an adopted country or rather for them, in the words of Thomas Hardy happiness is an occasional episode in the drama of pain. Rushdie feels this trauma in the land where he is living and he expresses his grieves through his characters. This is not only the story of the narrator Rai, Vina Apsara and Ormus Cama who have the same sense of belongingness as they have left their birth places but unable to quit birthroots.

The Enchantress of Florence is Rushdie's last adventure where he gives the sketches of two kinds of diaspora, i.e, one immigrant and other emigrant. Both of them suffer with the same problems in their accepted countries. Mogor, who arrives India from Florence, declares himself a distant relative of Mughal Emperor Akbar. But later he is exposed and he has to flee. The case is the same with Qara Qoz; she leaves her home for the betterment for Europe but succumbs to several problems. Both the protagonists suffer the crisis for individuality. Against the popular belief, the novelist has introduced a white immigrant and given his experiences that he comes across in India. He makes sure that not only a colonized person suffers this trauma of estrangement but also the same is the condition with the so-called occidentalists.

The narrator of the novel Mogor himself is the first victim of identity crisis. He is a traveller from the Medici and his claim to have a blood relationship with the emperor of Mughals is in the phrase of David Gates "a literal manifestation of the connection between East and West". He adopts different names at different times. In Florence, he was Uccello di Firenze, which he abandoned like the "abandoned skin of a snake" and Niccolo Vespucci that he left at the time of his arrival to India and became the self-styled Mogor dell Amore. And this Mogor dell Amore as defined by Father Acquaviva "is no name at all . . . It means a Mughal born out of wedlock. It is a name that dares much and will offend many. By assuming it he implies that he wishes to be thought of as an illegitimate prince" (93). Eventually, he proves his illegitimacy and as displaced has no vibrant future, he has to flee like the colonial empire; as Rushdie states in the voice of Akbar: "The English had no future on this earth . . . (and) would surely be erased from times record before very long" (98).

Being uprooted is one of the several aspects of postmodern era that fascinates Rushdie much. He celebrates the uprootedness of Mogor, disintegration of Qara Koz. As longing for belonging is one of the premier themes of diaspora and postcolonialism, all the characters of Rushdie loom between two worlds: one is indigenous and the other is adopted. Both struggle in their newly arrived countries and eventually both are compelled to leave their adopted countries.

Despite several miseries that are being faced by the immigrants and migrants one fruitful result of this wandering is that the boundaries that existed between the countries have been demolished. Authors of this class have attempted to bring both the hemispheres closer together. In the novel Argalia realizes the reason of Qara Koz's coming to the West, as he says:

> She comes here of her own free will, in the hope of forging a union between the great cultures of Europe and the East, knowing she has much to learn from us and believing too, that she has much to teach. (276)

This dream of diasporic authors, to a certain extent, has come to be true. Now the wall of Berlin ceases to exist and people are free to view the world according to their own perception and point of view.

Works Cited

Herwitz,Daniel &Ashutosh Varshney. *Midnight's Diaspora: Encounters with Salman Rushdie.* New Delhi: Penguin Books, 2009.

Rushdie, Salman. *Grimus.* London: Vintage Books, 1996.

______. *Midnight's Children.* London: Vintage Books, 2006.

______. *Shame.* London: Vintage Books, 1995.

______. *The Ground Beneath Her Feet.* London: Vintage Books,2000.

______. *The Enchantress of Florance.* London. Jonathan Cape, 2008.

______. *Imaginary Homelands: Essays and Criticism,1981-1991.* London: Granta, 1991.

Salgado, Minoli. "The Policies of Palimpsest in *The Moor's Last Sigh*". *The Cambridge Companion to Salman Rushdie.* Ed. Abdulrazak Gurnah. Cambridge University, Press, 2007, 153-168.

22

Salman Rushdie as a Children's Writer: Reading *Haroun and the Sea of Stories* and *Luka and the Fire of Life*

— Ved Mitra Shukla

Sir Ahmed Salman Rushdie, born in India in 1947, is an English Booker Prize-winner author. With the publication of *Haroun and the Sea of Stories* in 1990, he made his way in the realm of children's literature. Recently he has included one more fanciful fiction in the list of his children's literature, i.e., *Luka and the Fire of Life* (2010). He wrote *Haroun and the Sea of Stories* for his elder son, Zafar, who was ten years old two decades ago. The book was written after the publication of *The Satanic Verses* (1988) which was banned in India. In 1989, the supreme leader of Iran and some Muslim scholars also issued a *fatwa* to kill the writer as well as the publishers of the book due to *The Satanic Verses* controversy. It is believed that his work, *Haroun and the Sea of Stories*, is a representation of his feelings and thoughts of that time. And, thus, there is an allegorical theme. Similarly, the latest one is gifted to his young son, Milan, and also full of autobiographical elements. However, the remarkable point is that in the name of gifting his sons, the writer has provided a valuable service to the world of children's literature.

In the present time, there is a long list of such writers who are constantly writing for children. As far as the place of Rushdie among the children's writers is concerned, it may be a sort of overstatement to include his name in the writers' list of the first water. But, among the Booker Prize winner Indian English novelists in the present scenario, he is the only author who has intentionally penned some works for the children. There are many attributes which are essential for the children's literature. There are also many types of the children's literature. It may be divided on the basis of technique, tone, content, etc., and in this way, categorized into six categories: (1) picture books, (2) traditional literature, (3) fiction, (4) non-fiction, (5) biography, and (6) poetry (Anderson 2006). On the basis of different interests of children according to their ages, another type of categorization is possible. In the present paper, there is an attempt to examine the books (*Haroun and the Sea of Stories* and *Luku and the Fire of Life*) from the children's literature viewpoint. Keeping in mind the objective, the paper also tries to trace out some issues which make the books successful.

Rushdie did a lot in order to provide true pleasure to his readers through the books. Due to the different interests of children aged 0-18, it is not an easy task to write a winning book for children. While he was "writing *Luka and the Fire of Life* for his youngest son, Milan, he grew worried about a character called Nobodaddy – a devil who assumes the figure of Luka's ailing father in the book" (Galehouse 8). In an interview, he shares it:

> I was worried that Nobodaddy might be too frightening. There are no boys in America pretending to be Luke Skywalker because they all want to be Darth Vader – so we know children respond well to the scary, wicked characters. But what 12- and 13-year olds don't like is to be disturbed. Being scared can be delicious, but being disturbed can be upsetting. I worried that Nobodaddy might be on the wrong side of that line. But I gave Milan the first couple chapters of the book, and he said Nobodaddy was his favorite character. ... It gave me permission to just go for it. (Galehouse 8)

Thus, by genre, his works written for children are fictions which are full of fantasies and adventures. The works were written by the author for his own sons, and gifted to them when they were

13 years old. As a result, these are appropriate for children aged 13-18, and fall into the category of young-adult fiction. It is also noteworthy that the same atmosphere and repetition of some important characters in the latest one proves it the sequel of the earlier published book, *Haroun and the Sea of Stories*. Launching the book-series or sequels has been a frequent trend in the field of children's literature, that is also followed by Salman Rushdie.

Both books, *Haroun and the Sea of Stories* and *Luka and the Fire of Life*, revolve around a family headed by a storyteller, Rashid Khalifa. There are also some common themes which has been popular in the world of children's literature. Filial love is one of some common themes in both of the books. In the first one, Haroun with his father, Rashid, and mother, Soraya, lives in the country of Alifbay, a very sad city. Due to its saddest sadness, the city has forgotten its own name. Rashid Khalifa is famous for his "never-ending stream of tall, short and winding tales" that spreads cheerfulness throughout the sad city. His fans call him "the Ocean of Notions", and for his rivals, he is "the Shah of Blah". He is loved by the political leaders. In fact, the leaders have no credibility of their own among the people of the city. Therefore, they try to engage him in their political rallies in order to attract a large audience. His son, Haroun, is anxious to know where his father's stories come from. Soraya does not find herself happy with Rashid because he has no touch with hard ground realities.

One day Soraya runs off with Mr. Sengupta who is her neighbour. The extreme mental suffering of losing his wife and Haroun's questioning the usefulness of stories are too much for Rashid to bear. He opens his mouth, and finds that he has lost his talent of story-telling. Haroun decides to bring back to him his talent of story-telling. He starts his adventurous journey and reaches Kahani, Earth's second moon kept invisible by a P2C2E (Process Too Complicated To Explain). It is the Ocean of the Streams of Story, i.e., the source for all storytellers who subscribe through P2C2E. The process is controlled by the Walrus who is the Grand Comptroller of the city of Gup (a land of perpetual sunshine). Unfortunately, Khattam-Shud, the Prince of the dark and silent land of Chup, is polluting the Sea of Stories. Haroun leads the way in a brave attempt to save the Sea of Stories with Iff, the Water Genie; Butt the Hoopoe, a mad bus driver; and Mali, a Floating Gardener, and some other interesting companions. Finally, he is successful. We find that Soraya has come back to her farmer life, and Rashid has regained his talent of story-telling due to Haroun's adventurous journey.

Similarly, the second book, *Luka and the Fire of Life*, revolves around Rashid Khalifa's 12-year-old youngest son, Luka, who has accidentally disregarded a powerful supernatural being. In retaliation, the shape-shifter puts Luka's father into a deep and dangerous sleep. To save his father, Luka, following his elder brother's heroic adventures, begins another adventurous, and exploratory journey. He enters the Magic World from where he steals the Fire of Life with the help of Nobodaddy, Dog the bear, Bear the dog, the Insultana of Ott, etc. in order to revive his father. Finally, the story ends with the promise of happiness. In this way, it is right to say that the filial love is a common theme running in both of the texts.

The concept of 'home' has been a celebrated theme in the works of the transnational writers. In other words, a mental or emotional state of refuge or comfort through the construction of imaginative 'home' is frequently found in the works of such writers. Rushdie as a transnational writer also confesses that the subject of home is naturally found almost in all his works. Hence, he is aware that children as well as adults get pleasure from stories that narrate about going home. The author utilizes his talent in order to allure children in the present books composed for the children. He says:

> The subject of home is something which is, to some degree, in everything I've written. Where is it? Is it a place you make up

> yourself? All of us have an idea of home that changes – a home we're born into and, later, a home that we make. In this book [*Luka and the Fire of Life*], it's an attempt by Luka to preserve the home. (Galehouse 9)

Along with the themes of filial love and 'home', there are some other themes like the art of story-telling and its utility, allegorical theme (an account of Rushdie's life and contemporary society represented through the fables), etc. which are common in both texts. Story-telling and its utility can be taken as a dominating theme in the stories. In fact, both stories revolve around a story-teller, i.e., Rashid Khalifa. In *Haroun and the Sea of Stories*, the writer expresses his views on the talent of story-telling at many times. For instance, we note in the beginning of the novel that Haroun often takes his father's stories as lots of different tales juggled together. He thinks of his father as a juggler. In the mid of his adventurous journey, he realizes how the juggling is a kind of story-telling:

> It occurred to Haroun that Blabbermouth's juggling reminded him of the greatest performances given by his father, Rashid Khalifa, the Shah of Blah. 'I always thought storytelling was like juggling,' he finally found the voice to say. 'You keep a lot of different tales in the air, and juggle them up and down, and if you're good you don't drop any. So maybe juggling is a kind of storytelling, too.' (109)

In order to illustrate the passage, Rama Kundu writes:

> The supposedly trivializing comparison between storytelling and juggling gains significance in the theoretical context of the discourse which involves the idea of story-telling as a balancing act towards harmonizing the varied heritages that an author has got to handle. (148)

In *Luka and the Fire of Life*, there are also many examples which bear testimony to the importance of story-telling in the world. During his exploratory trip of the Magic World, Luka suggests to the badly-behaved gods that the original alternate reality is to give ancient stories a modern touch or look:

> Wake up and smell the coffee, old-timers! You're extinct! You're deceased! As gods and wonderful creatures, you have ceased to be! ... Listen to me: it's only through Stories that you can get out into the Real World and have some sort of power again. When your story is well told, people believe in you; not in the way they used to believe, not in a worshipping way, but in the way people believe in stories – happily, excitedly, wishing they wouldn't end. You want Immortality? It's only my father [a storyteller], and people like him, who can give it to you now. (181-182)

However, in the latest novel, it is interesting to read how the writer merges the earlier employed themes with the narrative in a differentiated manner, and presents his latest story with a fresh appearance. In the answer of the query, it is well explained metaphorically through the fable of the fish in the writer's own novel, *Haroun and the Sea of Stories*, that new stories are born from old and it is the new combinations that make them new:

> Iff replied that the Plentimaw Fishes were what he called 'hunger artists' – 'Because when they are hungry they swallow stories through every month, and in their innards miracle occur; a little bit of one story joins on to an idea from another, and hey presto, when they spew the stories out they are not old tales but new ones. Nothing comes from nothing, Thieflet; no story comes from nowhere; new stories are born from old – it is the new combinations that make them new. So you see, our artistic Plentimaw Fishes really create new stories in their digestive systems.... (86)

The concept of internationalism is not new in academic discourse about children's literature because of the successful attempts made by Paul Hazard (who gave the concept of a 'universal republic of childhood') like scholars. Positively, it is necessary for young readers to experience a range of different cultural understandings, otherwise their perception of their own remains narrow and impoverished. In this context, Latrobe writes:

> Today's children perceive the world from the perspective of photographs taken in outer space. They understand the concepts of lands and waters without national boundaries—boundaries that were never capable of limiting the flow of air or ocean currents or ideas. It is therefore especially appropriate that the highest prizes for children's literature should be international, representing the universality and diversity of children and their literature and offering young readers books and ideas that flow as freely as ocean currents. (Latrobe 101)

Rushdie also believes in the concept of internationalism. He takes recourse to some specific ways through which he merges this concept with the narratives. For example, in both of the stories, he deliberately interconnects literary and cultural heritages from across the globe with each other in order to prosper the idea of internationalism in the children's literature. In *Luka and the Fire of Life*, he presents a mythological adventure. During his adventurous trip, Luka faces ancient gods of Greece, Rome, South America, Scandinavia, Japan, Egypt, India, and other cultures as both friends and foes. His language also works as an effective tool for this purpose. Words are used from various languages which not only represent the different cultures, but also allure the international readership. It is also noteworthy that due to the popularity of the books among the children, and atmosphere of the stories which suit modern technology, the writer has received many suggestions from the videogame companies for converting the stories into videogames (Galehouse 9).

To conclude, Rushdie creates his literature in a broad framework. Therefore, there may be other angles from which the books may be read or examined. But, without a doubt, it may be said that with the publication of the present books, the writer has entered into the arena of international children's literature with the purpose of securing 'the fire of life'.

Works Cited

Anderson, Nancy A. *Elementary Children's Literature*. Boston: Pearson Education, 2006.

Galehouse, Maggie. "A Father's Gift Becomes a Magical Story." *Houston Chronicle* 28 Nov. 2010: 8-9. Print.

Hazard, Paul. *Books, Children and Men*. Trans. M. Mitchell. Boston: The Horn Book, 1944. Print.

Hunt, Peter, ed. *International Companion: Encyclopedia of Children's Literature*. New York: Routledge, 2004. Print.

Kundu, Rama. "Rushdie's Story of 'The Sea of Stories': Text as an Echoing Space." *Brno Studies in English,* A Journal of the Dept of English and American Studies, Masaryk Uni, Czech Republic, 32, 2006: 143-159. Print.

Latrobe, K. "Children's Literature: International Perspectives." *World Literature Today Magazine* 75, 2001: 98-101. Print.

Rushdie, Salman. *Haroun and the Sea of Stories*. New Delhi: Penguin Books in association with Granta Books, 1990. Print.

______. *Luka and the Fire of Life*. London: Jonathan Cape, 2010. Print.

23

Interrogating the Metanarratives on Indian Independence with Reference to Partition Narratives

— Raj Sree

Caught in the liminality of abandonment, of belonging nowhere, certain things appear trivial, and their loss remains unrecorded, forgotten. In comparison to the large forces of history and society, personal effects become ludicrous, disposable and preposterous. Situating *Lajwanti* by Rajendra Singh Bedi and Jamila Hashmi's short story *Exile* within the tradition of partition fiction, this article interrogates the grand narratives which create a grand history excluding localized, real events. The article further foregrounds the incoherence of Partition narratives which very well express and interpret the cataclysmic event. Placing these two works in the context of postmodernism and its critique of metanarratives, this article brings into light, the hidden memories and stifled silence of the survivours.

While India celebrates Independence every year and Independence history exists publicly, the particularities of Partition, the individual and cultural memories of it, are barely spoken or written about. It continues to live in the private, in silence. The ambivalence towards 1947 is visible in India among Indian English writers in the fact that less than 20 works of fiction have been written about this traumatic upheaval that affected the lives of most people in the two countries.

In August 1947, at the moments of its independence, India was also partitioned into two countries, Pakistan for Muslims and India as a secular state (but mostly for the Hindus). This partition resulted in the largest transaction of humans across state borders: 12 million refugees crossed the borders in a space of a few months, leaving behind their ancestral homes, their lands, most of their material possessions, and even their family members who had opted to stay. Of these, 10 million crossed the Punjab and two million crossed in Bengal. The death toll through slaughter, contagious diseases, and malnutrition is estimated at two million. Of these, 75,000 women were abducted and raped on both sides of the border. The intensely happy and victorious moment of independence has a deep trauma at its underside: India is a nation unachieved. Narratives giving voice to these aspects of Indian history is essentially postmodern in content and style.

The aesthetic of the postmodern text is based upon the gap between presentation and reality. Writers on Partition fiction are aware that in writing there exists a gap between thinking and writing that the story the writer is about to tell us somehow escapes language:

> Never before have I been so aware of the rift between thinking and writing. For the past few days, in fact, I have begun to feel that the story I am trying to tell is somehow incompatible with language, that the degree to which it resists language is an exact measure of how closely I have come to saying something important and then when the moment arrives for me to say one truly important thing, I will not be able to say it. (*The Invention of Solitude*, 32)

This aesthetic of the sublime, 'the unrepresentable', is based upon Kant's idea of the difference between our faculty to present something and conceive of it. In Partition narratives the sublime is based upon the reality which strikes the author as stranger than we think, and he wishes to incorporate these instances of inconceivable events into his text. Thus the 'unrepresentable' portrayed in these texts evades a clear-cut theoretical framework.

The men of letters and others took some time in registering the event of Partition and its aftermath. The first well-known novel on the Partition, Narayan Sanyal's *Balmik* (part of a trilogy) was published only in 1955; but thereafter, it was followed by a wave of novels in the 1960's and 70's by writers like Jyotirmoyee Devi (*Epar Ganga Opar Ganga*, 1967), Prafulla Ray (*Keya Patar Nouko*, 1970), Sunil Ganguly (*Arjun*, 1971), Atin Bandopadhyay (*Nilkontho Pakhir Khoje*, 1971) and Gour Kishore Ghosh (who wrote a trilogy over two decades - *Jal Pare Pata Nare*, 1978; *Prem Nei*, 1981; and *Pratibeshi*, 1995). All of these were well expressive of the trauma of the victims of partition. For instance, Jyotirmoyee Devi's novel (1947) is a searing commentary on Partition itself, and on history's erasure of women from its annals. It is also a powerful admonition of patriarchy's hypocritical obsession with women's sexual purity. Sutara's story is "the Story of woman" or "the Stree Parva" (The Woman Chapter) that the author believes has never been written, because all history is recorded by men.

While Partition has been a recurrent motif in Indian-English fiction right from the 1950s it is primarily Amitav Ghosh, who, in three of his six novels (*The Shadow Lines*, 1988; *The Circle of Reason*, 1986; and *The Hungry Tide*, 2004) has dealt, in varying degrees, with the aftermath of Partition on the Bengal border. However, partition imbued the collective conscious of Indians with a lot of images and metaphors related to mass slaughter and sexual violence and abandonment. There are certain images from the past which have always haunted the national consciousness. Partition was a very violent experience for everybody in the Punjab and the nearby states. Chance killings, fires, dead bodies were frequent sights. There were periods of four and five days at a stretch during which not a single train reached Lahore or Amritsar without bloated, butchered corpses, stinking and silent apart from the buzzing of flies. As these 'moving coffins' rolled into railway stations, blood would seep out from under the doors of the silent compartments, dripping like water flowing out of a refrigerator on a hot day. The first Partition novel in English, Khushwant Singh's masterly *Train to Pakistan* uses one of these trains of death, as they became known, as its grisly central image.

As we celebrate the Independence days of Pakistan and India in August, we seldom think of the bitter memories in the eyes of those who saw the events unfolding at the time of the first Independence-day. Those memories are often stifled by the metanarratives that followed the Independence. *Lajwanti* by Rajendra Singh Bedi and Jamila Hashmi's short story *Exile* are among the few counter narratives which give voice to the untold memories of Partition.

Many literary narratives bring out this anguish. When the entire family decided to migrate, no amount of force or persuasion could make the Amma of Ismat Chughtai's story *Jadein* ("Roots") leave her haveli. But then after everyone had left, she swayed in distress thinking of her near ones who were in exile and perhaps in a state of anguish. The old lady, "Bebe", of Joginder Paul Urdu story *Dariyaon Pyas* ("Thirst of Rivers") carried her ancestral haveli in her mind across the borders. She clutched the haveli in the grip of her hands, as it were, by carrying the keys of the haveli on her person all the time, close to her heart. Krishna Sobti's Shahni of the Hindi story *Sikka Badal Gaya* too resisted the uprootment from her haveli. The writer poignantly captures the torment of the elderly woman who is pushed into migration when her very identity is founded on home and kinship within that house. To her, discarding this home meant discarding her self. *Lajwanti* and *Exile* can be placed along this tradition of writing.

Rajinder Singh Bedi (1915–1984) was an eminent progressive Urdu writer, playwright and a Hindi film director, screenwriter and noted dialogue writer. He is considered as one of the greatest twentieth century progressive writers of Urdu fiction, and secondmost prominent Urdu fiction writer, after Saadat Hasan Manto, and like Manto he is most known for his haunting Partition of India tales.

Rajendra Singh Bedi in *Lajwanti* focuses not just on the horror of partition but the aftermath, what it did to the civilians and especially women who were raped and abandoned by both the parties. More than 75,000 women were abducted and raped during Partition. Bapsi Sidhwa's novel *Ice Candy Man* details the victimization and suffering of women in that chaotic time. Rajendra Singh Bedi and Jamila Hashmi give an account of what partition did to women with psychological depth and intensity. Their works rail against the victim hood and loss that characterize the narratives of localized events, and powerless beings, emphasizing that from small things grow unbridled significance and large, humanistic meaning and even a history which goes often unrecorded.

Lajwanti by Rajendra Singh Bedi is a heart-wrenching portrayal of the gender aspect of the partition. It touches individual readers deeply; many find it profound beyond its poetics. Its literary power stems from a particular narrative deployment of the abject and the traumatic. Literature thus connects trauma and the abject to create testimony, intertextual acts of (religious) witnessing performed by authors and addressed to a laity of readers. The narrative of *Lajwanti* and *Exile* exhibits the general characteristics of trauma. Cathy Caruth Cathy Caruth is Winship Distinguished Research Professor of Comparative Literature and English and chair of the Department of Comparative Literature at Emory University. She receives her Ph.D., notes the common "delay or incompletion in knowing" that is often present in trauma (5). These characteristics of trauma are found in the content of *Lajwanti* and *Exile* but gain further force and significance by being repeated in its narrative structure. Events, especially the most traumatic ones, are referred to over and over again. Specific details and phrases are repeated; related dreams are recounted; scenes are iterated and reiterated, fragmentally, in various stages of completion, but always "absolutely true to the event" (Caruth 5). The traumatic structure of the narrative forces readers to experience the trauma of the

Partition as if we are already subject to it, as though meaning had slunk slunk out of things and left them fragmented, disconnected. The trauma of Partition often involves psychological and social aspects because it is bound up with the betrayal and the treachery of the nation, the so-called protector of the citizens. "There were fires, killings, mass hysteria. Suddenly, humanity was lost and people were not the same any more," says Nusrat Soofi, who was only 15 when she was compelled to leave the warmth of her home in Kolkata to Chittagong, then East Pakistan

After two years of Partition when the governments of India and Pakistan decided to heal some wounds by tracing abducted women on both sides and returning them to their homes they did not realize that they could be creating another problem: many of these women may had been married with children and may had resigned to their fate when they were once again uprooted and asked to re-live the trauma of Partition. The other problem was whether their families back home would accept them now that they had lost their 'chastity'. A wife-beater Sunderlal in *Lajwanti* becomes a social activist and gets elected as secretary of the newly formed "Rehabilitation of Women" committee. He is elected to this post because his own wife Lajwanti has been abducted during those dark days of Partition. Every morning he would swear to himself, "... If I ever find her again if I ever again do, I shall honor her and give her a place in my heart..."(16). But on the other hand in *Exile*, the woman who comes back to her kin is rejected bruatally.

Narian Bawa in the story represents those who oppose the rehabilitation of women who offers the rusty example of Ram rejecting Sita from his "ideal kingdom". So entrenched is the notion of protection of "honour" of their women in each of the communities, that women were forced to either commit suicide to pre-empt the humiliation of getting sexually assaulted and dishonoured, or they were actually murdered. Ashish Nandy, Veena Das, Mushir-ul-Hasan and others recount the bizarre sexual violence suffered by women—their bodies mutilated and disfigured, their breasts and genitalia tattooed and brandished "with triumphal slogans", their wombs knifed open, foetuses killed, rampant raping —all this male savagery using the woman's body as an easy object to dishonour the other community. Ironically to save guard their self-respect, the members of the target community too, preferred to kill their women. This savagery is often shadowed by the overpowering presence of the grand narratives celebrating the feats of freedom fighters.

When Lajo returns back Sunderlal becomes gripped by an unknown fear at once. Lajo stands before him trembling with hope and despair. Sunderlal finds Lajo unlike what he imagines. She looks much healthier and fair and he like, other husbands, thinks "...if she had been comfortable and happy there why did she agree to return?"(26).

Sunderlal fails to identify the signs of pain and anguish on the face of Lajo. He starts calling his wife "Devi", although what she really desires is a little genuine love as opposed to the worship that he offers. He raises her to such a pedestal that it becomes difficult for her to come to equal terms with life. She is never the same Lajo again. She wants to share so much with Sunderlal but he is not ready to listen. She desperately struggles to tell her side of story to him so that she can feel clean again. But he always shrunks from her and she longes for an ear who can listen to her story. Her sorrows remain locked up in her breast. The story which commences with lots of promise ends again on a sad note where a man fails to understand the point of view of woman sufferings. As a result the long silence between Sunderlal and Lajo cannot be broken.

The emotionally insulated Lajo is a victim of abduction but she is recovered by her husband who is himself one of the leaders of the group mobilized to recover Partition women-victims and rehabilitate them in their homes. There is an incipient feminist consciousness working within this story. The story focuses on

Lajo's consciousness as she suffers quietly to see how she has been transformed and venerated as a Devi, a goddess, by her husband after she is recovered and they come together after 1947. She is no longer Lajo to him. She becomes Lajwanti, ironically, the one who will withdraw like the "touch-me-not" with any touch.

The notion of honour and purity of woman is so deeply internalized that even the spokesman for the rehabilitation of women, Babu Sunderlal of Bedi's story cannot come to accept "the defiled Lajo" back into their normal relationship. In a way, venerating her as a goddess becomes a strategy to distance himself from her. The wife in Lajo has to die an unnatural death. Life has to be redefined. Bedi records the popular sentiment in the story "There were some amongst these abducted women, whose husbands, parents, brothers and sisters refused to recognize them. Why didn't they die? Why didn't the take poison to preserve their virtue and honour? Why didn't they jump into a well? Cowards, clinging to life so tenaciously! (16) The writer exposes the hypocrisy as well as the callousness of the world of men who denied their women a normal life, either by brutalizing them or deifying them.

But on the other hand, in Jamila Hashmi's short story *Exile* the abducted woman is not welcomed back into the community. Sadia's story in *Aur Kitne Tukde* which is directed by Kirti Jain is based on Jamila Hashmi's story *The Exile.* The narrator of the story, a maid, is an orphan because of Partition. She is abducted. Her abductor after killing her parents being her to his house. Pushing her into the courtyard he proclaims, " 'Look, Ma, I have brought you a Bahu. She is tall and good looking of the girls who fell into our hands tonight. She was the prettiest. She will be you slave. There were no songs and dance, no celebration to welcome her.' No one greeted her at the door, no mehndi, no sindhoor yet she was a bride. Day in and out she desperately longs to see her relatives and friends whom she left behind. She sat outside the door of the house everyday with her bundle of hopes and starred longingly down the lane."

This was the irony of Partition days. The narrator of *Exile* wants to be with her family and friends whom she has left behind, and Lajwanti, though returned, is still facing an identity crisis among her own near and dear ones and in her own country. "How a world which was so familiar had suddenly become a world of strangers. *Exile* is no doubt one of the most accomplished stories on Partition dealing with the trauma and psychological aspect of fairer sex. The narrator knows very well that no one will accept a woman who has been despoiled, yet she longs for her brother every day, her eyes turned to stone. The distance between her and her relatives have widened with the passage of time which is now difficult to fill. When the soldiers from the other country come looking for abducted women she surprises the readers; she realizes that the city of dreams, which she had built, has crumbled into dust and vanished. Her life has taken roots in Sangraon and the roots have spread wide and deep. We accept her to reach out for freedom but she can't afford to forget the fact that she has become a mother. She is no longer her old self. She realizes that the only option left for her is to hide from the soldiers in the land of her captors, rather then going into exile for a second time. Unlike Lajo, this 'Sita' accepts Ravana's house.The permanently banished Sita of Jamila Hashmi's story has to reformulate herself after she has been wrenched from her own kinship support.

There were a large number of women who were not "recovered", women who apparently reconciled to the new circumstance, but they carried within themselves the gnawing sense of the irreparable loss of a perfect past. To get a glimpse of the inner self of such a woman's mind, Jamila Hashmi's oft quoted story *Exile* comes to one's mind. The protagonist of the story is doomed by memory and the inability to forget. The desirable past is unrecoverable. The inner monologue is a recalling of that past which counterpoises itself with the present. It is in the present that she has children from her "abductor" who has actually married her. She reacts inwardly to his mother who addresses her as "bahu" and creates a semblance of order. But this

Sita, unlike the mythical Sita, as the story tells us, has had to accept "Ravana's home". Suspended between her past and the present, she is in fact banished from her own selfhood. This is yet another kind of death seeking regeneration, a replanting. The story ends thus: "Life too flows on, carrying with it, as it always does, the smell of death."

Jamila Hashmi's protagonist may have the surface-appearance of an inert object, but the writer catches the throb of her consciousness in the sad monologue that runs all through the story. Her tottering personal identity comes together through her recalling. What is enshrined in her memory is gradually unfolded – as if to recall, readjust and reorder herself in the new context of her children, a new reality and a fresh area for rooting.

The trace of colonialism in India's postcolonial situation complicates the possibilities of a clear resolution. In *The Nation and Its Fragments*, Partha Chatterjee theorizes that "evolving nationalism in India has required Indians to develop a politics that is split between inner and outer, material and spiritual " (6-10). In his view, it was acceptable to emergent nationalists to accept material aspects of the colonizing Western culture, provided that Indians held firmly to their own traditions in the inner, spiritual realm. But Partition narratives unlike the Indian Writing in English cannot be located with in this tradition.

Partition narratives strengthens the connection of literature with the sacred, a connection in which literature becomes a kind of metadiscourse that subsumes confession and testimony, acts which, in the presence of an audience, are productive of power. The narrative style of *Lajwanti* by Rajendra Singh Bedi and Jamila Hashmi's short story *Exile* is that of a traumatic memory. It is an authorial testimony as to the effects of nation, state, sexuality, and gender on the human and social body.

Lajwanti by Rajendra Singh Bedi and Jamila Hashmi's short story *Exile* may be read as works of its time in the sense that Felman claims that we are now in "the age of testimony" (5). As sacred literature, fictional testimony, these works draws on the power of the abject to witness the traumas of contemporary history as the authors interpret them. Traumatic memory patterns inspire not only the content but also the narrative structure. *Lajwanti* and *Exile* double the descriptions of the abject and traumatic responses to it, and concentrate on literary power, which accounts for its dramatic effect on individual readers and its widespread success. Albeit in another context, Felman questions whether testimony is "a simple medium of historical transmission, or [...] in obscure ways, the unsuspected medium of a healing" (9). These works seems to share the "urgency to communicate, a problem of repression, poverty, subalternity, struggle for survival" with testimonial writing (Beverley 26), (12) which implies a desire for social healing. It remains to be seen whether its power will remain beyond our era of testimony or whether its testimony will further the healing of the body politic that it addresses. Its reception by, and interaction with, the histories of Indian Independence and millions of individual readers will determine its effect in that regard.

These works allow us to witness trauma's effects through our experience of the narrative structure. This may give readers some access to the trauma's effect as well since, as Caruth insists, "the pathology consists [...] solely in the structure of its experience or reception" (4). Felman discusses a "relation between trauma and pedagogy" (1), which permits testimonial literature to create educational opportunities by inducing "crises" in readers (53). This may, partially, account for the feeling that reading such literature can "change our lives". This testimonial nature of Partition narratives induces such a crisis in the reading of the text. A conscious effort to discern women as victims of the Partition 1947 raises the curtain to the uncontrolled release of a bizarre male violence on the one hand and a nerve-wrecking dismembering of the female body and self on the other.

Typical of postmodernist fiction, Partition narratives too seems to reflect the fact that the writer has become tired of trying to explain a disjointed and Godless universe. It has become a necessary means of organizing and interpreting the world as a consequence of the ideological failure of the 'sacred master plot' or the metanarrative in the terminology of post-modernists.

As a postmodern text, both these narratives avoid the end, closure. This makes it clear that like a postmodern theorist, the writers of *Lajwanti* and *Exile* reject the notion that the text's narrative is dominated by knowledge of end: the end which can finally determine the meaning, closing sentence as signifying totality:

> The closer you come to the end, the more there is to say. The end is only imaginary, a destination you invent to keep yourself going, but a point comes when you realise you will never get there. You might have to stop, but that is only because you have ran out of time. You stop but that does not mean you have come to the end. (*In the Country of Last Things* 183).

Works Cited

Bedi, Rajinder Singh. "Lajwanti" Tr. Muhammed Umar Memon. *An Epic Unwritten: The Penguin Book of Partition Stories from Urudu.* New Delhi: Penguin, 1998. 14-29

Beverley, John. "The Margin at the Center: On Testimonies". *The Real Thing: Testimonial Discourse and Latin America.* Ed. Georg M. Gugelberger. Durham: Duke UP, 199623-41.

Caruth, Cathy. "Introduction". *Trauma: Explorations in Memory.* Ed. Cathy Caruth. Baltimore: Johns Hopkins UP, 1995. 3-12.

Chatterjee, Partha. *The Nation and its Fragments: Colonial and Postcolonial Histories.* New Jersey: Princeton UP, 1993.

Felman, Shoshana and Dori Laub, M. D. *Testimony: Crises of Witnessing in Literature, Psychoanalysis, and History.* New York, state, United States.

24

Theorizing the Saga of Lost Dreams from the Perspective of Postmodernism

— Nancy S. Rethinam

Arundhati Roy's first novel *The God of Small Things* (1997) became an international bestseller and won the prestigious Booker Prize. It created a new space for Indian literature and even gave way to much controversy and divided critical opinion. Arundhati Roy portrayed the life in a modern society in which hegemonic power is reproduced by a mix of force and ideological influence from an emergent postmodern social formation.

This article attempts to place *The God of Small Things* in perspective within the larger framework of postmodernism and Indian Literature in English. *The God of Small Things* can be placed along the tradition of Mulk Raj Anand, Salman Rushdie, Anita Desai, etc. A brief account on Indian literature in English helps us to understand the text better as a nothing can be understood in isolation. Simultaneous with Narayan's pastoral idylls, Mulk Raj Anand gained recognition for his writing set in rural India; but his stories were harsher, and engaged, sometimes brutally, with divisions of caste, class and religion.

Among the later writers, the most notable is Salman Rushdie, born in India, now living in the United Kingdom. Rushdie with his famous work *Midnight's Children* (Booker Prize 1981, Booker of Bookers 1992, and Best of the Bookers 2008) ushered in a new trend of writing. He used a hybrid language –

English generously peppered with Indian terms – to convey a theme that could be seen as representing the vast canvas of India. He is usually categorised under the magic realism mode of writing most famously associated with Gabriel Garcia Marquez and other postcolonial writers.

Vikram Seth, author of *A Suitable Boy* (1994), is a writer who uses a purer English and more realistic themes. Being a self-confessed fan of Jane Austen, his attention is on the story, its details and its twists and turns. Shashi Tharoor, in his *The Great Indian Novel* (1989), follows a story-telling (though in a satirical) mode as in the *Mahabharata* drawing his ideas by going back and forth in time. His work as UN official living outside India has given him a vantage point that helps construct an objective Indianness. Other authors include Manoj Das, Vikram Chandra, Anita Desai, Kiran Desai, Arundhati Roy, Gita Mehta, Chitra Banerjee Divakaruni, Upamanyu Chatterjee, Raj Kamal Jha, Jhumpa Lahiri, Bharti Kirchner, Khushwant Singh, Vijay Singh, Tarun Tejpal, Amit Chaudhuri, Amitav Ghosh, Vikas Swarup, Rohinton Mistry, Suketu Mehta, Kiran Nagarkar, Dr Birbal Jha, Bharati Mukherjee, Mysore N. Prakash, Lakshmi Raj Sharma and C.R. Krishnan.

Chaudhuri feels that after Rushdie, Indian literature in English started employing magical realism, bagginess, non-linear narrative and hybrid language to sustain themes seen as microcosms of India and supposedly reflecting Indian conditions. He contrasts this with the works of earlier writers such as Narayan where the use of English is pure, but the deciphering of meaning needs cultural familiarity. He also feels that Indianness is a theme constructed only in IWE (Indian Writing in English) and does not articulate itself in the vernacular literatures. He further adds "the post-colonial novel, becomes a trope for an ideal hybridity by which the West celebrates not so much Indianness, whatever that infinitely complex thing is, but its own historical quest, its reinterpretation of itself". The renowned writer V. S. Naipaul, a third generation Indian from Trinidad and Tobago and a Nobel Prize laureate, is a person who belongs to the world and usually not classified under Indian literature in English. He evokes ideas of homeland, rootlessness and his own personal feelings towards India in many of his books. Jhumpa Lahiri, a Pulitzer Prize winner from the US, is a writer uncomfortable under the label of IWE. Recent writers in India such as Arundhati Roy and David Davidar show a direction towards contextuality and rootedness in their works. Arundhati Roy, a trained architect and the 1997 Booker Prize winner for her *The God of Small Things*, calls herself a "home grown" writer. Her award winning book is set in the immensely physical landscape of Kerala.

The God of Small Things is about a family living in India after the Declaration of Independence. The story isn't told in chronological order but it is revealed bit by bit to the reader. Rahel and Esthappen (Estha) are seven-year-old fraternal twins. They are living in Ayemenem with their mother Ammu and her brother Chacko, their grandmother Mammachi and their great-aunt Baby Kochamma. Their father Baba lives in Calcutta. Ammu left him when the twins were two years old.

The family is expecting the arrival of Margaret and Sophie Mol, Chacko's ex-wife and daughter, who are living in England. Since Margaret's second husband Joe had died in a car accident, Chacko invited them to spend Christmas in India in order to get over the loss. When they have arrived, Sophie Mol is taking centrestage. So Rahel and Estha stroll around on the river bank and find an old boat. With Velutha's help they repair it and frequently cross the river to visit an abandoned house on the other side. Velutha is an untouchable, whom Ammu and Chacko have known since their childhood. Their family have given him the opportunity to visit a school and employed him as a carpenter and mechanic in the family's pickle factory.

During the guests' stay Ammu is more and more attracted by Velutha. One night they meet at the river where they sleep with each other. As it is not possible for an untouchable to have a relationship or even an affair with somebody from a superior caste, they have to keep their meetings secret. But one night Velutha's father observes them and, feeling humiliated by his son's overbearing behaviour, reports everything to Mammachi and Baby Kochamma. As a consequence they lock up Ammu in her room. There Rahel and Estha find her and, through the locked door, ask her why she's being locked up. As she is angry and desperate, she blames the two children that without them she would be free and they should go away. Hurt and confused they decide two run away and stay at the abandoned house. But Sophie discovers the twins' plan and demands to be taken along. While the three are crossing the river, which has risen from heavy rainfall, their boat capsizes. Rahel and Estha are able to reach the other shore but Sophie cannot swim and is carried away by the current. After a long search for Sophie, the twins go to the abandoned house and fall asleep on its veranda. Neither do they see Velutha, who is sleeping on the veranda nor does he notice the twins' arrival. Earlier that night, Velutha had visited the house of Ammu's family, not knowing that their affair had been discovered. When he arrived Mammachi insulted him and chased him off.

In the morning the children's absence is detected. Then they receive the message that Sophie Mol has been found dead by the river. Baby Kochamma goes to the police and wrongly accuses Velutha of attempting to rape Ammu and kidnapping the children. When the police find Velutha sleeping on the veranda of the abandoned house, they beat him up so heavily that he almost dies. The twins wake up and observe the whole procedure. At the police station they are forced by Baby Kochamma to confirm the wrong statement which she has made. In the following night Velutha dies in prison.

After Sophie Mol's funeral Ammu and the twins have to leave the family's house because Chacko, manipulated by Baby Kochamma, accuses them of being responsible for Sophie Mol's death. Estha is sent to his father in Calcutta where he attends school and later college. Ammu is forced to leave Rahel in Ayemenem in order to look for employment. But Ammu is not able to earn enough for a living and so she dies of bad health a few years later alone in a hotel room.

Rahel returns to Ayemenem at the age of 31. She hasn't seen Estha since they were separated after Sophie Mol's funeral. She married an American and moved with him to Boston. After their divorce she has been working to make a living. Now Rahel returns to Ayemenem because she wants to see Estha, who has already returned to their family's house. During his stay in Calcutta he someday stopped speaking. After spending a whole day together in Ayemenem, Rahel and Estha, sister and brother, are sleeping with each other.

The fact that Estha has stopped speaking and that Rahel and Estha sleep with each other are only two aspects in which one can see how deeply hurt they still are by the events with Velutha and Sophie Mol that happened long ago.

In the context of postmodernity the definition of identity has been strongly influenced by globalization, an economic, social and cultural process that made originally steady cultural borders permeable to outer influences. In today's world the concept of identity has consequently been adjusting itself to a new reality that constantly evolves and mutates as a result of continuous structural and institutional changes. Post modernism negates fixed identities and in *The God of Small Things*, Arundhati Roy negates fixed identities. For instance Estha and Rahel are presented from different vantage points and the reader finds it difficult to confer a fixed identity to them. Even Ammu is a very complicated character with multiple identities.

Contradicting the solipsistic conceptions of Enlightment theories, a subject's identity in the post modern context is no longer unified and stable, self-centred and parted from social context. In opposition, it is undefined and decentralized. It is the result of new life forms that inhibit individuals to have a fixed, essential and permanent identity. Roy tries to decentralize patriarchal norms of marriage, love and brother- sister relationships in controversial terms. To challenge and deconstruct the existing societal norms, she brings in Marxist ideology and agenda.

Placed in the face of contemporary social diversity and different cultural systems, each character integrate multiple identity constellations, some even contradictory, which are continuously formed and transformed. In a social context of continuous exchanges like presented in *The God of Small Things*, characters inevitably experience a great variety of developments and metamorphosis or even feel different identifications over the course of their lives. And this is a circumstance that unquestionably corroborates the post modern thought that identity is indeed a very complex topic, which should be, first and foremost, perceived as a plural and dynamic idea.

Postmodernism recognizes that it is impossible to have a coherent centre. Centre is constantly under erasure. Though Roy tries to foreground socially marginalized characters and tabooed subjects like incest, she do not allow them to occupy the centre as centering and decentring are continually postponed. She questions and challenges the dominant ideologies and attitudes prevalent in South India.

Like a post modernist theorist, Roy foregrounds smaller, localized things and events, forsaking grand and globalised narratives of caste and gender. "Little events, ordinary things, smashed and reconstituted. Imbued with new meaning. Suddenly they become the bleached bones of a story" (32). "The air was full of Thoughts and Things to Say. But at times like these only the Small Things are ever said. The Big Things lurk unsaid....."

> ...In some places, like the country that Rahel came from, various kinds of despair competed for primacy. And that *personal despair*

> could never be desperate enough. That something happened when personal turmoil dropped by at the wayside shrine of the vast, violent, circling, driving, ridiculous, insane, unfeasible, public turmoil of a nation. That Big God howled like a hot wind, and demanded obeisance. Then Small God (cosy and contained, private and limited) came away cauterized, laughing numbly at his own temerity. Inured by the confirmation of his own inconsequence, he became resilient and truly indifferent. Nothing mattered much. Nothing much mattered. And the less it mattered, the less it mattered. It was never important enough. Because Worse Things had happened. In the country that she came from, poised forever between the terror of war and the horror of peace, Worse Things kept happening."
>
> ...Instinctively they stuck to the Small Things. The Big Things ever lurked inside. They knew that there was nowhere for them to go. They had nothing. No future. So they stuck to the small things...

They had to put their faith in fragility. Stick to Smallness. Each time they parted, they extracted only one small promise from each other.

> 'Tomorrow?'
> 'Tomorrow.'

That is perhaps the technique of the novel, in a nutshell. It proceeds from small material things, and inchoate notions, that bloom or explode into large uncontrollable passions, or transcendental ideas on humanity and society. A small baby, smelling of milk and urine, as Sophie Mol does, holds such power over Chacko's heart that upon her life and death pivots the sanity and meaning of a man's life, as well as the lives of his dependents, Rahel, Estha and Ammu. And this in turn is a technique which gives the novel a post modern approach to reality.

Roy's method of storytelling echoes that of the kathakali dance, an art that narrates the Great stories, or ancient myths, of Keralese folk history. They demonstrate the seemingly paradoxical concern with both attention to detail and the transcendental humanism that mounts from those same, significant details. Perhaps, they subscribe to the belief that, as Ludwig Mies van der Rohe put it, "God is in the details." The kathakali dance and its mythic storytelling switches smoothly between the minuteness of detail to humanist tragedy of the highest order:

So when [the kathakali dancer] tells a story, he handles it as he would a child of his own...

> He can fly you across whole world in mintues, he can stop for hours to examine a wilting leaf. Or play with a sleeping monkey's tail. He can turn effortlessly from the carnage of war into the felicity of a woman woshing her hair in a mountain stream. From the sensuousness of a woman with a baby at her breast into the seductive mischief of Krishna's smile. He can reveal the nuggest of sorrow that happiness contains. The hidden fish of shame in a sea of glory. He talls stories of the gods, but his yarn is spun from the ungodly, human heart.

Roy's novel functions on the same technique, swooping into the intricacy of intimate situations, and drawing back to paint an enlarged landscape of humanity and the world that it constructs for itself. There is a God in small things, the novel insists, embodied in the marginal Black Man of Velutha, in the hidden narratives of women, children and untouchables.

Moreover the grotesque permeates the story of *The God of Small Things* from the very beginning, when Rahel imagines the ceiling-painter dying on the floor, "blood spilling from his skull like a secret." We learn later that this is Velutha, dying alone and wrongfully accused in the police station. The grotesque takes precedence throughout the story precisely because it is not allowed to do so by the characters. That is, it is the manifestation of the ugly secrets that the family refuses to acknowledge, and since they are forbidden from being acknowledged openly, they are forced to seep into the world of "Small Things" through language, dreams, and daydreams.

Two repeating grotesque images are of Velutha's broken body and Sophie Mol's drowned corpse. They are the proverbial skeletons in the family's closet, willed to be nonexistent but unable to be forgotten. Therefore they become macabre images that haunt the characters, especially Rahel and Estha. Also, sex and violence are connected in a grotesque way in the novel. The first instance of this combination is in Estha's molestation; his first sexual experience is a terrifying violation. And when it is safe on the riverbank, Ammu's and Velutha's affair is crystallized and beautiful, but once it is discovered, it quickly becomes associated with violent death. Finally, when Estha and Rahel make love, their incest is grotesque. Roy portrays the act of lovemaking as beautiful, but it is made bizarre by the fact that Rahel and Estha are siblings—twins, no less—and that they are doing so out of "hideous grief." It is as though in order to overcome all their grotesque secrets, Rahel and Estha must perform a grotesque act. The grotesque, that Roy presents, borders on Julia Kresteva's abject, which is essentially a post modern and post structuralist concept.

Tirhankar Chanda argues that "the most significant intertext [of *The God of Small Things*] is that of the archetypal return of the exiled subject to his native land" (43). Certainly Chacko, Ammu, Velutha, Estha, and Rahel all bear the marks of their absences. Even Pappachi came to Ayemenem late in life after trips abroad and a working life spent in Delhi. This return of the native suggests the importance of centre and also the metaphysics of presence. What is present gains importance only by virtue of what is not present (absent) in the novel.

Roy risks the ire of nationalists by criticizing some traditional aspects of Indian society directly, although *The God of Small Things* also gestures to the plethora of complicated and traumatic historical strands that entwine to produce the contemporary situation. Her language is typically Rushdean and her stylistic tricks like capitalizing significant words and running together other words are also essentially postmodern. As this story focuses on two children and their impressions of the world, Roy uses various techniques to represent the children's viewpoint and their innocence. One technique that Roy employs is the capitalization of certain words and phrases to give them certain significance. Similarly, the children will restate things that the adults say in a new phonetic way, disjoining and recombining words. This echoes the children's way of looking at the world differently from the grown-ups that surround them. They place significance on words and ideas differently from the adults, thereby creating a new way of viewing the world around them. They pick up on certain feelings and ideas that the adults around them either fail or refuse to recognize, and give new significance to things that the adults may or may not ignore for their.

The reality into which she invites the reader is one of forsaken citizens, the prevailing status of untouchable, and the greed of political figures. Many critics argue Roy ministers to Western ideals because her novel is, as they claim, anti-communist. Others allege *The God of Small Things* is simply a story about love, caste, and sexuality in India. But it is above these things. It is a counter discourse on the metanarratives of caste, gender, patriarchy and sexuality.

Works Cited

Ahmad, Aijaz. "Reading Arundhati Roy Politically." *Frontline*. Aug. 8, 1997: 103-8.

Chanda, Tirhankar. "Sexual/Textual Strategies in *The God of Small Things*." *Common wealth Essays and Studies* 20.1(1997): 38-44.

Roy, Arundhati. *The God of Small Things*. Toronto: Random, 1997.

25

Culture of Consumerism as Reflected in Chetan Bhagat's *One Night @ Call Center*

—Yatri D. Dave

In this modern era, literature is also becoming modern. Being very popular writer Bhagat himself provided very typical modern test to readers. In his famous *Fiction Night @ Call Center*, he mainly deals with youth and the power of modern technology. Here the researcher will mainly focus on trends and techniques of modern world. Now multi-capitalism and consumerism took place in literature also. This fiction deals with consumerism which shows how to attract customers for their selling of products. Characters were also played crucial role in this particular way. The whole fiction is based on One Night's Story.

Six characters work together in the BPOs. They help US companies in sales, service and maintenance of their operation. In the globalized world youth also wants all kinds of comforts for their life. Six people by the growth of the novel become victim of major problems. Our Indian youth is ready to sacrifice many things for economic empowerment, and the youth suffer a lot in the call centre for money which hide their abilities and produce nothing, and youth sacrifice their social and private life for the sake of wealth. Still they are not satisfied with their job. The main aim of presenting this culture is only to provide information about suffering of youth in a manner of getting high salary. Here in this way researcher will mainly deals with different sides of novel. This novel is also converted in Bollywood film named "Hello".

A global issue is a broad description that is often used to explain matters of great social concern that affect human populations locally and that are shared among diverse human societies within our global community. Consumerism describes the shift in American culture from a producer-oriented society in the nineteenth century to a "consumerist" society in the twentieth century. Changes in domestic demographics and advances in industrialization, manufacturing, transportation and communication, all contributed to the change. Consumerism also contributed greatly to the liberal thrust of the Progressive Era and spawned a long-running trend of consumer advocacy and consumer protection legislation. A post-war boom in technology sped the transportation of goods with a device called a steam brake. The same technological boom affected other areas of the economy. Industrial workplaces boomed. Plants made steel, locomotives, rail cars, trolleys, wagons, textiles, clothing, furniture, and new electrified appliances such as the first American refrigerators and washing machines.

The social transformation was not easy, and it bore heavily on those at the bottom arc of the cycle—the workers, both industrial and agricultural. In the industrial workplace, employees faced long hours—often 12 or more per day—in sweaty, dangerous conditions. Pay was low, and employees had little recourse against employers, who protected their own pocketbooks rather than their workers. Industry owners felt no obligation to recompense employers injured on the job or the families of workers killed in workplace accidents. Consumerism is the equation of personal happiness with consumption and the purchase of material possessions. The term is often associated with criticisms of consumption.

> It is true of dress in even a higher degree than of most other items of consumption, that people will undergo a very considerable degree of privation in the comforts or the necessaries of life in order to afford what is considered a decent amount of wasteful consumption; so that it is by no means an uncommon occurrence,

> in an inclement climate, for people to go ill clad in order to appear well dressed. (Thorstein 44)

This paper tries to elucidate the nuances involved in the consumerism and its effect on Indian society. It tries to throw some light on benefit gained by peoples in society with the literary aspects. The aim of this paper is to enlighten the reader about the complications of this system without going into technicalities. In all it is an analysis of consumerism in India. A general attempt has been made to understand this system. And in our Indian system the consumer has six rights given for his protection from exploitation from the shopkeepers or sellers. Consumer exploitation means mistreatment or cheating with consumer by adulteration or in any other unfair form. In the novel of Chetan Bhagat *One Night @ Call Center* he uses this kind of trend for aware people who are losing their identity by gaining more comforts and goods for the sake of their life.

One Night @ Call Center is based on the story of the six different characters who are working together in the BPO. They, suffer lot in their life. Bhagat deals with the new treatment of social civilization through which they acts in their life. The story begins with a train journey from Kanpur to Delhi. During the journey, the author meets a very beautiful girl. The girl offers to tell the author a story on the condition that he has to make it his second book. After a lot of hesitation, the author agrees. *ON@CC* is a tale about the events that happen one night at a call centre. Told through the views of the protagonist, Shyam (Sharman Joshi), it is a story of almost lost love, thwarted ambitions, absence of family affection, pressures of a patriarchal se-up, and the work environment of a globalized office. Shyam loves Priyanka, Vroom loves Esha, Esha wants to be a model, military uncle wants to talk to his grandson they all hate Bakshi, their cruel boss.

One of the key elements in the development of a consumerist nation would be uniformity and speed in manufacturing. A post-war boom in technology sped the transportation of goods. Consumer is the king of market, if he is getting exploited than the market will be ruined. Businesses have realized that wealthy consumers are the most attractive targets for marketing their products. The tastes upper class their lifestyles, and preferences trickle down to become the standard which all consumers seek to emulate. The not so wealthy consumers can purchase something new that will speak of their place in the tradition of affluence. A consumer can have the instant gratification of purchasing an expensive item that will help improve their social status. Popular fiction aims at the entertainment of the people in mass. The purpose of the fiction is to amuse the readers and not to make them think more. Here Bhagat has tried to give the readers such ambience. By presenting the recent phenomena of day-to-day life of middle class people, he has kept behind a humorous classification to take pleasure in. The popular fiction does not refer much philosophical or ideological issue. As it is explained it is purely written for the sake of entertainment it does not present deeper sense, instead it talks about the outer layer of human beings. If it presents philosophical or ideological issues, they are just to provide more pleasure and entertainment.

One of the salient features of this novel is that all the characters experience a dramatic and disturbing event during the night when they receive a call from God. Shyam is very upset to learn that Priyanka is engaged to a person called Ganesh Gupta, who works at Microsoft in the US. To add to his woes, he is horrified to learn that Bakshi had cheated him, and Vroom, by submitting the *Troubleshooting Website* to the Boston centre as his own without crediting himself and Vroom. Priyanka is first happy when she is engaged to Ganesh Gupta, who works for Microsoft but becomes furious when she hears that her parents have planned her marriage the very next month, which she feels is too early. Both her mother and Ganesh press her to agree to this proposal. She is even more saddened by the fact that Shyam was eavesdropping on her conversation with Ganesh. When

Vroom and Shyam show her that Ganesh had forged his pictures to hide his baldness, she disapproves Ganesh for having cheated her.

Esha had earlier done a compromise by sleeping with a designer to get a modelling contract. However the guy turned out to be opportunistic as he betrays her by telling her she can't become a model due to her height. He also tries to console her by sending her some money. Esha feels terribly betrayed and tries to suppress the mental pain by inflicting herself with physical pain by purposely cutting her skin. Vroom is shocked to learn that Bakshi has cheated him and Shyam by submitting their work as his own. To add to his miseries, he overhears Esha telling the other girls that she had slept with a designer to get a modelling contract. Radhika, who loved her husband very much, is shocked to learn about his dark side. When Vroom calls up her husband portraying as a radio jockey and asks him to dedicate roses and a song to someone special, he chooses his girlfriend Payal over his wife. Radhika who listens to this gets terribly upset as her husband has betrayed her. Military Uncle tries to be nice to his son and grandson. But when he sends some pictures via mail to his grandson, his son loses his cool and asks him to keep out of his life. This leaves Military Uncle heartbroken.

The phone call from God is one of the salient features in the novel. The author has represented God as a friendly figure rather than a boss. He is shown as speaking in modern English rather than the stereotypical pure English or Latin commonly used for God. The circumstances in which the characters of the novel get a phone call from God are discussed in the book issued by Chetan Bhagat in order to cheer them up, all the lead characters of the novel decide to go and enjoy themselves at a night club. After having fun for a while, they leave for office. Midway through the journey, Vroom starts to feel nauseated after drinking alcohol and so they stop and venture out. Vroom throws up and also breaks the window-pane of a shop, setting an alarm off. They rush out of the place in fear. While returning, they face a life-threatening situation when their Quails crashes into a construction site hanging over a mesh of iron construction rods. As the rods began to yield slowly, they start to panic. They are unable to call for help as there is no mobile phone network at that place. In this situation, Shyam's mobile phone starts ringing. The phone call is from God. He speaks to all of them and gives them suggestions about how to improve their lives. After that, God also advises them on how to get their vehicle out of the construction site. The conversation with God motivates the group to such an extent that they all plan together to teach their boss a lesson.

It is similar in the sense that the story is universal. Even if one removes the call centre setting, the characters remain identifiable. The style of writing is the same — there is a message, but there are laughs aplenty. The difference is in the time span. It is much more challenging to write a story that is set in just one night. The whole story takes place on one memorable night at their call centre in India. Since their customers are based in the US, these call centres operate during the night. The job pays well, but is rather mind-numbing. You are required to read out the responses from a pre-written script. Even your name is changed to something which Americans can pronounce easily.

This call center is in the verge of getting down sized. The bad boss takes the credit for work done by his subordinates and gets himself placed in Boston while more that 40 percent of the employees are going to be fired. At this juncture, they get a call from god. No, that was not a typo; they get a call from GOD. He helps them introspect and discover what they really want in life. The rest of the story is how they save the call center and get even with their nasty boss. The solutions are rather simplistic. If it is really a book for grown-ups? Maybe it is reflective of the generation whose story the book tells. People who have been rudely shoved from their Mills & Boons and thrust into a larger than life adult world. You can see some of those confusions in the characters of the book. Like Priyanka who is upset that her fiancé hid the fact that he was bald but seems to have no qualms about the affair she had with Shyam. Esha, who sleeps with an agent who promises a modeling contract in exchange? There is an interesting twist at the end of the book. Remember the stunning lady in the train who is narrating this story to the author.

The novel presents day-to-day life of people in general; it doesn't deal with hi-fi philosophical thoughts and issues. It's about people like you and me, presents problems of yours and mine. Along with problems it focuses on some nostalgic feelings and happy moments, as a common person has. It is more interesting because the novel is centered on the contemporary world of India's new generation. Bhagat has avoided heavy plot construction; instead he has used simple plots, like the picture of call center and picture of Shyam's dates with Priyanka at different places. The life is very complex, but Bhagat has presented it in a very simple way with easy language. It is a simple story, told in an interesting manner. In one of the interview Bhagat said that even a moderately educated person has the right to enjoy a book. Books are for everyone, not just for high society snobs. My language is simple, and that is the biggest appeal of my books. Thus using simple language Bhagat target large number of readers, and he has succeeded in that mission. Finally if one has to have a peep into the new generation, their jobs, life, attitude, values and their dreams, which makes the fiction popular, he must read *One Night @ the Call Center.*

Chetan Bhagat may not use many big words, but he does have a big idea. The interactions amongst his six protagonists make for pleasurable, highly entertaining reading—until the novel turns into a screed against their profession. For, Bhagat, it turns out, doesn't like call centres. He sees them as soul-destroying sweatshops soaking up the talents and energies of young Indians who could and should be doing better for themselves and their country. The book's denouement inveighs against young Indians wasting their time catering to the unreasonable and petty demands of American customers — customers so stupid that an instructor teaches call centre trainees the formula, "10=35": "Remember, a 35-year-old American's brain and IQ is the same as a 10-year-old Indian's... Americans are dumb, just accept it as Bhagat mentions", this at the time of launching of this book.

Demeaning and unproductive is Bhagat's theme which dominates the entire novel. Because of demeaning and unproductive situations, all six characters find their lives worthless at the call center. He takes a dim view of the back office work, his cardboard characters do not harbor much ambition in life either - one gives in to sexual exploitation to become a fashion model, another gives in to her mother's insistence that she marries a software engineer in the United States. Vroom says that we are sacrificing an entire generation to service their call centre. "A call center job is not any better than a sweat shop. Is this the best our young people can do" (Bhagat 208). He says defending the theme in which the character finds their work demeaning and unproductive. Bhagat insists that these jobs waste the full potential of bright young people who take them up out of financial compulsion.

This novel has some issues of social criticism. Bhagat has a self-righteous and self-important streak that undermines much of his possibly valid social criticism. Claims of intellectual superiority hardly mask the pathetic inferiority complex they all seem to suffer from. He tries to sketch the human conditions that every human life is in pit. They don't know why they are here, and also don't know how to come out from it. Human race is always in a hope that somebody will come to help People only blame their situation but never think about the deeds which brought them there and never try to get out of this situation themselves. Every human have the inner power which if used properly and at time one can easily get out of such situation. Here in this novel also all characters are waiting for help. They are lucky enough that God

Himself comes to help them and explain to them the importance of oneself. God asks them how many calls they attain in a day at the call centre. Vroom says 100 or 200 as per the rush of the day. God in return tells them that at this moment they are attaining the most significant call the lost important call of the world "The inner call".

Chetan Bhagat has used supernatural element to solve the problems of each of them. He has used different kinds of device to control critical situation of human lives. In India, we have theory or ideology of 'Inner Voice', that is, the soul's voice, many people believe in this theory. At last, Chetan Bhagat leaves thought in the mind of reader through the narrative technique that GOD is not there but whatever he has suggested at that place, the reader can replace their Military Uncle.

Generation gap is seen everywhere in the novel. While many may suffer the angst this novel so effectively depicts, most see a job in a call centre as a passport to a better life, one offering more possibilities and choices than were available to the previous generation. These young Indians may keep unsocial hours, neglect their family obligations, drink excessive cocktails with names like "Long Island Ice Tea", and date each other with a casualness that horrifies their parents. But they are part of a social and economic revolution that is enriching and transforming India, mostly for the better. Consumerism is the movement seeking to protect and inform consumers by requiring such practices as honest packaging and advertising, product guarantees, and improved safety standards. Six people in the BPO are doing and providing the same thing to their customers. For this they have to put up with different irresponsible people. In literature authors deal mostly about the social, myth and philosophical aspects, but with the advancement of technology and global commercial trend, there is a shift in literature towards consumer orientation. This novel has advocated these new trends in literature through the varied situations of BOPs and call centre settings. It is not merely the story of six characters but it is more a story of global marketing trends and social transformations.

Work Cited

Aaker, David A. and George S. Day, eds. *Consumerism: Search for the Consumer Interest.* New York: The Free Press, 1974.

Bhagat, Chetan. *One Night @ Call Center.* New Delhi: Rupa Co., 2005.

Fox, Richard Wightman, and T.J. Jackson Lears, ed. *The Culture of Consumption: Critical Essays in American History, 1880–1980.* New York: Pantheon Books, 1983.

Lee, Martyn J., ed. *The Consumer Society Reader.* Malden, Mass.: Blackwell Publishers, 2000.

Velben, Thorstein. *The theory of leisure class: an economic study of institutions.* Dover Publications, Mineola, NY, 1994.

26

The Avante-Garde Experience of Silence in Ambai's "Yellow Fish"

— Paula Hayes

The short story, "Yellow Fish," by Ambai (C.S. Lakshima), is a work of postmodern fiction. As a contemporary author, Ambai (b. 1944 in Tamil Nadu) is well-educated, holds a doctorate from Jawaharlal Nehru University, and publishes frequently on the subject of the relationship of women to images in theatre, film, and fiction. Starting with a short definition of postmodernism as an aesthetic movement that concentrates upon recognizing that reality is not static but ever-changing and that multiple perspectives of life should replace socially entrenched hegemonies, Ambai's short story "Yellow Fish" portrays the emotional pain and suffering of a woman's loss. Given that postmodernist fiction often seeks to explore the silenced voices of those socially oppressed, Ambai's "Yellow Fish" well represents such a postmodernist move; for, Ambai's stories are feminist in nature. To offer a synopsis, "Yellow Fish" is about a bereaved woman, Anu, standing on the edge of the sea, watching the fishing boats come to shore and the fishermen at their work. When a spotted fish is thrown away, she flashes back to the death of her baby daughter, Jalapa. But, Anu is also the narrative voice in the story, and as such the story is told from the too-oft underrepresented female perspective.

"Yellow Fish" is positively simplistic, elegant, and shorn of any unnecessary words; as a minimalist narrative it could easily be classified as avant-garde. The narrative vision of the story is driven forward primarily by images, not action. Ambai shuns conventional fictional standards of using action (plot) and characterization as means of developing the theme of the story; instead, what creates the sense of 'movement' or progression in "Yellow Fish" is established by a strong sense of *what is not said, what is left untold*, which in turn produces the aesthetic effect of articulating silence on the page. It is a seemingly impossible feat to use words to convey non-meaning, to express silence. It is a paradox at best to think of a narrative text as capable of depicting the non-representational; for, how can silence be adequately represented with language when to be silent is the opposite of to speak? Yet, it is precisely this strange accomplishment Ambai carries out in "Yellow Fish."

The story of "Yellow Fish" opens with an image of the sea. There is a swirl of colour and as readers we 'see' or construct a mental *impression* or portrait of the sea in our minds before we find out any cause, reason, or purpose for the exploitation of the sea as image. In fact, Ambai wants to draw our inner eye in toward the sea, almost literally it seems. She writes in the opening of the story, "High summer. Already the sand feels hot. It will not hold its wetness. Away, to the left of the shrunken sea, the sand spreads like a desert. Yet the eye is compelled by the sea alone." Why does she want us to so exclusively focus on the sea? As the story unfolds, we as readers are able to determine the 'why' behind the need to create the sea as a primary symbol; it is because, as the narrative voice in the text reveals, the sea holds the sacred mysteries of life and death. And particularly, the sea houses the unforgotten death of the narrator's premature baby, Jalapa, who died in a hospital incubator after being born kicking and leaping in this world and sucking for air.

The connection between the sea and Jalapa in "Yellow Fish" creates a semiotic strategy reminiscent of what feminist literary theorist, Julia Kristeva, describes in *Revolution in Poetic Language* as the linguistic maternal body as a point of exit from social constraints (social fears, social paranoia, social hysteria). Kristeva describes the maternal body as figuratively an entrance into a place where the natural world is accepted. According to her postmodern feminist theories, socially it is the case that modernity exists as oppositional to the natural world; thus, the female body is feared and denied in modern societies because the female body is representational of nature and an ever-present reminder of life and death (what we fear most). Modernity, wanting to deny the realities of life and death (through the creation of institutional structures that seem to replace the reality of time as cyclical events), must therefore shun and exclude the female presence from its vision. Ambai in "Yellow Fish" uses fragmented images that the readers, must in turn, construct and re-construct, to represent the fragmentation of the female presence in modernity. But the use of fragmented images also goes a step further toward the sheer emotional depiction of a woman in a state of isolated grief. Ambai is concerned with representing female "mind and memory." Her concerns include the accurately giving voice to how women actually feel, think, and see the world. How does a grief-stricken mother perceive the world as she walks through it with her sense of loss and absence?

> Black hands. Brown wood of the boats. Between the meshes of the nets, white bellied fish. Crowding near, the colours of the saris press gently but firmly. Painted troughs. Dry sand. An extraordinary collage of colours, on the shores of the wide-spread sea. A composition that imprints itself on the mind and memory.

As readers, when we initially approach "Yellow Fish," all we know for the first half of Ambai's story is that there is a sea, and is beautiful and magnificent, compelling even, and that a white fishing boat has arrived by the shore. We know that fishermen are emptying their strained and overarched nets. We also know that in the process of the fishermen cleaning out their catches of fish for the day that one lone fish, a yellow fish, is tossed carelessly and remorselessly onto the sand. The yellow fish, left apart from the other fish that will be used, will die on the sand if not rescued. The female narrator, Anu, is overwhelmed with sympathetic emotions for the fish's plight; this allows for her own consciousness to drift back in time to the place of memory. In the seat of consciousness, where memory is somehow housed, the association is made in her mind between the flopping, dying yellow fish, as it gapes its mouth open wide for air (but in need of water), and that of her premature daughter's hours of life inside an incubator.

Anu's memory of her daughter's tiny mouth opening and closing, and its near sucking motions, as she tried to open herself to the world around her, only to not survive, becomes tightly unified in the story with that of the fish's motions on the sand. The more that the narrator, Anu, watches the fish open its mouth to try and find life (but only move closer to death), the more she recalls with anguish the death of her daughter, "The mouth closes; closes and opens, desperate for water. Like Jalapa's mouth."

It is at the moment in the story where memory of the beloved daughter overlaps and is placed onto the sight of the yellow fish wriggling on the sand that the story turns to reveal another sad feature—the narrator recalls how when her daughter passed away she was cremated, and how she asked for the urn to be opened so that she could see the ashes. Thus, in the story, symbols become overlaid, one on top of the other—the symbol of the fish's open mouth becomes overlaid with the memory of the baby girl's open mouth as she lay dying, and both mouths then become linked with a third open mouth, the open mouth of the cremation urn.

The story ends with an encounter of happenstance, as the narrator comes across a young boy whom she asks to throw the fish back in the sea for her. But, the story's ending leaves the reader wondering: why didn't the narrator take the initiative and toss the fish back into the sea herself? Why did she feel the need to wait on someone else to do so? And, had fate not intervened by sending the boy to her to do this task for her, what would have become of the yellow fish? Would it have been left out in the vast openness of the sands to die, all the while the woman standing and watching?

Of course, as readers, we can infer that the narrator—whose consciousness binds the story together for us—is too struck with the flood of feeling that has swept over her and with the memory of the loss of her small daughter that she is practically immobilized and unable to act as she might otherwise normally act. Thus, we would not take her lack of actions in the story as a fault against her nor even hold her truly accountable for almost letting the fish die; rather, we should perceive her in the story as *equal to consciousness*, to having, in fact, melded into a state of consciousness, a state of reflection, of almost, nearly pure emotive being. Anu is a symbol of consciousness in "Yellow Fish." Throughout the narrative, she remains in a mental condition of seeming to exist as disembodied, just as the sea is a symbol of disembodiment; the only attention given to physical bodies in the story are those of fish and of the dead baby girl.

The narrator, Anu, is also an expression of *sentience*. Yet, because her memories focus so much on a fleshly life, of actually being-in-this-world, we as readers yearn for her to be capable of more than she is. But if nothing else, we as readers can understand why the narrator would possibly need to see herself as extension of the impersonal sea; for, she recalls through the unforgiving function of memory, it was she who asked that her daughter's ashes be scattered at sea. To return to the sea, is to return to life; thus, for the yellow fish to return to the sea is for the fish to regain its life. There is a degree of resurrection experienced in the symbolic return to the sea, as the sea becomes the symbol for the emergence of life and its waters associated with the living waters of a woman's body.

The question, then, becomes: what is meant by the story's revelation of openness? One answer is that the openness of the three mouths (fish, daughter, and urn), that is symbolically carried in the story through the motif of the yellow fish, is intended to express the sacred dimensions of silence. Depicting silence in a work of art is also an avant-garde practice. It is difficult to discuss postmodern literature as a whole, and this is for the simple fact that there are so many branches of the postmodern. There is not one gigantic 'grand narrative' that can describe postmodernism nor explain to readers what postmodern literature is. But, there are many divisions and hence many paths to be taken in postmodernism and one such path is that of the avant-garde. But what is the avant-garde? Richard Kostelanetz in *The Avante-Garde Tradition in Literature* defines the movement in the following way:

> The term *avante-garde* refers to those out front, forging a path that others will take. Initially coined to characterize the shock troops of an army, the epithet passed over into art, in part because the dissemination of art resembles in certain respects to the progress of an army. Used precisely, the term avante-garde should refer to work that satisfies three discriminatory criteria: it transcends current artistic conventions in crucial respects, establishing a discernible distance between itself and the mass of current practices; second, avante-garde work will necessarily take considerable time to find its maximum audience; and third, it will probably inspire future, comparably advanced endeavors. ...As a temporal term, avante-garde charaterizes art that seems to be 'ahead of its time '—art that is beginning something—while 'decadent art, by contrast, stands at the end of a prosperous development (3).

Following Kostelanetz's definition, what is the battle of the avant-garde feminist writer? What portends the "probably inspire[d] future" that Ambai envisions? In the easiest of terms, the answers are: there is a desire for the recovery of the natural world as relational (in a semiotic, symbolic, and narrative sense) to the female body as well as a recovery the formerly silenced voices of women; hence, the right of women to define the perimeters of their bodily, physical spaces socially, as well as define their psychological and emotional lives, privately.

There are many theories about how postmodernism uses silence as a means to construct meaning in texts, but a seminal theory dates back to Ihab Hassan's *The Dismemberment of Orpheus: Toward a Postmodern Literature* (1971). In the opening chapter of the book, Hassan expounds upon 10 characteristics or tenets of the postmodern use of silence in a work of art. It is the suggestion, here, that her tenets of the postmodern use of silence are applicable to Ambai's short story, "Yellow Fish."

Hassan's first tenet states that "Silence refers to an avant-garde tradition of literature" (13). As has already been established, Ambai's story qualifies as avant-garde; for, she is unconcerned with sticking to the traditional or conventional means of constructing a narrative. Plot is primarily ignored; there is scant attention given to action in the story. Characters remain indistinct, ill-defined beings. In the place of plot and characterization, there is an emphasis upon time, consciousness, memory, and the meaning of the *'other's'* body as perceived by a distant, detached, disembodied purveyor. In "Yellow Fish," the detachment of the narrative voice gives us, as readers, a portrait of the world as fragmented, disjointed, broken, and undesirable. The scenes in "Yellow Fish" are impressionistic and imagistic in a way that emulates how consciousness culls pieces of empirical reality to create a sense of how things appear to the self.

> Bodies and hands darkened by the salt wind, the men will spread their nets and start sorting the fish the minute the boats come in. Now the fish will splash into plastic troughs, round eyes wide open. The unwanted ones are thrown away. There is a general murmur of tired voices, rising for a split second, then falling.

It is important to recognize Ambai's work as avant-garde; for, not only does it employ the textual strategy of using silence on the page to express the feelings of the underrepresented and minority positions of those historically oppressed, the work is avant-garde, too, because it is reverses the reader's expectations. Avant-garde work deliberately and poignantly seeks to dispel the traditional concepts of what defines a text. For example, as readers we may go to a text with the idea in mind that what the characters speak, what they 'say,' will convey the whole or at least the bulk of the narrative's meaning. But in Ambai's work, her use of avant-garde style makes it possible for readers to find places within the text where silence has been represented. What is not said in the story becomes as important and meaningful as what is said.

Hassan's second tenet of the postmodern states, "Silence implies alienation from reason, society, and history, a reduction of all engagements in the created world of men, perhaps an abrogation of any communal existence" (13). We see an example of alienation as well as a portrait of the communal order in "Yellow Fish" when the narrator describes the bustle of the fisherman. The fish in the story are a symbol for communal life and of the social; thus, nature offers in the story more hope for the communal than can be found in the world of human activity. In one sense, the fishermen violate the communal order of nature by *discarding* what humanity deems as unusable—this is a violation because *in the natural order everything has a purpose.* It is the fishermen who break this code of nature by casting aside what they do not want, "A yellow fish is thrown away on the sand." But in spite of this act of careless disregard, the fishermen are oblivious to the portent of the fish being cast away, "The men carry on sorting their fish quickly and efficiently." The female narrator, on the other hand, is able to 'see' what the men are unable to perceive.

> Of that palest yellow that comes before the withering and falling of leaves. It has black spots. As I stoop to watch, it begins to shudder and leap. The mouth gasps; gasps and closes. It shudders and tosses on hot sand.

In Ambai's story, the fish are also symbolically representative of individuals in society who are cast away, discarded as lacking value—those who are ignored, forgotten, abused, even reprimanded. Anu, as a woman belongs among a class of the forgotten and abused, and so her position in the social world allows her to not only empathize for the senselessness of throwing away an imperfect fish; more so, her position permits her to literally see the world in a different light, in a changed hue. She can see the fish's blemishes, but this does not stop her from longing for its safety. She stops her gait and watches the fish's movements. Because the female narrator's activity of watching the fish is drawn in such a way to connect in the story with her daughter's death, so the violation of nature becomes linked to the violation of a baby girl's death. In the description of the baby girl's death, it is as though the quickness of her entrance into the world is a type of violation as well; thus, her "too soon" entrance must be overcome by her eventual return to the realm of the cycle of life and death. The scene starts off with an image of the dying fish's open mouth but then moves into images of the baby girl.

> Too hasty infant Jalapa. She pushed and bumper her way out into the world. Her name had already been decided. She who rises from the waters. Lotus. Jalapa. They had to put her in an incubator. I stood outside the room constantly, watching her. Her pale round mouth. Her round eyes. Sometimes she would open and close her mouth, as if sucking. The ashes which Arun brought back from the electric crematorium were in small urn, a miniature of those huge earthenware jars of Mohenjadaro and Harrapa. Its narrow mouth was tied with a piece of cloth.

For the narrator, her daughter's ashes buried inside a cremation urn is a violation too. The ashes must be permitted to return to the natural world and join the cycle of the life and death processes, not remained sealed. For, just as the daughter's name is associated with the life of waters, so even her urn is associated with the places of the origins of civilization and of culture. But for the female narrator, it is as though the daughter's ashes are deemed *as* valueless *until* the moment when the ashes are returned to nature, when the ashes are disseminated into the sea, "the ashes [of the baby daughter] were in this very sea."

Also in Ambai's story, silence is portrayed by the fact that the fishermen lack words; they do not need a language to chuck aside what they do not want. Their bodies form an action, a rhythm of work that is shown to exist without the need for the exchange of dialogue; silence calls attention to their activity, which in turn calls attention to their desecration of nature. Hassan's third tenet of the postmodern is "Silence also betrays separation from nature, a perversion of vital and erotic processes. The symptoms range from misogyny to necrophilia. Man rejects the earth and abhors woman; he detaches himself from the body" (13). Thus, given this relationship of a male rejection of nature (the fishermen's rejection of certain unusable fish), so we find in Ambai's story that there is a rejection of the maternal, a denial of the woman's body. The female narrator in the story cannot allow her daughter's urn to remain closed (the mouth of the urn had to be reopened); by freeing the ashes and returning the body to the waters of the sea, so the female narrator is shown to unleash the maternal waters of life. What is separated from and taken out of maternal waters must eventually return to them; but, the world of male activity, of work that works against nature is a world of the abomination and fear of the female element.

Hassan's fourth tenet of the postmodern is that "Silence demands the self-repudiation of art which aspires to event, dream, nonsense, or number", and so it is that "Art, rejoining brute matter or pure ration, pretends to become anti-artist; between these extremes, it discovers cunning equivocations" (13). Ambai's story is an example of anti-art and of a portrait of the anti-artist; for, the only protagonist in "Yellow Fish" is the female narrator who is a kind of anti-hero or anti-artist. She is shown to overthrow ritual, to throwaway tradition, and to live off of the epiphenomena of what consciousness constructs for itself in relationship to the natural world, while rejecting the constraints of the social world. The social world is, in fact, shown to exist as a mirage in "Yellow Fish." And the female narrator moves in the story in a dream-like state. This leads us to Hassan's fifth tenet, "Silence requires the periodic subversion of forms. At times, the resulting anti-forms feign a formlessness that nothing made or perceived by man can ever possess," and given if this is true, "*Still, anti-forms oppose control, closure, statis, telos, and historic pattern*" (13; emphasis mine). The female narrator cannot stop the Jalapa's disappearance from the world, and her acceptance of this fate shows a sharp contrast to her husband in the story; for, he wants to keep Jalapa's ashes locked inside the urn. But the female narrator wants to release Jalapa's ashes; thus, embracing movement and *resisting control, closure, and stasis.*

The sixth tenet of Hassan's theory of postmodern expression brings silence and the use of language into a direct relationship with another; for he writes, "Silence creates anti-languages. Some are utterly opaque, others completely transparent. These languages transform the presence of words into semantic absence and unloosen the grammar of consciousness" and so "They accuse common speech" (13). What is an anti-language? An anti-language does not refer to nonsense; rather, it refers to any use of words that draws attention to counter-hegemonies. In Ambai's "Yellow Fish," an anti-language is established that calls for the reader to approach more closely the language of the maternal. The only dialogue used in the story is that of a woman's speech with that of a male. It is significant that what breaks the silence in the text is a woman's voice, her words seen as an intrusion, a forced entrance into tradition, thereby rupturing the stasis of tradition. As the female narrator questions her husband, the conversation unfolds to represent the anti-language of the maternal longing for openness, both the literal opening of Jalapa's urn and the figurative, emotional openness that is to be found in the desire to be understood by another.

> "Why is the mouth closed?"
>
> "What mouth?"
>
> "The mouth of the urn. Open it."
>
> "Anu. It only contains ashes."

> "I want to see. Open it."
>
> "Anu."
>
> "Open its mouth. That mouth..."
>
> Loud racking sobs. The cloth was removed to reveal the urn's tiny mouth.

Hassan's seventh tenet states, "Silence fills the extreme states of the mind—void, madness, outrage, ecstasy, mystic trance—which ordinary discourse ceases to carry the burden of meaning" (13). There is no mysticism in Ambai's story, but there is a quiet madness permeating the sobs of Anu's discourse with her husband. Thus, left alone on the sands of the sea, she must ask a stranger to perform the task she cannot perform—to toss the fish back. In the scene, a second anti-language is established; that of the fish's leaping movements of recovery as it returns to the sea. A boy's "snorting" laughter, a fish's quick movements—these are all part of the story's anti-language.

> A fisherboy is on his way back from splashing the waves. He comes when I summon him in Marathi,
>
> "Ikkade e, come here."
>
> "Will you throw this yellow fish back into the sea?"
>
> A quick snort of laughter.
>
> I run after him. He places it on the crest of an incoming wave. For a moment, it sputters, helpless, like a drunk who cannot find the way home. Again it opens it mouth to the water, taking it in. Then a swish of the fin tail. An arrogant leap.

Additionally, Hassan's eighth tenet is that "Silence de-realizes the world. It encourages the metamorphosis of appearance and reality, the perpetual fusion and confusion of identities, till nothing—or so it *seems*—remains" (13). The ninth tenetis "Silence turns consciousness upon itself, altering the modes of its awareness; or else condemns the mind to repetitions of the same solipsist drama of self and anti-self", and this creates the situation described as "Thus, the transvaluation of values or their complete devaluation ensues" (13). And lastly, the tenth tenetis "Silence presupposes, at times, apocalypse, the dissolution millennial vision of non-human perfection" and so results in "Thus the total accusation of life may yield to its opposite, and the affluence of being flood the abyss" (14). In a highly simplistic way, an apocalyptic end is found in Ambai's conclusion; this apocalyptic dimension is not forcibly visible, rather it is subtle.

> Once again it swishes its tail and swims forward. You can see its clear yellow for a very long time. Then it merges into the blue-grey-white of the sea.

The postmodern abyss we, as readers, uncover is contained in the final merging together of the sea, the fish, and Jalapa's ashes. The abyss is contained in the emotional world of a woman's feelings.

Works Cited

Ambai. "Yellow Fish" *Passages: 24 Modern Indian Stories*. Ed. Barbara H. Solomon and Eileen Panetta. New York: Penguin, 2009. (ebook)

Hassan, Ihab. *The Dismemberment of Orpheus: Toward a Postmodern Literature* Oxford: Oxford University Press, 1971.

Kristeva, Julia. *Revolution in Poetic Language.* New York: Columbia University Press, 1984.

Index